THE TREATMENT OF DRINKING PROBLEMS

a guide for the helping professions

GRIFFITH EDWARDS

MA, DM, FRCP, FRCPsych, DPM,
Professor of Addiction Behaviour and
Honorary Director, Addiction Research Unit,
Institute of Psychiatry, London;
Honorary Consultant Psychiatrist,
the Bethlem Royal and Maudsley Hospitals

GRANT MCINTYRE
MEDICAL & SCIENTIFIC

Copyright © 1982 by
Grant McIntyre Ltd
90–91 Great Russell Street
London WC1B 3PY

First published 1982

Photoset by Enset Ltd
Midsomer Norton, Bath, Avon
and printed and bound
in Great Britain by Billing & Sons Ltd
Worcester

DISTRIBUTORS.

Throughout the world except North
America and Australia
  Blackwell Scientific Publications Ltd
  Osney Mead, Oxford, OX2 0EL

Australia
  Blackwell Scientific Book Distributors
  214 Berkeley Street, Carlton
  Victoria 3053

British Library
Cataloguing in Publication Data

Edwards, Griffith
  The treatment of drinking problems:
  a guide for the helping professions.
  1. Alcoholism Treatment
  I. Title
  616.86'106 RC565

ISBN 0–86286–019–9
ISBN 0–86286–020–2 Pbk

Contents

III. TREATMENT

Acknowledgements

This book has drawn freely on those two major resources which must be the foundations of any treatment text – the worlds of clinical experience and of scientific research. It is those twin origins of the book which point to the two overlapping groups of people whose help must be specially acknowledged.

Firstly I want to thank those many clinical colleagues with whom I have worked over the last 20 and more years at the Maudsley and Bethlem Royal Hospitals. The continued sharing of discussion in the immediate setting of casework has been invaluable, and the fund of ideas from which I have borrowed reflects the contributions of staff members too numerous to mention by name. Under this same clinical heading I must also acknowledge what has been learnt directly from those many patients who have actively shared in the search for better understanding.

As for acknowledging the help which I have received from the research world, the fellowship and stimulation which have come from working in the Addiction Research Unit have been essential to the writing of this book; though here again there are too many names for individual listing. I must also of course thank those many researchers in other institutions and parts of the world from whose writings I have derived so much.

In particular, I have to thank Dr D.L. Davies, who introduced me to the study of alcoholism and to the fascination of this subject. Valuable comments on draft chapters of this book were provided by many friends, and Mrs Julia Polglaze has not only seen each chapter through its drafts and typed the whole manuscript, but has as ever provided extraordinary support. Without her help, ideas would never have become a book. The text of the Twelve Steps, the AA Preamble and the AA Prayer is reprinted by permission of Alcoholics Anonymous World Services, Inc. Adam Sisman of Grant McIntyre has given much encouragement and useful advice, and finally I should like to thank Mrs D. Blake for the expert indexing.

Introduction ·

In many parts of the world today alcoholism is a large and threatening problem. In Africa and Asia rapid changes in the structure of society, and in particular the influences of urbanization, have meant that old social or religious controls over drinking have broken down at exactly the same moment as economic forces have led to breweries being established within the borders, or imported liquor being aggressively sold for the first time. In Western countries the affluence of the post-war years has bred a consumer society which has generated, amongst so many other demands, a demand for more drink. Prosperity seems to breed alcoholism as much as poverty, and we are as likely to find the problem among executives in the suburbs where there are two cars in the garage, as in the slums of New York or the ever-expanding shanty towns of South America. Alcoholism is a great leveller.

No matter what the culture, the *range* of drink-related problems is enormous. It is not just a case of 'alcoholism' presenting neatly at 'the alcoholism clinic', but of head injuries on Saturday night in Glasgow, a car driving of the road somewhere in West Africa, violence at the fiesta in a Mexican village. And these instances are but part of a virtually endless list of ways in which excessive drinking may acutely, occasionally or chronic-ally impair social and family functioning, physical health or mental well-being. There is no simple stereotyped picture of alcoholism which can in any way satisfactorily subsume the extraordinary range of its presen-tation. Diversity itself is, paradoxically, a leading common feature.

Another commonality between countries is that these presentations are made to a very large range of people. Many professionals besides doctors are likely to be closely involved in helping. In some countries it may be the social workers who take the lead, or it may be probation and parole officers and prison welfare officers who are actively contributing to treatment programmes. Nurses often play an important role, and also clinical psychologists and occupational therapists. In other countries the priest or the pastoral counsellor may be much involved, and increasing use

1

is being made of volunteers and of specially trained lay counsellors, some of whom may be recovered alcoholics. In large parts of the Third World the only available professional help is from the medical assistant or barefoot doctor, and with alcohol problems exacerbating many endemic health and social problems in the developing countries, ways must be found to help with drinking problems when there are only minimal professional resources.

FOR WHOM THIS BOOK IS INTENDED

The purpose of this book is to lay out in simple form the essentials for understanding drinking problems, for making an assessment of the individual and family, for giving appropriate help within one's own competence, and for making decisions on when to make professional referral and when to seek the advice of others. The position taken here is that the treatment of alcoholism is less arcane than has sometimes been made out. For instance, it is not necessarily or exclusively a matter of specialized in-patient units and intensive group therapy, or of prolonged out-patient psychotherapy. Provided the generalist is willing to learn about alcoholism, much of the real helping business can, for example, be conducted by the family doctor who knows how to make full use of a ten-minute talk, or the community social worker who finds the mother intoxicated at 11 am, or the probation or parole officer who has many other types of clients among his case-load. Over recent years alcoholism treatment has sometimes become too cultish, with its claims to specialism inflated, and these claims have undermined the confidence of the very people who ought to have been giving the front-line help. At the same time the expansion of specialist services to an extent where they could cope with the whole potential case-load has remained an absurdly impossible dream in most countries.

A stress on the role of the generalist should not be taken to mean that there is nothing very special to be learnt. A syllabus must be developed to teach the basic knowledge, attitudes and skills needed by the generalist if he is to deal appropriately with drinking problems. Once interest has been aroused, continued case experience is implicitly self-education. This book is also, of course, concerned with the needs of the person who is going to take a more specialized interest in alcoholism. But whether the reader is generalist or specialist, no book stands as a teaching aid in isolation; it is a tool which can find its full use only in the context of continuing casework with patients, discussion, further reading and, where possible, the stimulation which comes from courses and summer schools.

Finally, the intention has been to write a book which deals with basic and general principles that are of importance in very different cultural settings. There can be no such thing as treatment which is 'culture free'; help for drinking problems must be in alignment with general patterns of help-seeking. Nevertheless, many of the ideas in this book, if critically 'translated' by the clinician with intimate knowledge of his own territory, can be seen as relevant to the practical problems which we all encounter when we sit down and talk with the next patient or client, whatever our country. There is indeed in this regard an immense need to share experience between countries.

THE GENERAL PLAN OF THIS BOOK

Following this introductory chapter, material will be grouped into three major sections. Chapters 1 to 8 are headed 'Background to Understanding'. 'Assessment' is dealt with in Chapters 9 to 12, while Chapters 13 to 20 are put together under the heading of 'Treatment'. In the paragraphs below some signposting of the book's structure is given, certain important emphases established, and core terms defined.

WHY DO SOME PEOPLE DRINK TOO MUCH?

This is a question of great concern to preventive health, and obviously it is also of importance to individual casework. But to suppose that the therapist can work on a model as mechanistic and rational as a discovery of *the* cause, which then proposes *the* solution, is unreal, although the patient may fantasize that this is the case. This book therefore includes a discussion on analysis of causes in so far as they may bear on the practical business of treatment (Chapter 1).

WHAT COUNTS AS A DRINKING PROBLEM?: THE DEFINITION OF TERMS

Too often in the past only the advanced case was recognized as having a drinking problem. The 'real alcoholic' was accepted as cause for medical concern, but anyone who failed to fulfil the alcoholic stereotype would be turned away from the clinic. In fact it seems likely that the majority of excessive drinkers who will be encountered by the social worker, the community nurse or the family doctor will be manifesting problems which do not look at all like the advanced clinical case. Any teaching which is designed exclusively in terms of the clinic's experience and the clinic's working methods will therefore be poorly fitted to the needs of such workers.

This book is concerned with how to help people with drinking problems of any and every type or degree. There is a need, though, at this stage for a definition of terms which can offer a basic framework for classification. The word 'alcholism' will be used throughout in a general sense to describe damage to the individual's health or impairment of his social and family adjustment caused by the use of alcohol, whether that damage is acute or chronic. This term has been employed in many different ways over more than a century, and although some authorities would still wish to give it a restricted meaning (only severe or repeated damage perhaps, or only addiction), usages have become so uncertain and conflicting that to try to give the word more precise meaning seems rather a lost cause. In any case a term of broad meaning is much needed.

Alcohol is a drug which potentially can induce dependence, or in older and familiar terms it is a drug of addiction. The clustering of signs and symptoms which define the dependent state is described as the alcohol dependence syndrome, and this syndrome is delineated in Chapter 2. But the phrase 'alcohol dependence syndrome', though scientifically exact, is unduly cumbersome for repeated or everyday use, and instead we will often use 'dependence' or 'being dependent'.

The dependence syndrome is undoubtedly of importance to the work of anyone who seeks to help patients with drinking problems. It is an idea roughly coterminus with what many people would call 'the disease of alcoholism', or with the Alcoholics Anonymous notion of what counts as alcoholism. The person who works with drinking problems must learn to recognize this syndrome in all its degrees, stages and variations, to appreciate the subjective meaning of dependence for the person who is suffering from the condition and its significance for the family who are seeking to cope with this problem, and must know what treatment goals the condition proposes and how this disorder is appropriately treated. What is required is indeed an old-fashioned clinical skill of the type which the good doctor or the good nurse would always have possessed as regards, say, the understanding of what it meant to have contracted pneumonia, that is, they recognized the faces of the condition, knew its time course, could see the condition in its context and knew what could be done to help. To use this physical analogy may seem false when alcohol dependence is obviously a condition with psychological and social as well as physical aspects. The analogy is, though, in many ways apt: what has to be cultivated is a *feeling* for a condition, and an awareness of how it will be coloured by context.

Although the dependence syndrome is of importance, it should by no means be the exclusive idea for understanding people with drinking problems. People may experience acute or chronic trouble as a result of their drinking and not be suffering from this syndrome. That a drunk man is repeatedly violent or steals, or that a drunk woman falls downstairs, are important facts in their own right, whether or not the syndrome is present. The approach adopted in this book therefore proposes that a distinction should be drawn between 'alcohol-related problems' on the one hand, and the 'alcohol dependence syndrome' on the other. The person who is suffering from the syndrome is likely to be drinking at such a level as to have incurred a range of disabilities, but there are also many people who will have experienced similar disabilities but who are not dependent. This statement catches up a vitally important idea which is the basis for a simple and ordered approach to the understanding of the seemingly endless complexities of case presentation. The types of problems which may be caused by drinking are discussed in several different chapters: family problems in Chapter 3, other social complications in Chapter 4, psychiatric complications in Chapter 5, and physical complications in Chapter 6.

WOMEN WITH DRINKING PROBLEMS AND OTHER SPECIAL PRESENTATIONS

Over the last few years there has been an increased interest in women with drinking problems, which goes some way to redress previous neglect. The presentation and treatment of alcoholism in women is discussed in Chapter 7. Some other special presentations are discussed in Chapter 8 – the young alcoholic, for instance, and the elderly patient with a drinking · problem.

THE IMPORTANCE OF ASSESSMENT AND FORMULATION

An emphasis on the importance of thorough initial assessment is an essential part of the philosophy of this book (Chapter 9). Assessment is, however, seen not as an impersonal business of data-gathering carried out to satisfy the professional needs of the therapist, but as an interaction between patient and therapist which is in itself the initiation of treatment. Assessment is a live and dynamic undertaking, and its whole purpose is betrayed if it accidentally becomes the dull compilation of case-notes for compilation's sake. (Case-notes within that latter formula are neither worth making nor worth reading.) Assessment with the spouse deserves separate consideration (Chapter 10). To give meaning and shape to the assessments, it is necessary that a formulation on the basis of the information which has been gathered should be made under headings (Chapter 11). However, it must not be assumed that every patient with alcoholism comes forward to treatment with his condition already declared, and case identification and screening are therefore important issues (Chapter 12).

THE NATURE OF TREATMENT

The initial emphasis must be on defining, on the basis of co-operation with the patient himself, what are to be the goals of treatment (with the goals being negotiated rather than imposed), and on discussing with the patient how those goals are to be worked towards. The emphasis should be on putting the responsibility back onto the patient, and restoring his sense of autonomy and possibility. The treatment philosophy which is favoured here is purposefully rather low-key, characterized by a willingness to expect, to demand, to wait, to point out or to challenge, rather than a willingness to plunge in with intensive help which covertly reinforces the notion that recovery is the therapist's rather than the patient's responsibility. Chapter 13 deals with treatment of withdrawal, and Chapter 14 goes on to discuss at length the basic treatment concepts. The important place that Alcoholics Anonymous may play is discussed in Chapter 15, with an emphasis on the need for the professional to learn how to co-operate fruitfully with this organization.

Chapter 16 then provides discussion of certain special techniques – behaviour therapies, deterrent drugs (disulfiram and calcium carbimide), and formal psychotherapies. Although this book puts emphasis on the importance of basic issues such as goal-setting and the use of the therapeutic relationship, it should be appreciated that the appropriate deployment of special techniques may play an important part within a total treatment programme.

The question of whether some patients can aim for controlled drinking rather than abstinence should not be seen as contentious once the probable heterogeneity within any 'alcoholic' population is understood. However, to determine what goal is most appropriate for a particular patient demands very careful decision-making. Therapies aimed at a normal drinking goal are discussed in Chapter 17.

Much of the therapeutic work discussed in this book is envisaged as feasible within an out-patient setting. The assumption that whenever possible it is preferable to treat patients within their natural environment is so implicit in the discussion of both basic and specialized techniques, and of work either towards abstinence or controlled drinking, that it would be redundant to offer a special chapter dealing with out-patient care. However, the in-patient unit still has an important if revised place, and the role of a multi-purpose in-patient unit is discussed in Chapter 18.

CO-OPERATION AND SERVICE ORGANIZATIONS

There may be occasions when the help which the alcoholic needs can be provided by one person alone, but on many other occasions a number of different people will be involved in the helping process. It may be a matter of a therapeutic team working together in continuous and organized fashion (either a hospital or a primary health care team), or of *ad hoc* arrangements being set up between different agencies and individuals. In practical terms it amounts to the telephone call at the right moment, the informative letter with copies sent to the right people, the case conference called on the right day, proper trust between voluntary and statutory organizations, and the cultivation of a sixth sense as an inherent part of casework, which makes the therapist *always* check whether these sorts of communication are in good repair. Chapter 19 discusses the questions of co-operation and communication, and the design and functioning of alcoholism treatment services.

STAYING CLOSE TO REALITIES

In writing any book about treatment there is always the danger of gradually being edged towards portraying things in terms of an ideal world where treatments are rationally proposed, patients obligingly get better, and the treatment team is always happy. Such a picture is sadly remote from many working days and Chapter 20 deals therefore with a number of familiar ways in which things may go wrong and discusses how they may be put right.

REFERENCES

At the end of most chapters references are given which have been selected as likely to be useful to the reader who has not got endless time to spend in the library but who wants to take his reading a stage further under any heading. In constructing these lists the emphasis has been particularly on major journal reviews and book chapters rather than research papers. Referencing is restricted to English language publications but with a fair mix of British and North American sources. It was felt that lists of this sort were more appropriate for the purposes of this volume than a full referencing in the conventional academic fashion.

VOCABULARY

This book is written for people who work within the traditions of many different helping professions, and different professions have to an extent their own vocabulary, loaded with special meanings. Strangely, the helping professions possess no common vocabulary relating to certain core issues, for instance, are the people whom we are seeking to help to be referred to as 'patients' or 'clients'? A choice which pleases one group of professions may suggest bias to another, and this book uses the word 'patient' in the hope that the text itself gives evidence of sensitivity to those considerations which have led social workers usually to prefer the other term. Throughout the book the person who gives the help is referred to as 'the therapist'.

Finally, 'he or she' has become mandatory, particularly to the American reader, as the replacement for 'he' when the pronoun is used in the open sense. This book follows the older convention that the male pronoun is taken to mean either sex, unless the context suggests otherwise. And it is again hoped that the text itself gives evidence that due and proper sensitivities have in practice been shown.

REFERENCES

HISTORICAL

Booth W (General) (1890) *In Darkest England and the Way Out.* London: Salvation Army.

Glatt MM (1958) The English drink problem: its rise and decline through the ages. *British Journal of Addiction*, **55**, 51–67.

Gusfield JR (1976) *Symbolic Crusade: Status Politics and the American Temperance Movement.* Urbana: University of Illinois Press.

Harrison B (1971) *Drink and the Victorians.* London: Faber and Faber.

Levine HG (1978) The discovery of addiction. *Journal of Studies on Alcohol*, **39**, 143–174.

Pan L (1975) *Alcohol in Colonial Africa.* Helsinki: Finnish Foundation for Alcohol Studies.

Williams GP and Brake GT (1980) *Drink in Great Britain 1900–1979.* London: Edsall.

Winkler AM (1969) Drinking on the American frontier. *Quarterly Journal of Studies on Alcohol*, **29**, 413–445.

INTERNATIONAL PERSPECTIVES

Edwards G (1979) Drinking problems: putting the Third World on the map. *Lancet*, **2**, 402–404.

Edwards G and Arif A (eds.) (1980) *Drug Problems in the Socio-cultural Context.* Geneva: WHO.

Hawks DV (1980) The meaning of 'Treatment services for alcohol-related problems' in developing countries. In: Edwards G and Grant M (eds) *Alcoholism Treatment in Transition*, pp 199–204. London: Croom Helm.

Moser J (1974) *Problems and Programmes Related to Alcohol and Drug Dependence in 33 Countries.* Geneva: WHO.

Moser M (1980) *Prevention of Alcohol-Related Problems: an International Review of Preventative Measures, Policies and Programmes.* Toronto: Addiction Research Foundation on behalf of WHO.

World Health Organisation (1973) *Existing Patterns of Services for Alcoholism and Drug Dependence.* Copenhagen: WHO Regional Office for Europe.

World Health Organisation (1980) *Problems Related to Alcohol Consumption: Report of a W.H.O. Expert Committee. Technical Report Series 650.* Geneva: WHO.

GENERAL BACKGROUND

Armor DJ, Polich JM and Stambul HB (1978) *Alcoholism and Treatment.* London: Wiley.

Chafetz ME, Blane HT and Hill MJ (eds) (1970) *Frontiers of Alcoholism.* New York: Science House.

Davies I and Raistrick D (1981) *Dealing with Drink.* London: British Broadcasting Corporation.

Edwards G and Grant M (eds) (1977) *Alcoholism: New Knowledge and New Responses.* London: Croom Helm.

Edwards G and Grant M (eds) (1980) *Alcoholism Treatment in Transition.* London: Croom Helm.

Edwards G, Gross MM, Keller M *et al* (1977) *Alcohol-Related Disabilities.* WHO Offset Publication No. 32. Geneva: WHO.

Glatt M (1975) *Alcoholism: A Social Disease.* London: Teach Yourself Books.

Grant M and Gwinner PDV (eds) (1979) *Alcoholism in Perspective*. London: Croom Helm.

Hore B (1976) *Alcohol Dependence*. London: Butterworth.

Kessel N and Walton H (1965) *Alcoholism*. Harmondsworth: Penguin Books.

Madden JS (1979) *A Guide to Alcohol and Drug Dependence*. Bristol: Wright and Sons.

Mendelson JH and Mello NK (eds) (1979) *The Diagnosis and Treatment of Alcoholism*. New York: McGraw Hill.

National Institute of Alcohol Abuse and Alcoholism (1981) *Alcohol and Health: Special Report to the U.S. Congress*. Washington D.C.: U.S. Government Printing Office.

Pattison EM Sobell MB and Sobell LC (eds) (1977) *Emerging Concepts of Alcohol Dependence*. New York: Springer.

Robinson D (ed) (1979) *Alcohol Problems: Reviews, Research and Recommendations*. London: Macmillan.

Royal College of Psychiatrists (1979) *Alcohol and Alcoholism, Report of a Special Committee*. London: Tavistock.

Schukit MA (1979) *Drug and Alcohol Abuse: A Clinical Guide to Diagnosis and Treatment*. New York: Plenum Medical.

Sherlock S (ed) (1982) *Alcohol and Disease*. London: Churchill Livingstone.

PART I
BACKGROUND TO
UNDERSTANDING

Chapter 1
Causes of Excessive Drinking

That a single, isolated cause should ever exist for a person's excessive drinking is unthinkable. There is always a multiplicity of causes. Not only do several causal factors operate at any one time, but present causes influence drinking behaviour which was shaped by factors in the past. It would be wrong therefore to interpret the reasons for excessive drinking discussed in this chapter as mutually exclusive influences. It is necessary to see these factors as interactive both in cross-section of time and longitudinally.

EXCESSIVE DRINKING FOR THE DRUG EFFECT

That alcohol is a drug which has the capacity at least in the short term to remove or allay wide varieties of unpleasant feelings, is vital to understanding why some people drink heavily. Those feelings can sometimes be given labels, for instance, anxiety or depression. Frequently, however, the unpleasant states which the person habitually experiences cannot easily be given conventional labels, although they may still be potent reasons for that individual's drinking. Life may seem boring or unrewarding, suffused with a sense of emptiness, or there may be a chronically uneasy feeling of frustration and restlessness. For the person who is insecure or who doubts his own worth, drinking may temporarily remove these feelings. Feelings of masculinity and power can be enhanced by intoxication. The person who is drinking too much is frequently using alcohol either as a drug to alter his perception of a world which he finds difficult, or to alleviate feelings about himself with which he finds it difficult to live.

Unfortunately, if alcohol is to produce any of these wanted effects it is likely to be needed in quantities which will exceed safe drinking, and as alcohol only gives temporary relief the dose must be frequently repeated. But this short-term respite from unpleasant feelings can indeed be gratifying, and it is no use trying to persuade that person otherwise. Not

13

only is there the drawback that alcohol has to be taken in rather large quantities to sustain the wanted effects, but tolerance develops to alcohol so that ever greater quantities have to be consumed to achieve the desired ends. Furthermore, unwanted effects may then also come into play which exacerbate all the pre-existing troubles and defeat the initial objects. Excessive drinking can be the cause of 'bad nerves'; a person's drunken behaviour can itself make the world a hostile place and the consequences of his drinking may provide good reason for him to feel thwarted and a failure. The problems thus become circular.

Within the general theme of drinking for drug effect, a number of different reasons for the drinker finding alcohol attractive must now be separately identified.

(a) Personality

Some people may have character traits which make them easily anxious, or they may habitually be prone to feelings of depression. The list of such possible traits is extensive. What is needed is a willingness when assessing each individual patient to work out with him an understanding of why alcohol may be functional for relief of his particular constellation of difficulties.

In taking the view that a frequent cause of alcoholism lies in such aspects of personality, it is not being implied that all alcoholics suffer from 'neurosis' or 'personality disorder', nor that gross aberration in personality is either a necessary or a sufficient cause for development of excessive drinking. The sort of traits which are being discussed are only exaggertions of common facets of personality, and in every patient strengths and resources of character must also be taken into account. Sometimes, however, excessive drinking can develop in a person whose psychological constitution is very grossly disturbed, although even then it is necessary to understand that person individually and see what alcohol may do to relieve his psychological distress, rather than retreating to labels such as 'inadequate personality' or 'psychopath', which foreclose understanding. Assessment of personality is discussed again in Chapter 9, when the initial case assessment is considered in detail.

(b) Mental illness

Almost every type of mental illness may in some circumstances contribute to a person's beginning to drink heavily. Depressive illness and anxiety states can be predisposing, while hypomania, schizophrenia when it is accompanied by anxiety, and the pathological jealousy syndrome with its attendant anxious distress, all provide instances of conditions which generate mood disturbance and which can on occasion lead to excessive drinking. The importance of underlying psychiatric illnesses is discussed at greater length in Chapter 5.

(c) Distressful situations

A person may be anxious because he has a heightened tendency to anxiety as a character trait, or he may be anxious because of the mood disturbance consequent on a mental illness, and these are the two possibilities which have just been discussed. But a third possibility is that a person is put in a *situation* which produces distress. What constitutes a stressful situation for a particular person will be highly dependent on his personality, and stress may on occasion precipitate a depressive illness. A rather typical story is that of the man who is working long hours and carrying heavy responsibility but whose business has taken such a turn that he is now constantly warding off the threat of failure. Unprepared retirement, with its sudden emptiness of purpose, can also be a very stressful situation which may be met by drinking. A woman who has put everything into her maternal role and finds life depressingly empty when her children leave home may seek to repair her feelings by use of alcohol. A person locked in an unhappy marriage or someone who is widowed provide other instances of people in situations which carry risk of drinking. Such risks are especially threatening when there is a lack of alternative supports, a lack of more positive ways of dealing with things, or when there is some vulnerability in the personality. What is needed to bring on the drinking is usually a co-incidence of factors, with the stressful circumstances one part.

EXCESSIVE DRINKING FOR PSYCHODYNAMIC REASONS

Not only is alcohol a substance which may be used excessively because of its treacherously beneficent drug effects, but drinking may also have very important symbolic and subconscious meanings. It may be part of a play in which the drinker is caught up – a sort of stage property – and drinking may be repeatedly involved in important dynamic transactions between that person and others in his life. Varieties of such plays are infinite, but here is a woman with a drinking problem talking about her childhood.

> I can't think how I ever took to drinking myself when I remember what I went through in childhood. I hated the smell of the stuff. My father was more often drunk than sober, and my mother was stark terrified of him, would hide us away when she heard him coming home. What do I go and do? I follow exactly in his footsteps. I'm as nasty when drunk as ever my Dad used to be.

Psychodynamic meanings of excessive drinking will be further discussed in Chapter 16, in relation to formal psychotherapy.

EXCESSIVE DRINKING AND ENVIRONMENTAL INFLUENCES

What is under discussion here are not the environmental pressures which engender stress but rather those socio-cultural, economic, or immediate environmental factors which give approval to heavy drinking or put alcohol directly in front of the individual. These influences may be those of the childhood home, or of general cultural expectations which the adult has adopted as governing his attitude towards drinking. The immediate drinking influences of the job or the leisure environment, or other drinking pressures in the here and now may also be very relevant.

To understand any adult's use of alcohol it is certainly necessary to take note of his attitudes to drinking which his particular culture inculcated. His culture may for instance have taught that 'a real man' is 'a good drinker', while a man who drinks moderately or is an abstainer is suspect. When that person moves from his original culture to another part of the country or goes abroad, he takes these attitudes with him, while at the same time in the new environment he may be freed from previously controlling social and cultural influences. The national per capita alcohol consumption (the 'liquor supply') will broadly correlate with the incidence of alcohol-related problems, and this is a very important message for Public Health.

Take as an example the young Irishman who has grown up in a village where men are expected to drink and occasional drunkenness is not much disapproved of; until a rather late marriage (and even after marriage), the bar is the place where any man is likely to be found outside working hours.

But there is a limit to drinking set by low wages and there are the constraints of living in a rural community where everyone has an eye on his cousin's behaviour. If that man then emigrates to London, works on a building site and earns a wage which puts money in his pocket beyond any previous expectations, while at the same time he escapes from the scrutiny of the village to a world where employers, workmates and landladies are changing figures who do not provide any substitute system of support or control, it is hardly to be wondered that he is now a candidate for alcoholism. This is not to suggest that cultural predisposition will ever be the sole cause of heavy drinking. In the example just given, it is clear that present circumstances as well as culture of origin are operative. Personality will then often further interact, and obviously a range of factors must account for the fact that not everyone from a culture which is permissive towards heavy drinking is going to drink excessively. Family influences in so far as they may affect drinking through dynamic processes have already been mentioned, but the family is also a transmitter of cultural attitudes.

As regards influences in the patient's adult life which may be especially conductive to heavy drinking, occupation can play an important role. The job may make alcohol directly and cheaply accessible, or something about the style of life which that occupation entails may make drinking specially likely. Risks are obviously attached to working in a bar or any other setting where drink is sold, or in a distillery or brewery or any place where drink is manufactured and 'breakages' are countenanced as one of the fringe benefits. The restaurateur may drink heavily himself and ensure that his invaluable chef always has a bottle for the pouring, while the kitchen porter expects to get the dregs from other peoples' glasses. The pub pianist is stood drinks, which are lined up on the top of his piano. People who work in the entertainment world are often at risk, and in many occupations the bar may be the place to make useful contacts. The sales-man may see entertaining as essential to his obtaining business and he may drink along with his clients. The executive may enjoy an expense account and part of the prestige of his job may be a cocktail cabinet in his own room, while the directors' dining-room can encourage lunch-time drink-ing. Big wages, unusual working hours, much time spent waiting around and in London the opening times of Fleet Street pubs mean that people in the printing industry may encounter special drinking pressures. Journalists seem to be particularly at risk, and also casual labourers, who may be easily caught up in an environment conducive to drinking.

Members of the armed forces may be vulnerable, especially on retirement when they are suddenly freed from a structured set of social controls but with a pension and a taste for drinking. Medical doctors and merchant seamen are both prone to alcoholism. Anyone who is posted to work abroad in a locality where alcohol is relatively cheap may begin to drink more heavily. The list can be extended almost endlessly, for example, the street photographer who when it rains will retreat to the nearest pub for shelter and conviviality.

Leisure habits also deserve enquiry. The exposure may be as obvious as the fact that a patient centres his leisure on playing darts and is a member of a team which tours from pub to pub. His cricket or his football or his bowling may also be a focus for drinking. Clubs of every variety may be influences towards heavy drinking – the political club, the work club, the Prison Officers' club, the club in St James's, and so on. Drinking may be written into the social life of the student, with the Fraternity House or the bar in the Students' Union the hub of social activities. A family may change its drinking habits because of a new circle of friends, new patterns of entertaining, a different group of people with whom to play cards. But it is well to remember that the heavy-drinking barman may be behind the bar for reasons quite other than accident; he may have taken the job because he was already a heavy drinker, and working in a pub is for him as much a symptom of alcoholism as a cause of drinking.

FAILURE IN CONTROLS

That excessive drinking can be due not only to influences which excite drinking but also in part to a failure in controlling influences has already been illustrated by the example of the young Irishman coming to London. The same considerations are equally relevant to many other situations – the student suddenly freed from the constraints of home, the retired Petty Officer freed from naval discipline, and so on. That urbanization and rapid cultural change can overthrow old social conventions was noted in the Introduction.

The same theme arises again in relation to personality. The origins of a particular patient's drinking may in part lie in his character being such as generally not to give him very certain control over his own behaviour. This trait may be an extension of normal personality variation, and the patient may simply be a person of large appetites who enjoys his pleasures in large quantities and who does not care very much for tomorrow's consequences – his friends see him as a jolly extrovert and a good fellow. Alternatively, the personality development may be more obviously abnormal. We are seeing perhaps someone who has great difficulty in getting along with society because his sense of responsibility is in many ways subtly or grossly impaired.

A further instance of a situation where impairment of controlling influences can be important is mental retardation or organic brain damage due to any cause, but this is an issue which will be dealt with more fully in Chapter 5.

GENETIC INFLUENCES

Research on the genetics of drinking and alcoholism suggests that inheritance must not be discounted, but its influence depends on what other additional factors are operating to protect that individual from excessive drinking or to encourage heavy drinking. To talk about the percentage contribution of genetics in abstract terms is unreal. Inheritance will in most circumstances play rather a small part and parental example is generally more important than parental genes. But there may be other circumstances in which heredity is more potent, though the mode of operation may be through inheritance of a depressive tendency or high anxiety levels, rather than a direct transmission of a taste for alcohol or a metabolic predisposition.

EXCESSIVE DRINKING AS CIRCULAR PROCESS

When a person has a serious drinking problem, the reasons for his drinking may in part be self-perpetuating. If, for instance, a woman has lost her home, is ostracized by former friends and can only find companionship in the pub, any alternative to continued drinking may be hard to find. An extreme example of the same process is the destitute man who believes that a homeless and drifting life is the only existence to which he can adjust, that prison is a familiar and not objectionable place, and that the bottle-gang sitting out in the park is the only group which will welcome him when he comes out of gaol. Alcoholism can narrow the social alternatives to being an alcoholic, and this not only because of damages to social competence which drinking has directly effected, but also because of the way everyone now reacts to this person; no one is keen to give a job to someone with his record.

The circular process can involve psychological as well as social factors. The alcoholic can become damaged in his self-esteem, convinced of his worthlessness, caught up in a sense of guilt, profoundly pessimistic and of course clinically depressed. Drinking and its consequences engender these feelings, and then alcohol is used because there seems to be no other way of dealing with these same feelings.

Perpetuation of excessive drinking can also result from the brain damage caused by drinking. When a patient has gross alcoholic brain damage, the existence of this circular process may be sadly obvious. At the extreme he is someone who now cannot be trusted with a penny in his pocket and who will get hopelessly drunk the minute he leaves hospital. But minor degrees of alcoholic brain damage which are more difficult to detect may also be of importance in this regard.

And an enormously important cause of drinking perpetuating excessive drinking is the development of the dependence syndrome (Chapter 2). Whatever the complex of factors which originally led that person into heavy drinking, there is then something which can be seen as having a dynamic of its own.

BURNT-OUT CAUSES AND EXPERIENCES WHICH LIE DORMANT

Under this heading two rather subtly contrasting aspects of causation must be briefly noted. Firstly there is the type of case where the drinking is in its origins a legacy of the past but is now perpetuated by present influences. For instance, a woman who during early adulthood found herself handicapped by her shyness used alcohol to cope with these feelings. Seen 15 years later she is alcohol-dependent, and the dependence and many life circumstances are perpetuating her drinking. She may state that she is drinking because of her shyness, but if she ceases to drink she may be surprised to find that she has to a considerable extent matured out of that problem. Similarly, a patient who started to drink many years previously because of phobic symptoms may be surprised to find that when he stops drinking he can travel on buses and underground trains much more easily than he ever expected. A depressive illness, from which a patient has since completely recovered may also be an important reason for him becoming dependent on alcohol.

A second and very different situation is where, for instance, a man whose marriage breaks up and who is certainly not at that time a heavy drinker seems with rather surprising rapidity to raise his drinking to a high level. Questioning may then reveal that 10 years previously, and before he married and settled down, he had been in the merchant navy and had gone through long periods when he was drinking very heavily indeed and on the edge of dependence. It is as if being a drinker is a learnt skill which, like riding a bicycle, when once learnt lies dormant; the bicycle can be put away for years but it is usually easy to get on it and ride again.

CAUSES AND THEIR IMPLICATIONS FOR THERAPY

The precise manner in which an understanding of how this or that cause (or the interaction of causes) may be translated into implications for therapy will be discussed at many places in later chapters of this book. What must, however, be immediately apparent is that if the individual's drinking can result from such a variety and interplay of influences in the environment and aspects of personality, from needs for self-medication and from dynamic meanings given to alcohol, from forces in past and present, from primary and self-perpetuating processes, then a treatment approach which is narrowly conceived in terms of such simple propositions as, for example, alcoholism is *always* rooted in personality disorder, *always* due to lack of social skills or *always* the result of loneliness, is likely to be inadequate and misconceived.

REFERENCES

Barnes GE (1979) The alcoholic personality: a re-analysis of the literature. *Journal of Studies on Alcohol*, **40**, 571–634.
Blane HT and Chafetz ME (eds) (1978) *Youth, Alcohol and Social Policy*. New York: Plenum.
Brenner MH (1975) Trends in alcohol consumption and associated illnesses: some effects of economic changes. *American Journal of Public Health*, **65**, 1279–1292.
Bruun K, Edwards G, Lumio M *et al* (1975) *Alcohol Control Policies in Public Health Perspective*. Helsinki: Finnish Foundation for Alcohol Studies.
Cahalan D (1970) *Problem Drinkers*. San Francisco: Jossey-Bass.
Cahalan D and Crossley HM (1969) *American Drinking Practices*. New Brunswick: Rutgers Center of Alcohol Studies.

Cappell H (1975) An evaluation of tension models of alcohol consumption. In: Gibbins RJ, Israel Y and Kalant H (eds) *Recent Advances in Alcohol and Drug Problems*, Vol. 2. pp 177–210. New York: Wiley.

Edwards G (1971) Public health implications of liquor control. *Lancet*, **2**, 424–425.

Goodwin DW (1976) *Is Alcoholism Hereditary?* New York: Oxford University Press.

Heath DB (1976) Anthropological perspectives on the social biology of alcohol: an introduction to the literature. In: Kissin B and Begleiter H (eds) The Biology of Alcoholism. Vol. 4: *Social Aspects of Alcoholism*, pp 37–76. New York: Plenum.

Heath D (1980) A critical review of the sociocultural model of alcohol use. In : *Normative Approaches to the Prevention of Alcohol Abuse and Alcoholism*, Research Monograph No. 3, pp 1–18. Rockville: U.S. Department of Health, Education and Welfare.

Jessor R and Jessor S (1975) Adolescent development and the onset of drinking. *Journal of Studies on Alcohol*, **36**, 27–51.

McAndrew C and Edgerton RB (1969) *Drunken Comportment*. Chicago: Aldine.

McClelland DC, Davies WN, Kalin R *et al* (1972) *The Drinking Man*. New York: Free Press.

McCord W and McCord J (1960) *Origins of Alcoholism*. Stanford: Stanford University Press.

Mules JE, Hague WH and Dudley DL (1977) Life change: its perception and alcohol addiction. *Journal of Studies on Alcohol*, **38**, 487–493.

Plant MA (1979) *Drinking Careers: Occupations, Drinking Habits and Drinking Problems*. London: Tavistock.

Robins LN (1960) *Deviant Children Grown Up*. Baltimore: Williams and Wilkins.

Schmidt W (1977) Public health perspectives on alcohol problems with special reference to Canada. *Canadian Journal of Public Health*, **68**, 382–388.

Shield J. (1977) Genetics and alcoholism. In: Edwards G and Grant M (eds) *Alcoholism: New Knowledge and New Responses*, pp 117–135. London: Croom Helm.

Storm T and Cutler R (1975) Alcohol consumption and personal resources: a general hypothesis and some implications. *Journal of Studies on Alcohol*, **36**, 917–924.

Chapter 2
The Alcohol Dependence Syndrome

The ability to recognize the alcohol dependence syndrome is vital to clinical work, but a mechanistic approach to this diagnosis is quite insufficient. Dependence cannot be conceived as 'not present' or 'present', with the diagnostic task then completed. The skill lies in being able to recognize the subtleties of symptomatology which will reveal not only whether this condition is there at all but, if it exists, the degree of its development. What has then also to be learnt is how the syndrome's manifestations are being moulded in any particular instance by personality, by immediate environmental influence, or by wide cultural forces. There are certain basic themes but, as has been stressed in the Introduction, it is the ability to recognize and understand the variations on these themes that constitutes the real art.

Dependence fundamentally means an altered relationship between a person and his drinking. A man starts to drink for many reasons and when he is dependent, many of these reasons will still pertain; they are not wiped out because of the superadded fact of the dependence. But the dependence now provides reasons for drinking which are truly superadded, and which may dominate the many preceding reasons for drinking and heavy drinking. Dependence becomes a self-perpetuating behaviour.

If the therapist cannot recognize *degrees* of dependence, he will not be able to fit his approach to the particular patient, and sometimes he may then retreat into seeing 'addiction to alcohol' as a fixed entity from which all patients with drinking problems are presumed to suffer, for whom the universal goal must be total abstinence, and the treatment which is offered universally intensive. The needed skill is the development of a discriminating judgement which is able in each case to sense out the degree of dependence, identify the rational treatment goal for that particular person, and propose the treatment fitted to that particular person's problem.

How is dependence to be recognized? Rather than immediately presenting a case history, it is more useful first to analyze the individual elements which go to make up the total syndrome and to consider the recognition of each one of these elements in turn. This approach is taken only for the sake of clarity; when each element has been looked at separately, the picture has to be put together, and a case history will then be used to illustrate the picture in the round.

INDIVIDUAL ELEMENTS OF THE DEPENDENCE SYNDROME

NARROWING OF REPERTOIRE

The ordinary drinker's consumption and choice of drink will vary from day to day and from week to week; he may have beer at lunch on one day, nothing to drink on another, share a bottle of wine at dinner one night, and then go to a party on a Saturday and have a lot to drink. His drinking is patterned by varying internal cues and external circumstances.

At first, a person becoming caught up in heavy drinking may often widen his repertoire and also the range of cues that signal drinking. As dependence advances, the cues are increasingly related to relief or avoidance of alcohol withdrawal, and his personal drinking repertoire becomes increasingly narrowed. The dependent person begins to drink the same whether it is a workday, weekend, or holiday, the nature of the company or his own mood makes less and less difference. Questioning may distinguish earlier and later stages of dependence by the degree to which the repertoire is narrowed. With advanced dependence, the drinking may become scheduled to a strict daily timetable to maintain a high blood alcohol. More careful questioning will, however, show that even when dependence is well established, some capacity for variation remains. Change in personal circumstances, such as a new job or a different marriage, may for a time constrain the drinking. The syndrome must be pictured as subtle and plastic rather than as something set hard, but as dependence advances the patterns tend to become increasingly hardened.

SALIENCE OF DRINKING

The stereotyping of the drinking pattern as dependence advances leads to the individual giving priority to maintaining his alcohol intake. The wife's distressed scolding – once effective – is later neutralized by the drinker as evidence of her lack of understanding. Income which had previously to serve many needs now supports the drinking habit as first demand. Gratification of the need for drink may become even more important for the patient with liver damage than considerations of survival – 'a short life and a merry one'. Diagnostically, the progressive change in the salience given to alcohol is important, rather than behaviour at any one time. Typically, the patient relates that he used to be proud of his house but now the paint is peeling off, used always to take the children to football matches but now spends no time with them, used to have rather rigid moral standards but will now beg, borrow, or steal to obtain money for alcohol.

INCREASED TOLERANCE TO ALCOHOL

Alcohol is a drug to which the central nervous system (CNS) develops tolerance. The precise mechanisms are not yet known, but there is some sort of adjustment by the brain cells to continued alcohol exposure. Metabolic tolerance (increased liver clearance) makes a relatively trivial contribution. Patients themselves report on tolerance in terms of 'having a good head for liquor' or 'being able to drink the other man under the table'. Clinically, tolerance is shown by the dependent person being able to sustain an alcohol intake and go about his business at blood alcohol levels that would incapacitate the non-tolerant drinker. This does not mean that his functioning is unimpaired – he will be a dangerous driver – but because of his tolerance he will (unfortunately) still be able to drive.

Cross–tolerance will extend to some other drugs, such as barbiturates and minor tranquillizers, which means that the person who has become tolerant to alcohol will also have a brain tolerance to these drugs and vice versa. The rate of development of tolerance is variable, but the heavy drinker who is not dependent can manifest considerable tolerance. In later stages of dependence, for reasons which are unclear, the individual begins to lose his previously acquired tolerance and then becomes incapacitated by quantities of alcohol which he could previously handle; for the first time he may fall down drunk in the street.

REPEATED WITHDRAWAL SYMPTOMS

These vary with the degree of dependence. At first, symptoms are inter-mittent and mild; they cause little incapacity, and one symptom may be experienced without others. As dependence increases, so do the frequency and the severity of the symptoms. When the picture is fully developed, typically the patient has severe multiple symptoms every morning on waking; these symptoms may waken him even in the middle of the night. Questioning often reveals that the severely dependent patient experiences mild withdrawal symptoms (which he recognizes as such) at any time during the day when his alcohol level falls. Complete withdrawal is therefore not necessary to precipitate these symptoms.

To incur withdrawal symptoms an individual generally has to drink about half to one bottle of spirits a day for several years, although there are many exceptions to that imprecise rule, and in either direction. The patient often remembers rather exactly the dating of the period when he first began to experience withdrawal, and there is no necessary association with a sudden increase in alcohol intake.

The spectrum of symptoms is wide and includes tremor, nausea, sweating, sensitivity to sound (hyperacusis), ringing in the ears (tinnitus), itching, muscle cramps, mood disturbance, sleep disturbance, hallucinations, *grand mal* seizures, and the fully developed picture of delirium tremens. There are four key symptoms:

(i) Tremor

This nicely illustrates that it is *range* of experience that is essential to the report, rather than recording in the case-notes simply that the patient does or does not experience withdrawal shakes. Shakiness may have been experienced only once or twice, or very intermittently and mildly, or it may be experienced every morning and to a degree which is incapacitating, or with many intervening intensities and frequencies. As well as the hands shaking, there may be an awareness of facial tremor or, indeed, of the whole body shaking. The therapist has to cultivate an awareness of something equivalent to the Beaufort scale for wind strength and look out for the patient saying that he rattles his morning teacup against the saucer, that he has exchanged an ordinary razor for an electric razor or that, in the extreme case, he is forced to rely on the kindness of the barmaid to lift the day's first pint to his lips.

(ii) Nausea

The patient who is simply asked whether he vomits may well deny it. His experience, however, may be that if he attempts to clean his teeth in the morning he will make himself retch; or he may never eat breakfast because he knows it would be too risky. A common story is that most of the first drink of the day is regularly vomited back; at the extreme, the patient may keep a bucket by his bed.

(iii) Sweating

This may be dramatic: the patient may wake regularly in the early hours of the morning with soaking sweats. At the earlier stages of dependence, he may report no more than feeling clammy.

(iv) Mood disturbance

This symptom of withdrawal is important in its own right, and is not just a reaction to the physical distress. At the earlier stages of dependence, patients may phrase the experience in terms of 'being a bit edgy' or 'nerves not too good', but when dependence is fully developed they may use vivid descriptions to indicate a state of appalling agitation and depression. Often the anxiety seems to be characterized by a frightened reaction to loud noises or traffic (sometimes with a phobia of crossing the road), a fear of a friend coming up suddenly from behind, fright at 'the twigs on the trees rubbing together'. The over-sensitivity can be like that of a gouty patient who fears a fly alighting on his toe.

RELIEF OR AVOIDANCE OF WITHDRAWAL SYMPTOMS BY FURTHER DRINKING

In the earliest stages the patient may be aware that at lunch-time the first drink of the day 'help to straighten him up a bit'. At the other extreme a patient may require a drink every morning before he gets out of bed, as a matter of desperate need. As with withdrawal symptoms, relief drinking must not be conceived as only a morning event; the patient may wake in the middle of the night for the drink which will abort incipient withdrawal, and he may be well aware that if he has to go three or four hours without a drink during the day, the next drink is valued especially for its relief effect. Relief drinking is probably cued not only by frank withdrawal but also by minimal symptoms of subacute withdrawal, which signal worse distress if drink is not then taken. The dependent individual may try to maintain a steady alcohol level which he has learnt to recognize as comfortably above the danger level for withdrawal, and to this extent his drinking is cued by withdrawal avoidance as well as withdrawal relief.

Clues to the degree of a patient's dependence are often given by the small details he provides of the circumstances and timing of the first drink of the day, and his attitudes towards it. If he has time to get up, have a bath, dress and read the paper before that drink, then dependence is not very advanced. A housewife who finishes her morning chores before having her first drink is at a different stage of dependence from the woman who is pouring whisky into her first cup of tea. Someone engaged in relief drinking may have ritualized the procedure. He will go to the early-morning pub at 7 am, go straight up to the bar, where the barman will know immediately to give him his pint of cider, which he will grab at clumsily with both hands and drink down fast. He may go to the lavatory and vomit some of it back, but he can then drink a pint of beer at greater leisure, and he will know that within 20 or 30 minutes of walking into that pub 'the drink will have cured him'. The patient often relates that he knows the exact quantity of alcohol required for this cure and the exact time interval for the alcohol to take effect, and he reports also that the cure is repeatedly so complete as to be almost miraculous. Sometimes he reports what is presumably a conditioned effect: the mere fact of having a glass in the hand gives him some immediate relief.

That the dependence syndrome is a plastic condition rather than something immutable is brought out again by the way this particular element is shaped by social and personal factors. For the labourer the idea of keeping drink in the house may be so against subcultural expectations that he will always wait for the pubs to open (perhaps travelling specially to an early-morning market pub), rather than 'keep a drink indoors'. The man of rigid personality may endure considerable withdrawal for some hours rather than take a drink before lunch. Fully to understand what the patient reports always requires that these shaping factors are taken into account.

SUBJECTIVE AWARENESS OF COMPULSION TO DRINK

The conventional phrases used to describe the dependent person's subjective experience are not altogether satisfactory. For instance, awareness of 'loss of control' is said to be crucial to understanding abnormal drinking, and patients sometimes say, 'If I have one or two, I'll go on', or 'If I go into the pub, promises don't mean anything', or 'Once I've really got the taste of it, I'm away'. It is unclear, however, whether the experience is truly one of losing control rather than one of deciding not to exercise control. Control is probably best seen as variably or intermittently impaired rather than 'lost'.

Another complex experience which can too easily be wrapped up in conventional phrasing is the experience of 'craving'. The patient may describe it in unambiguous terms – he may be 'gasping for a drink'. The subjective interpretation of the withdrawal may, however, be much influenced by environment, and the patient who is withdrawing on a ward may not experience any particular craving. Cues for craving may include the feeling of intoxication, as well as incipient or developed withdrawal, mood (anger, depression, elation) or situational cues (being in a pub or with a particular friend).

Perhaps the key experience can best be described as a compulsion to drink (analogous, say, to the hand-washing of a compulsive neurosis), and the subjective experience of dependence may come close to fulfilling the classic psychiatric criteria for a diagnosis of compulsion. The desire for a further drink is seen as irrational, the desire is resisted, but the further drink is taken. The patient who is in a withdrawal state (or partial withdrawal) may report that he is compulsively ruminating on alcohol and that he has hit on the strategy of blocking these ruminations by bringing in other lines of thought. It is this feeling of being in the grip of something foreign, irrational and unwanted, which for the severely dependent patient seems to be the private experience that is so difficult to convey.

REINSTATEMENT AFTER ABSTINENCE

Patients usually find abstinence surprisingly easy to maintain, especially in a hospital with the usual cues for drinking removed. If later they again begin to drink, relapse into the previous stage of the dependence syndrome then follows an extremely variable time course. Typically, the patient who had only a moderate degree of dependence will take weeks or months to reinstate it, perhaps pulling back once or twice on the way. A severely dependent patient typically reports that he is again 'hooked' within a few days of starting to drink, though even here there are exceptions: on the first day he may become abnormally drunk and be surprised to find that he has lost his tolerance. But within a few days he is again experiencing severe withdrawal symptoms and drinking to relieve them, the subjective experience of compulsion is reinstated, and his drinking is back in the old, stereotyped pattern. A syndrome which had taken many years to develop can be fully reinstated within perhaps 72 hours of drinking, and this is one of the most puzzling features of the condition.

A 45-year-old window cleaner gave the following story. He had grown up in an old working-class area of his city, and identified himself with its culture. He saw the pub as being an essential part of that world, perhaps almost its centre. Before he had left school, he and his mates were going into pubs, and to brazen out the age question in the face of the barman's suspicions was proof of manhood. He had never worked other than as a window cleaner, and he said that most of his trade was picked up at the bar. When it rained, the pub was the obvious place to retreat. He was married with three children but left the entire management of the home to his wife. Everything therefore was so set up as to enable a man who 'always liked his beer' to sustain a minimum daily intake of 10 to 15 pints as easily compatible with his pattern of life.

About six years before he presented for treatment, he had begun for the first time to notice that his hands were a bit shaky in the morning – 'not too good for the job'. He started to drop into the pub immediately at 11 am opening and would have a couple of pints, which would relieve the shakiness and generally make him feel better. His daily intake of beer which had gradually increased over the years was now about 20 pints each day, but he never took alcoholic drink other than beer. The experience of withdrawal symptoms seems to have intensified fairly rapidly over a period of about 12 months, and he was able to identify a transitional phase as occurring five to six years prior to presenting for help, and separating his previous lifetime of 'liking the beer' from the last five years of 'being bad like I am now'.

He had now for three years experienced severe withdrawal symptoms every morning, and it was the retching and vomiting which worried him particularly – 'Alright when I'm lying flat, but as soon as I sit up in bed it starts, have to rush to the toilet, heave my heart out and it just keeps on like that.' He had heavy night sweats.

He did not at first directly mention the mood component in the withdrawal experience, and words like 'anxiety' or 'depression' were probably not part of his ordinary vocabulary. But he 'felt bad, sort of butterflies', and on closer questioning it was clear that each morning he was experiencing very unpleasant mood disturbance, although he did not spontaneously differentiate between physical and mental symptoms; it was all a matter of 'feeling bad, more than terrible'. Tremor was such that 'I'll knock over a milk bottle'. Withdrawal seemed only to be a morning experience, presumably because he otherwise kept his blood alcohol level constantly topped up.

Evidence for drinking to relieve withdrawal was certainly present, but here a colouring due to class-related attitudes was to be seen. He never kept drink in his own home, and this was a taboo which despite the intensity of his dependence, he was entirely unwilling to break. So far as he was concerned, 'bringing drink indoors' would have been a depravity. He therefore tried to stay in bed almost until the pubs opened, and would then be in the pub exactly at opening time. His needs were so well-known that the barman would have two separate pints of bitter drawn and waiting for him. He drank these pints more or less straight down, and during the first half-hour he would have a third pint. But by the end of the first 30 minutes he was feeling much better, and within the hour he was 'guaranteed right as rain'.

Evidence for drinking to relieve withdrawal was certainly present, but here a colouring due to class-related attitudes was to be seen. He never kept drink in his own home, and this was a taboo which despite the intensity of his dependence, he was entirely unwilling to break. So far as he was concerned, 'bringing drink indoors' would have been a depravity. He therefore tried to stay in bed almost until the pubs opened, and would then be in the pub exactly at opening time. His needs were so well-known that the barman would have two separate pints of bitter drawn and waiting for him. He drank these pints more or less straight down, and during the first half-hour he would have a third pint. But by the end of the first 30 minutes he was feeling much better, and within the hour he was 'guaranteed right as rain'.

The increased tolerance to alcohol had obviously existed for many years before this man developed the dependence syndrome; no naive drinker would be able to drink five or six pints of beer at lunch-time and then do an afternoon's work (and climb a ladder), as this man had done most of his working life.

The narrowing of drinking repertoire by the time he sought treatment had become extreme. From 11 am to 2.30 pm he was in the pub, and drank 10 pints of beer during that time. He came home and slept, returned to the pub at 6 pm, and drank another eight pints up to 10 pm, when he would always go home and take the dog out for a walk. He would, though, get back to the pub before closing time, and have a final two pints. Sometimes when he was a bit short of money his daily intake would fall a little below the regular 20 pints. There had been occasions when he was ill with influenza and had spent a week or 10 days at home, and he had then been completely off drink (with some hallucinatory experience during the first few days). Otherwise the drinking had followed this invariable pattern for the last three years.

The salience of drink-seeking over other considerations was witnessed by a number of features. Work would now have got in the way of his drinking, so he had largely stopped working, and drinking had really become his occupation. Provided he had money for his beer, nothing else mattered. he had previously always prided himself on 'giving the wife a good wage'; she now went out to work, and he took from her whatever money he could by wheedling or demand. He would 'take the rent money', and had broken into his own gas meter on more than one occasion. He had cashed an insurance policy. His drinking was also financed by sickness or unemployment benefits.

The subjective awareness of compulsion was very much sensed. He contrasted 'the old days' with his present. In the old days if there was a job to do, he went out and did it, and 'I drank but I didn't have to drink – now I have to drink'. He had often recently promised himself to cut down on his drinking and get back to regular work, but 'it's no good, the beer's really got a grip of me, and if I go into that pub I can't get out again. When I've got a pint, I'm thinking of the next pint.' He did not spontaneously use the word 'craving' but he was certainly aware of his great subjective need for the first drink of the day: 'If anyone stood between me and that beer I'd go mad.'

The fact that this man had on occasions been abstinent for 10 days or so because of minor illnesses made it possible to gain some information on reinstatement. As soon as he was able to get out of the house, his first walk would be back to the pub. He would tell himself that he 'wasn't going to drink in that bad way again', but full reinstatement of the whole picture nowadays only seemed to take about a week, and within two or three days of restarting his drinking he was again experiencing quite severe withdrawal symptoms. He summed things up by saying, 'Don't know what's happened really, but the drink's got on top of me.'

DEPENDENCE: INTERPRETING THE PICTURE

Given an awareness of the basic elements of the syndrome, when confronted with a history such as that given by the window cleaner, there is then the task of bringing this theoretical knowledge to bear on the understanding of a very individual story. Using that particular patient's history where appropriate as illustration, the matter can be discussed under a number of headings.

SENSITIVITY TO LANGUAGE

Casework is highly dependent on being alert towards meanings of words and nuances of phrase which are partly idiosyncratic to that one patient, but often also culturally endowed. If such alertness is neglected, a great deal of important information is passed over or misinterpreted. For people of different class or cultural backgrounds to find mutually comprehensible terms for describing subjective experience (for such an experience as compulsion there is no very satisfactory wording in common language), requires exceptional responsiveness, and a willingness to play phrasings backwards and forwards until there is a flash of mutual comprehension. The possibility of understanding will often be destroyed if such conventional terms as 'craving' or 'loss of control' are prematurely introduced. The live phrasing which is remembered from one patient's account may, though, on occasion seem immediately to reach another patient's experience, for instance, 'drinking one drink and thinking about the next one'.

ASSESSING THE COHERENCE OF THE PICTURE

The picture which emerges of any patient's experience of the dependence syndrome ought to be more or less coherent. If one element of the syndrome is well-established, another element should not be absent. For instance, if he patient reports that he is suffering from withdrawal symptoms but his recorded daily intake of alcohol is only the equivalent of eight pints of beer (say 150g absolute alcohol), the story does not fit properly together. Either some part of the information on which the picture is being built is inaccurate (the patient is perhaps under-reporting his drinking), or morning symptoms of some other origin are being interpreted as alcohol withdrawal symptoms. Inconsistencies are there-fore valuable observations in their own right. They should alert the diagnostician to make a closer investigation of the case. Coexistent drug-taking may often distort the picture. Sometimes a seeming inconsistency is accounted for by the strong influence of some special aspect of person-ality or culture, which are matters dealt with more fully below.

INFLUENCE OF CULTURE AND ENVIRONMENT

The dependence picture given by the window cleaner is typical of alcohol dependence as manifested by an Englishman from that particular social background. As ever, there were personal as well as social causes for the drinking, but the social factors were in this instance enormously important determinants of the years of heavy drinking which were the prelude to dependence, and these same factors then followed through to shape aspects of the dependence syndrome. For instance, a class-related insistence on not drinking in the house meant that a degree of dependence which would normally have resulted in drink being brought home and kept by the bed for morning relief was characterized instead by the patient's waiting for the pubs to open. True to class drinking habits, he drank only beer, despite the uncomfortable fluid intake. His stereotyped dependent drinking (like all his previous drinking) was centred round the pub, and pub opening hours. His whole present drinking pattern can be seen as an extension of ordinary 'pub drinking', rather than as something standing completely outside an ordinarily accepted social pattern. This man's peculiar and makeshift but real economic stability (his wife's earn-ings and the welfare benefits) also enabled his dependent drinking to be conducted in a steady fashion.

INFLUENCE OF PERSONALITY

Not much has so far been said about this man's personality, but there can be no doubt that there was play between his personality and features of his dependence. His responsiveness to cultural dictates is in itself evidence of a personality trait – he was basically a conventional person. The flat pattern of his dependent drinking, the rigidity of that narrowed drinking repertoire (the dog faithfully taken for a walk each evening), the exact daily repetition of the ritualized first two pints, might all be read as evidence of a rigid element in his temperament – he had always indeed been a very methodical window cleaner. The salience which he gave to his drinking when he had become dependent on alcohol was understandable as a simple extension of what had always been his detachment from the family; he had never really felt that responsibilities went beyond giving his wife a regular cash sum, and now he just retreated from that one obligation.

DEGREES OF DEPENDENCE

Although one element may be more or less developed than others (some-times as a result of unexplained variation or sometimes because of the impact of modifying social or personal factors), the coherent picture which emerges should be of a certain *degree* of dependence, with each element more or less in step. Thus if, as with the window cleaner, with-drawal symptoms are severe and experienced every day, it is to be expected that there will be a well-established pattern of relief drinking, with full realization that a given amount of alcohol will relieve these symptoms whithin a fixed time. Tolerance will obviously be well-developed if severe withdrawal is experienced, although around this stage in the history some evidence of declining tolerance might begin to appear. The narrowing of drinking repertoire reported by this man was commen-surate with his other symptoms, and it would, for instance, have been surprising if with this degree of dependence he had been drinking much less at weekends than on weekdays. The daily alcohol intake would be expected to be not less than 300g. The salience he accorded his drinking fitted in with the total picture. The subjective awareness of compulsion was typical of this degree of development, and if someone with this duration of severe withdrawal experience and regular intentional relief drinking did not report a sense of severe compulsion, one would assume that the history had not been taken sufficiently carefully. And quite typically, the syndrome was for him rapidly reinstated after a few days abstinence.

It is not easy to set up any absolute rules for grading the overall severity of dependence, but it would be a fair guide to say that if anyone has experienced withdrawal symptoms on a more or less daily basis for five years, and engaged in regular relief drinking in response to those symptoms over the same period (with other elements congruently developed), he will be extremely severely dependent on alcohol. If he has experienced withdrawal symptoms on no more than a few occasions, but been aware that alcohol usefully brought relief (even without intentionally bringing forward the first drink of the day), an early case of dependence must be diagnosed. Between those two extreme pictures there are many gradations, rather than fixed degrees. A history of an attack of delirium tremens is clinching evidence of severe dependence, but discussion of alcohol-related and dependence-related mental illness will be postponed to Chapter 5.

THE TIME ELEMENT

To discuss the severity of dependence inevitably introduces consideration of the significance of the time element. The longer someone has been putting himself through repeated cycles of withdrawal and relief, the more severe the dependence he will have contracted. Note has, however, also to be taken of the rapidity or gradualness of the transition between heavy drinking and dependence, and of the age at which dependence developed. The window cleaner had sustained a pattern of heavy drinking for many years before the dependence syndrome started to be seen, and this is perhaps typical of a history where the determinants of drinking are largely cultural. Why dependence should at a certain phase in his life have become manifest is unexplained, but presumably the answer lies in some as yet unexplained biological process. Whatever the underlying causes, it is however rather typical for the man with a long-standing heavy alcohol intake to be able to identify a transition period of about 12 months during which the dependence symptoms had their onset and a quickly mounting severity. With other cultures, personalities and patterns of drinking, dependence may arise earlier or later in life, after longer or shorter alcohol exposure, and may then advance with greater or lesser rapidity.

In summary, fully to understand the individual's dependence, the present picture has to be related to its evolution over time, and the determinants of that evolution identified.

DEPENDENCE: THE LATER STAGES

The therapist needs to be familiar with the pictures which can evolve of dependence in its later stages. A patient may continue to drink dependently and at a heavy level for many years, and when one sees him again after a 10-year interval the account in the old case-notes can seem, astonishingly, to be the description of the present – nothing has changed. But if the patient neither dies nor stops drinking, sooner or later the presentation is likely to evolve toward the breakdown of the old picture and a much more fragmented type of drinking.

There are a number of themes within this evolution which can be identified:

(i) Dependence gets progressively worse

We are referring here to the dependence disorder *per se,* rather than to the surround of alcohol-related disabilities which are certainly likely at this stage to occur with increasing severity. The withdrawal symptoms may have plateaued at much the same level for many years or have gradually worsened, but at a certain phase there will probably by a rapidly mounting intensity of morning distress. The patient may, for example, report an appalling experience of shakes or almost suicidal disturbance in mood each morning, and he himself speaks aghast of these agonies. The immediate morning drink is a matter of terrifying urgency. Hearing voices, seeing things, frightening half-waking dreams, may all be frequently experienced on a come-and-go basis, or the patient may experience a series of attacks of frank delirium tremens.

(ii) Gross and incapacitating intoxication becomes more common

Reference has already been made to the late-stage possibility of an actual decline in tolerance. A patient reported his experience in the following terms: 'That last year, whenever I started to drink, I got so drunk that I literally didn't know night from day, just a haze. It would get so I couldn't go into any bar because I was just an embarrassment, and I was falling over in the street, brought home by strangers.'

The loss of tolerance may at the extreme be so severe that the patient is manifestly intoxicated after only a pint or two of beer. Brain damage often underlies this picture. Gross and repeated amnesias become common. But although loss of tolerance and accompanying brain damage are usually the major factors lying behind this 'getting very drunk', other factors may also be involved, such as the fear of withdrawal leading to desperate and misjudged efforts to top up the blood alcohol, or a searching after the good feelings that alcohol used to give but no longer provides.

(iii) Drinking makes the patient feel very ill

The patient finds that he can no longer drink in his previous continuous manner because after a few days of drinking he now feels so ill that, despite the threat of withdrawal symptoms, his suffering forces him to desist. The mounting intensity of the morning withdrawal certainly contributes to this general feeling of distress, but this distress is likely to be compounded by the consequences of various alcohol-induced physical disorders, for instance, gastritis, liver disease, or chronic pancreatitis.

The total result of these various factors is that the patient moves towards a pattern of short, acute and incapacitating bouts, each of them a chaotic and devastating experience. This end-result seems in large measure to be determined by the progression of the dependence itself – by the march of incompletely understood physiological and psycho-physiological processes. However, social and environmental factors must, as ever, also be taken into the analysis: marriage break-up and the loss of every constraint and support can make for further inevitability.

MANY VARIATIONS OR A FEW SPECIES? THE JELLINEK TYPOLOGY

The window cleaner whose story was used to illustrate how understanding of the dependence syndrome can be reached provides a history of only one particular person's dependence, and it cannot adequately represent the whole range of pictures of dependence which will be encountered. There are an infinite number of ways in which the dependence syndrome and its degrees of development may be moulded in their manifestations by secondary factors; and it is not helpful to pick out particular sub-patterns and accord them the status of distinct 'species' of alcoholism. Setting up a neat and absolute listing of 'types of dependence' would go completely against the central concept of one clearly identifiable syndrome, which is moulded into different patterns by a variety of forces which have in each instance to be understood. Over time and with changing circumstances, any particular individual's presentation of the syndrome may vary greatly.

To reject the notion of 'species of alcoholism' is, however, to go against one of the accepted systems of the last 20 years or so: the Jellinek typology of alcoholism. E.M. Jellinek was an American scientist who made profoundly influential contributions to the study of alcoholism. As usually quoted and simplified, his system sets out a fivefold species categorization:

alpha alcoholism: excessive drinking for purely psychological reasons without evidence of 'tissue adaptation'.

beta alcoholism: excessive drinking which has led to tissue damage, but where there is no dependence on alcohol.

gamma alcoholism: excessive drinking where there is evidence of tolerance and withdrawal, a peaky and fluctuant alcohol intake, and marked 'loss of control'. (Jellinek saw this as the pattern typical of Anglo-Saxon countries.)

delta alcoholism: excessive drinking where there is again evidence of tolerance and withdrawal, but with a much steadier level of alcohol intake. rather than the patient manifesting 'loss of control', he would exhibit what was called 'inability to abstain'. (The pattern was seen as typical of France and of other wine-drinking countries.)

epsilon alcoholism: bout drinking, or what used to be termed dipsomania.

Jellinek's typology deserves careful scrutiny. Study of his original writing shows that his views on categorization were considerably more subtle than would be supposed from the oversimplified extracts from his thinking which later became the popular basis for a typology. For instance, the distinction he drew between gamma and delta alcoholism showed an obvious awareness of the need to take into account the shaping influence of culture. When he discussed epsilon alcoholism he noted that the picture might be the result of the fragmentation of a previous pattern of continuous drinking by the influence of Alcoholics Anonymous membership. He did not see his five-part typology as exhaustive, but said that all the other letters of the Greek alphabet might be needed in addition, and then some other alphabets besides. And yet because of its attractive simplicity, it is the typology which is widely known, with Jellinek's insistence on the arbitrariness of a restricted focus on these few patterns usually ignored.

MORE ORDERLY OR MORE CHAOTIC DEPENDENT DRINKING

Jellinek's contrasting identificates of gamma (loss of control) and delta (inability to abstain) species point to an important aspect of drinking behaviour which shows variation between cases. He was, however, describing extreme types, and today the best use of his insights is to note the dimension of variation to which his ideas potentially drew attention, rather than to accept the notion of contrasting ideal types with nothing in between.

Some alcohol-dependent patients drink predominantly in a chaotic fashion. When they start to drink they go on to a variable and uncertain upper limit of blood alcohol. Others, although suffering from alcohol dependence of similar severity, usually so order their drinking that they attain much the same high blood alcohol level every day and one with which their tolerance can cope; they do not overshoot the mark, albeit that the mark is an abnormally high one. Although it is possible to meet patients who seem to conform to one or other extreme stereotype – always losing control on the one hand, unable to abstain on the other – more careful enquiry usually reveals that, even with the seemingly clear-cut and stereotyped case, patterns are more varied than first meets the eye. A man who now appears to be drinking in a choatic fashion is only doing so since he lost his job and his marriage broke up; before then his dependence manifested itself by heavy continuous drinking through the business day, followed by armchair drinking in the evening. A man who appears to be drinking predominantly in a controlled fashion may similarly reveal that there are patches when his drinking is much more peaky and uncertain in its patterning; when his wife goes off and leaves him at home during her yearly trip to visit her parents, temporary removal of her restraining influence means that he will then drink late into the night while the money lasts, not bother to get up in the morning, not be over-concerned about work. And in addition to those cases which at initial meeting appear extreme then seldom conform closely to a stereotype when more fully analyzed, there are many cases which even at first sight are obviously presenting with a mixed pattern. The true variety of patterns will be missed if all that is available to the diagnostician's thinking is a few pigeon-holes.

MORE CONTINUOUS OR MORE INTERMITTENT DRINKING

Jellinek again picked up an obviously important dimension when he contrasted epsilon (bout) drinking with other types. But again the reality is degrees of variation, raher than any absolute contrast between dependent patients who drink unfailingly every day and those who drink unfailingly in sharply demarcated bouts.

The degree of intermittency which often will be found in reality to characterize supposedly 'continuous' drinking is surprising. Even the skid-row drinker, who is superficially pictured as someone who drinks with relentless continuity, will usually be found to have several months of more or less voluntary abstinence during any year, even leaving aside the enforced abstinences during imprisonment; he may have abstained because he was 'too sick to drink', because he had temporarily settled in a job, ot because he was living in a hostel where drinking was not allowed.

The person who at first presents with seemingly clear-cut bout drinking will often on closer questioning give a previous history of dependent drinking cast in a much more continuous pattern. That a move towards a pattern of short bouts is very common at the most advanced stages of dependence has already been noted, but bout drinking can also emerge as the predominant mode earlier on in the drinking career. Remorse, mood swing, physical distress, mounting pressure from a wife, the need to get back to work, running out of money, the general practitioner's calling at the house, Alcoholics Anonymous friends coming to the rescue, may all mean that such a person may at any stage begin intermittently to pull out of his drinking. He relapses, pulls out again – and hence 'bout drinking'.

The boutiness of the drinking is not witness to his suffering from a unique *species* of alcoholism, but to the many and complex influences which are once more moulding the presentation of the same core dependence syndrome. Careful history-taking may reveal that bouts are beginning to be more or less frequent in their occurrence, or more or less prolonged in their duration, and enquiry may then also identify the shift in the play of influences which brings these changes about. The coherence of the dependence picture should be such that the patient who is highly dependent will be able to swing his drinking repertoire only between bouts of heavy dependent drinking and intervening periods of total or near-total abstinence. The less dependent person will have bouts with hazier edges, and intervening periods of non-dependent drinking which gradually edge again towards establishment of dependence.

What has been said here about patterns of drinking seeks squarely to meet the complexity of clinical reality as it will actually be found. If the diagnostician goes about his business with open eyes he will not see what is before him in terms of a limited typology, but only in terms of great and continuously unfolding variation. However, the complexity need not be overthrowing. The clinical task is not the false simplicity of putting drinking patterns into pigeon-holes; it is, though, remarkably straightforward. The real task is to describe each individual's drinking pattern as it in reality exists, and then to try as best as possible to identify the influences which shape this pattern.

WHY AN UNDERSTANDING OF DEPENDENCE MATTERS

Having discussed the diagnosis of dependence, the manner in which degrees of the syndrome's development are to be identified, and the way in which personality and environment may shape the presentations, an obvious question then comes up – what is the practical purpose of such diagnostic work, the gain from developing this kind of diagnostic skill? The answers are several.

The realization that there exists such a condition as alcohol dependence, and an understanding of the personal implications of this diagnosis, may greatly contribute to the relief of the patient's sense of muddle and bafflement. It can contribute to a helpful framework for personal understanding, and enable him to come to terms with a condition to which he has previously reacted only with very understandable confusion. The fact that alcohol is a drug which can produce dependence – 'a drug of addiction' – often comes as a surprise to the patient's family as much as to the patient himself. The diagnosis and the accompanying understanding can then, for the family too, mean a way of restructuring a reaction to a situation which previously engendered only confusion, fear or anger. The wife begins to realize that there is something more than 'weakness of will' that has to be understood, that expecting her husband 'to drink like other people' may not be possible.

For the therapist, the utility of such knowledge lies partly in what it carries in the way of empathy for that patient's experience. The knowledge is also needed when negotiating with the patient the treatment goal for the drinking itself and the wider aspects of treatment. Therapist and patient negotiate shared understanding, and on the basis of shared understanding they work out together the best treatment approach – the therapist is not the dictator. But to operate in such a manner there must be the foundation of shared and factually correct understanding of what has to be dealt with, and a comprehension of what is meant by dependence may be an important part of the basic shared understanding. Baldly to impart no more than the diagnostic label – a sort of magisterial sentencing – is not what is meant by building up understanding. The implications of the diagnosis of dependence and its degrees for setting treatment goals and design of treatments will be taken up much more fully in subsequent chapters.

Furthermore, it would be useful health education if the public in general were aware that alcohol had dependence potential. The public need to know more of the dangers and the danger signals, what dependence can mean for themselves or someone in their family, for someone at work or someone they meet in the pub. Understanding of alcohol dependence should, without over-dramatization, become part of ordinary awareness.

DEPENDENCE IN CONTEXT

Dependence is a highly important clinical reality, and understanding of all its implications is one essential part of the therapist's competence if he is to deal with drinking problems. But nothing which is being said should be misinterpreted as implying that dependence is everything. Dependence only exists in a personal and social context, and it would be an absurd abstraction ever to see things otherwise. Furthermore, and as has already been stressed, many patients with drinking problems are not suffering from the dependence syndrome. That latter fact in itself is good reason for seeking to develop the skill to recognize the presence of dependence in any of its degrees; one needs to be able confidently to recognize when dependence is not present.

REFERENCES

Chick J (1980) Is there a unidimensional alcohol dependence syndrome? *British Journal of Addiction*, **75**, 265–280.

Criteria Committee, US National Council on Alcoholism (1972) Criteria for the diagnosis of alcoholism. *American Journal of Psychiatry*, **129**, 127–135.

Edwards G (1974) Drugs, drug dependence and the concept of plasticity. *Quarterly Journal of Studies on Alcohol*, **35**, 176–195.

Edwards G and Gross M (1976) Alcohol dependence: provisional description of a clinical syndrome. *British Medical Journal*, **1**, 1058–1061.

Hodgson R (1980) The alcohol dependence syndrome: a step in the wrong direction? A discussion of Stan Shaw's critique. *British Journal of Addiction*, **75**, 255–263.

Jellinek EM (1960) *The Disease Concept of Alcoholism*. New Haven: Hillhouse.

Jellinek EM (1952) Phases of alcohol addiction. *Quarterly Journal of Studies on Alcohol*, **13**, 673–684.

Keller M. (1972) On the loss of control phenomenon in alcoholism. *British Journal of Addiction*, **67**, 153–166.

Littleton JM (1977) The biological basis of alcoholism: some recent experimental evidence. In: Edwards G and Grant M (eds) *Alcoholism: New Knowledge and New Responses*, pp 107–116.

Shaw S (1979) A critique of the concept of the alcohol dependence syndrome. *British Journal of Addiction*, **74**, 339–348.

Stockwell R, Hodgson R, Edwards G *et al* (1979) The development of a questionnaire to measure severity of alcohol dependence. *British Journal of Addiction*, **74**, 79–87.

World Health Organisation (1981) Nomenclature and classification of drug- and alcohol-related problems: a WHO Memorandum. *Bulletin of the World Health Organisation*, **59**, 225–242.

Chapter 3
Alcoholism and the Family

Someone with a drinking problem often has family links waiting to be reactivated or feelings which are still potent, even though the contacts have gone. Much more frequently, however, a drinking problem will intensely involve the family as well as the patient. The spouse and the children are the people commonly drawn into the play, but parents, brothers, sisters, uncles or aunts or grandparents may in some way be involved. The nature of the involvement can be in terms of that person experiencing the adverse impact of the drinker's behaviour, in terms of the family's interaction in the genesis of the drinking problem, in terms of the family member's unhelpful connivance with or encouragement of the drinking problem, or most positively in terms of that person being able to aid the processes of recovery.

The present chapter will give a groundwork description of certain important aspects of family interaction, while full discussion of therapeutic implications will be postponed to later chapters of this book.

THE SPOUSE

At the outset it is necessary to emphasize that the spouse may be the husband of the alcoholic woman, as well as the wife of the man who is drinking. Although the initial discussion will largely be in terms of the wife as the non-alcoholic spouse – for this is indeed the commoner situation – many of the considerations would apply equally to the reverse circumstances. (A later section will focus on the husband of the woman alcoholic.)

A HISTORY FROM THE SPOUSE IN HER OWN RIGHT

The assumption is too often made that the purpose of taking a history from the spouse is solely that of obtaining 'independent information'. What is frequently forgotten is the need to take a history from the spouse as a person in her own right. The result is that after months have gone by it is suddenly realized that treatment is proceeding on the basis of much being known about the patient while the wife remains a cipher, and their interaction is hence inexplicable. No one has bothered to see this woman in terms of her own being, and her own needs and expectations. Treatment of the patient is handicapped, and the fact that the wife herself needs help is overlooked.

What has to be overcome is a subconscious social constraint – the feeling that it is embarrassing to ask a woman whose role is presumed to be that of someone coming to the clinic to talk about her husband, then within that definition to talk about herself. The constraint may emanate more from lack of confidence on the therapist's part than from any reluctance on the wife's part to talk about herself. Indeed, the interview may soon reveal that the wife has a great pressure of need to talk about herself. How the initial history is to be taken from the spouse in terms that honour her in her own right is fully discussed in Chapter 10.

THEORIES OF THE 'ALCOHOLIC MARRIAGE'

A number of different theories have been put forward to explain what may happen in a marriage where one partner is an alcoholic. Each of these approaches can at times give useful understanding, but certain stereotyped descriptions of the alcoholic's wife which have gained currency over recent years have no general validity.

One of these theories is that the wife actually wishes her husband to be an alcoholic. The fact is noted that a proportion of wives had a father who was an alcoholic, and it is argued that the wife then marries an alcoholic with whom she can continue to enact her unresolved dynamic problems. She will subtly or overtly hamper treatment, persuade her husband to discharge himself prematurely from hospital, and tell him that a few drinks will not do him any harm. She will even buy the drink for him and bring it back to the house, and she will indicate to him that 'he's horrid now he's sober'. If the husband persists in his recovery, the wife herself may in terms of this theory then decompensate and develop a depressive illness.

There can be no doubt that marriages are occasionally encountered which astonishingly resemble such a bizarre picture as that just given, and where it is a reasonable supposition that the wife is subconsciously willing the husband's drinking. She married him knowing he was an alcoholic, she gains from seeing him as weak and inferior, has enjoyed taking over the management of home and finance, and wishes to have her expectations confirmed that men are dirt. She likes to show how badly she is used, enjoys mothering or dominating, and so on. But cruel mistakes result from being so persuaded that this is the picture of *the* alcoholic marriage, and from forcing all such marriages into interpretations in these terms. For instance, the truth of the matter may be that when the husband began to drink excessively the wife inevitably then had to make the choice between letting the home go to rack and ruin or taking much of its running into her own hands; it can be seen, therefore, that her seeming 'dominance' is merely adjustive.

Some research has suggested that the wife's reactions go through a predictable sequence of stages. The evidence does not in fact support the notion that all wives follow exactly the same pathway, but certain phases can sometimes be recognized. At the beginning there is the reluctant and groping admission that drinking is indeed a problem, and then the first attempts to control or prevent the problem behaviour. The family begins to be socially isolated, partly as a protective strategy; invitations are refused, people are not encouraged to call, relatives are not visited. Later, the wife may go into a phase where she begins to realize her strategies are not working, that things are getting worse rather than better, that her reserves are being worn down. She may start to fear for her own sanity, and a feeling of hopelessness sets in. Sexual contact is diminished or ceases, and there is a general and continuing sense of estrangement, fear or anger. At this stage or earlier, the wife may begin to feel that 'something must be done'; she tries to persuade her husband to look for help. If no improvement follows the marriage may either break up, or continue for years in a phase characterized by strategies which might be called *circumvention*:

> It's terrible really, but I suppose we've all got used to it. We'll all go to bed before he comes in at night and I'll pretend to be asleep when he comes into the room. I tell the kids just to keep out of his way. Sometimes he gets back early but if we're in the sitting-room watching the television, more often than not he just goes out to the kitchen. I take the children on holiday, he doesn't come, and frankly we don't ask him.

Given that the ordering of phases may vary widely, it is still useful to try to make an assessment of the *coping style* which the wife is at any stage employing, for such knowledge can be useful in therapy. One such style is exactly the circumvention (or withdrawal) employed by the woman who has just been quoted. Contact is so far as possible minimized, and there is emotional as well as physical avoidance. Another style is that of *attack*: the wife tries to control her husband's behaviour by scolding, shouting, threatening to leave him, or on occasions even by physical assault. She lets him know that she is contacting a solicitor. Drink is poured down the sink. *Manipulation* embraces a number of behaviours, such as seeking to shame the drinker, with the woman showing her own distress or emphasizing the children's suffering, while the wife herself may get very purposely drunk 'to show him what it's like'. *Spoiling* may be another approach: the spouse nurses him through his hangovers, keeps the dinner warm for him whether he is drunk or sober, or promises him special treats if he will ameliorate his behaviour. A further style is that of *constructive management*: she retains her own sense of worth and protects and looks after the family by making sure that finances are in as good order as possible while she goes out to work. She makes sure that the children go short of nothing, and herself paints the house and cares for the front garden. *Constructive help seeking* is a pattern characterized by behaviour such as the wife going to see the family doctor and asking him to speak to the husband, she finds out about Alcoholics Anonymous and leaves some pamphlets around for the husband to come upon, or goes along to the public library and reads books on alcoholism, so as to help her own understanding.

These various styles seldom exist in pure form, and there are other types of behaviour which do not go under any of these headings. The choice of style may be influenced by the way in which the particular woman generally copes with life, by class expectations, by the type of behaviour which the husband is manifesting, and by the duration of the problem. The coping style employed at a particular time may be a response in a sequence of experiments in which the wife is searching around, trying first one tack and then another.

WHAT IS THE WIFE HAVING TO COPE WITH?

The special stressfulness of a situation where there may often be social isolation rather than social support, and where there are no guidelines, has already been noted. A frequent additional feature is the stress imposed by the unpredictability of what is going to happen; the wife does not know whether when the husband gets back from the pub he will be in a sentimental or maudlin mood, or whether he will be in a raging temper and have at her with his fists. The exhaustion which can be engendered by the experience of dealing with continuing distress and peaks of crisis over a period of years can be the wife's dominant complaint.

Fundamentally the wife is having to cope with the problems both at the emotional and at the reality level. The emotional problems include anxiety, fearfulness and misery. Often there is an element of self-doubt or self-blame; she wonders whether the problem has arisen because she is a bad wife and has sexually or in some other way failed her husband. She may also be perplexed by the acute conflict in the feelings which she develops towards her husband; she married this man because she loved him, and yet now she at times feels almost murderous towards him. There is often also a sense of emotional deprivation and of loss; the man she married has disappeared. She herself begins to feel in some way diminished in her worth, or disgraced.

At the reality level the problems can be tangibly threatening; there is the risk of eviction if the rent is not paid, or his violence may result in serious damage. More commonly it is the host of minor reality problems which have to be coped with: no housekeeping money this week, no money to pay the electricity, the neighbours complaining about the doors being slammed when he got home last night, constant rowing, his jealousy, his dirtiness or his wetting the bed.

It would, though, be a mistake always to picture such marriages in extreme terms. Extremes of suffering certainly occur with sad frequency, but there are all gradations. Sometimes, indeed, the husband's deportment when drunk causes little distress; he is a bit silly and argumentative, tends to fall asleep in the chair after supper and can be difficult to get to bed, but in a drunken sort of way he remains polite and is never violent. He regularly hands over the housekeeping money, and if there are the finances to cushion the effects of his drinking, and a job which is secure, some of the more distressing reality problems will not be so evident.

The types of hardship which the wife may encounter are discussed in more detail in relation to taking the 'independent history' from the spouse (Chapter 10).

MARRIAGES WHERE THE WIFE IS ALCOHOLIC

As was stated at the beginning of this chapter, most of the principles which apply to understanding the situation where the husband is the alcoholic apply equally well when it is the wife who is the patient. There are, though, certain additional aspects to the marriage problem which may then develop, many of these relating to the generally punitive attitudes towards the female alcoholic which many cultures can evince, and which are more fully discussed in Chapter 7. The husband's reaction may be coloured by a primitive disgust at his wife's behaviour, or by fear of social disapprobation and of the family being disgraced by a drunken woman. His feelings can lead to violence. To work through these feelings so that the husband is less frightened of what is happening and less blindly condemnatory may be the necessary prelude to any constructive changes.

If the husband is employed and the woman is the housewife and mother, he may find himself drawn into a managing role within the family to compensate for the wife's impaired competence. If, though, he is also trying to keep going in a demanding job, he may find the double demands difficult to cope with, and the welfare of the children may be a particular worry. Failure of the woman to fulfil her expected roles sets neither greater nor lesser problems, though in some ways different, than a man's role failures. Sometimes the husband will seek to solve the family's plight by rather purposely promoting an elder daughter to the central female role within the household.

Another difference relates to the fact that economically it is often easier for a man to leave an alcoholic wife than for a wife to leave her drinking husband. Despite continued suffering she may hold back from separation because she does not see an alternative way of providing a roof to shelter herself and the children. The husband can more readily see separation from his wife as an option, either taking the children with him or surrendering his responsibilities.

MARRIAGES WHERE BOTH PARTNERS ARE ALCOHOLIC

This extraordinarily difficult situation is sometimes encountered. The story is usually that of someone with a drinking problem marrying someone else with an established and evident drinking problem. For one or both partners it may be a second marriage. They met perhaps in a bar or even in a hospital ward, and it is a marriage of convenience between drinkers. Their only shared interest is drinking, they have no knowledge of each other's sober beings, and are, sadly, likely to drag each other down further. Alcoholism does, though, sometimes develop in both partners in an already established marriage. Quite often the development is not simultaneous, but the wife seems to follow in the husband's footsteps, her drinking being in part perhaps a reaction to the stress of the husband's behaviour. Another type of marriage is where the partners have met at Alcoholics Anonymous, are both committed to 'recovery', and are able to give each other much support.

In general, where both husband and wife have a serious problem, it can be very dificult to reach them with any effective help. If they met in a pub and each purposefully married a drinking partner, the therapist may encounter a baffling lock of pathological motivations. In such instances all that may be possible is to make the offer of help, try to maintain some sort of monitoring contact, and wait for the happening which can provide the therapeutic opening – one partner going into hospital with a physical illness, for example. Where the alcoholism has developed during the marriage, rather than its being the very foundation of the marriage, the possibilities for therapy are usually more hopeful. Both partners may then simultaneously be able to seek help, or it may be necessary to start with the partner who is more motivated. If therapy can capture the potential for mutual understanding which can exist between partners who have shared the same problem, an initially difficult situation can be turned to special advantage.

HOMOSEXUAL COUPLES

Problems similar to those which occur in a marriage are encountered when one partner in a steady homosexual liaison is an alcoholic. A rather common story seems, however, to be of the partner who is more emotionally dependent and more insecure beginning to drink heavily at a period when he fears that the relationship is going to break up:

> I'd get home from work, and after I'd had a drink I'd start doing the cooking. All the time I was cooking the dinner I'd be wondering – is he coming home tonight? Who is he with? What lies is he going to tell? Not like the old days! So while I was cooking I'd have a few more drinks. By the time he came in I'd be all ready for a row.

But this is by no means the only pattern of homosexual relationship in which the drinking problem can develop. And the basic social expectations and social pressures which can be influential in persuading married couples to try to keep their marriages going do not always operate to the same degree for the homosexual couple, so that the therapist may find that he is helping such people through the dissolution of their relationship.

CHILDREN

For the children in the alcoholic marriage to be entirely forgotten by the therapeutic team is sadly all too easy. Their names and ages are noted in the initial history-taking, out of the corner of an eye there is the awareness of their continued existence, but the parents are the focus of attention and are taking up all the therapeutic time. There is the vague feeling that 'more ought to be done about the children', but the intention is all too seldom honoured.

DAMAGES WHICH CAN BE INFLICTED

The variety and extent of damages which can be inflicted are varied and must depend on the personality of the child, the degree of emotional support provided by either parent, the variety of other social and emotional supports which may be available, and the age of the child when the alcoholic parent developed the drinking problem. Of great importance is the actual behaviour of the parent when intoxicated; if there is continued rowdiness, arguments or violence, the impact will be far more adverse than in those instances where drunkenness is not associated with verbal or actual aggression. A drinking problem of whatever degree or nature which as its end-result produces what can in summary be described as a bad home atmosphere is attacking the centre of what family life should be able to give to a child. This is the kind of family where the social worker will report that 'you know there is something wrong as soon as you go in at the door'. Whether it is more damaging for the mother rather than the father to be the alcoholic is uncertain, and there may be a different impact on the boys and the girls in the family. If a parent when drunk continuously picks on a particular child, scolding him, finding fault, demeaning him, or hitting him, then that child is immensely at risk.

The psychological damages, and the social disabilities which can result, very much interact. At the psychological level, one effect may be a general and non-specific raising of the anxiety level in that child. He is anxious in his relationships, both inside and outside the home, anxious in the school setting, with consequent learning and social disability, and may develop overt neurotic or behaviour symptoms. But as well as this general impact on psychological health, a variety of important dynamic processes related to psychological growth can be affected. The child may, for instance, be very basically deprived of a satisfactory role model when the same-sex parent is the alcoholic, and a disturbed or ambivalent relationship with the parent of the opposite sex may result in feelings which are later going to be acted out in other relationships, as has been discussed on pp. 15–16. Fundamental aspects of self-definition and of self-esteem may be impaired.

There is, though, little which is absolutely specific to the damaging psychological experience of the alcholic home, and much the same types of disturbance must often result in homes where, for instance, one parent is chronically or repeatedly psychiatrically ill. What may be more specific is that the experience of intense family conflict centred on alcohol leaves the child the conflicting attitudes towards drinking and drunkenness which are built into his psychological being as highly charged determinants of later feelings and behaviours (see p. 247). Part of the emotional damage is latently the risk of alcoholism.

The absence of emotional regard within the home can mean that a child will at an adolescent stage develop particularly rejecting attitudes towards the parents, and enter precipitously into identification with an adolescent peer group. Such an extreme version of a normal process is not necessarily harmful, but the children from such a disturbed home can be vulnerable to involvement with groups which are themselves disturbed and engaging in drug-taking or delinquency. Such associations may in part represent a revenge on the parents, or substitute comfort or excitement to replace the good inner feelings which are so lacking. There can, though, be no fixed predictions as to how a child from an alcoholic home will meet adolescence. Another outcome may be that the child is very clinging, desperately and anxiously involved in the home, tied to protecting the non-drinking parent, and unable to make any identification with other young people.

At any stage of childhood the possibility of actual physical damage must be considered. There is an association between alcoholism and baby battering, and in childhood and adolescence the risk of physical assault may continue; the damage is often no more than bruising, but the risk of more serious injury is not to be discounted.

There is little precise information on the long-term outlook for children who come from homes which have been severely or chronically afflicted by a parent's abnormal drinking. Seen 20 years later a reasonable guess might be that a percentage of such children would appear remarkably unhandicapped, while another group (perhaps 20 to 30 per cent) would themselves have developed drinking problems. Help for the child is discussed in Chapter 14.

DRINKING PROBLEMS AND FAMILY INTERACTIONS

Whether discussing the marriage or the children, what has essentially been argued in this chapter is that alcoholism will inevitably be embedded in a network of family interactions. Those interactions are in terms both of overt communications and direct impacts, and dynamic processes of great subtlety. The alcoholic influences the spouse's behaviour, which in-fluences the alcholic's behaviour, so that a sort of resonance is set up. And the children are not just passive recipients of what is done to them, but themselves actively participate. Not only are parents and children and other family members involved, but so also perhaps the wife's friend 'who is always dropping in'. Ever to become focused only on a single actor is to lose sight of the play.

REFERENCES

Gayford JJ (1979) Wife battering: a preliminary survey of 100 cases. *British Medical Journal*, **1,** 194–197.

Jackson JK (1954) The adjustment of the family to the crisis of alcoholism. *Quarterly Journal of Studies on Alcohol*, **15,** 562–586.

Kogan KL, Fordyce WE and Jackson JK (1963) Personality disturbances of wives of alcoholics. *Quarterly Journal of Studies on Alcohol*, **24,** 227–238.

Orford J (1975) Alcoholism and marriage: the argument against specialism. *Journal of Studies on Alcohol*, **36,** 1537–1563.

Orford J (1977) Impact of alcoholism on family and home. In: Edwards G and Grant M (eds) *Alcoholism: New Knowledge and New Responses*, pp 234–243. London: Croom Helm.

Orford J, Guthrie S and Nicholls P (1975) Self-reported coping behaviour of wives of alcoholics and its association with drinking outcomes. *Journal of Studies on Alcohol*, **36,** 1154–1163.

Orme TC and Rimmer J (1981) Alcoholism and child abuse: a review. *Journal of Studies on Alcohol*, **42**, 273–287.

Whalen T (1953) Wives of alcoholics: four types observed in a family service agency. *Quarterly Journal of Studies on Alcohol*, **14**, 632–641.

Wilson C and Orford J (1978) Children of alcoholics: report of a preliminary study and comments on the literature. *Journal of Studies on Alcohol*, **39**, 121–142.

Chapter 4
Social Complications of Excessive Drinking

In this chapter what is meant by 'social complications of alcoholism' will first be explored, and some specific types of complication then taken under headings. Complications which occur within the family – a very important type of social problem – have already been discussed in the previous chapter.

Convenient though it is to think in terms of three classical problem dimensions – physical, mental and social – this must not be allowed to obscure the fact that in the real lives of patients the dimensions are not separate at all. Problems in any one area lead to, and are exacerbated by, problems in the other areas. The clinical skill lies not just in making the detailed, one-dimensional assessment, but in putting the dimensions together.

Even as the social worker may sometimes be tempted by training, or habit of mind, rather to neglect the importance of the physical considerations in the equation (the psychiatrist is also sometimes vulnerable to the same charge), so may the physician occasionally be guilty of too narrow a concern with his patient's physical well-being at the cost of a proper awareness of the other dimensions. This chapter, as well as presenting some initial theoretical discussion, seeks therefore to provide, as it were, a sort of practical check-list of what should be borne in mind in the social sphere – a check-list which should be useful whatever one's particular professional affiliation.

THE CONCEPT OF 'SOCIAL COMPLICATIONS'

The idea of 'social complications' essentially implies a failure adequately to fulfil an *expected social role*. The failure may be in meeting expectations as, for example, family member, employer or employee, good neighbour, or law-abiding citizen. The results of such failures may be detrimental both to the individual and to those around him.

As for the alcohol-mediated processes which lead to such functional impairments, several factors usually interact. Excessive drinking may, for instance, at an early stage result in a hangover which makes it difficult to get to work, while intoxication may impair ability to manage the complexities of the job, and physical and mental impairment later make work impossible. More subtly the drink-centredness of the individual and the salience which continued drinking begins to acquire over other demands may mean that work ceases to matter very much, that this person moves indeed into an 'alcoholic role' which competes with any pre-existing roles.

And whatever the objective failures in role-performance, a secondary problem is likely to arise in terms of loss of reputation, and the way that others now think about and react to the drinker and confirm him in the alcholic role. A series of self-fulfilling prophecies may be set up and the process of amplification gets underway:

> 'I wrote 30 job application letters to various firms and told them I
> had been treated for alcoholism, was now sober, and wanted to find
> my way back with everything in the open. Didn't get a single
> interview. So next time I kept very quiet about my drinking, spun a
> yarn about that year off work, handed in two out-of-date
> references, lied on the medical form, and got the job. And then?
> They checked things out, I was fired on Friday, and yes, it's stupid,
> but I've been drinking. Just what they expected.'

The plea must therefore be that we become attuned to the subtleties of the *processes* which are involved in social disability and to the nature of the personal *experience* of such disability. And social complications will in reality almost inevitably involve and lie within a network of family and social relationships, rather than ever properly being seen as affecting just the one individual. Social *maladjustment* is ultimately, of course, only to be understood by an appreciation of the processes and multiple complexities of what passes as social *adjustment*.

So much then for an outline consideration of some general principles. The list of headings which follows attempts to deal with possible major areas of social problem experience. The ordering does not indicate precedence of importance, and the list is by no means exhaustive.

PROBLEMS AT WORK

The difficulty that a person with a drinking problem may encounter when seeking employment has just been instanced, and this example shows how stigmatization may compound the objective difficulties. The varieties of adverse influence that excessive drinking may have on work performance are many and costly. The impact is not limited to any one level of seniority in the employment hierarchy, and drinking problems are as likely to be found in the boardroom as on the shop–floor.

There are common features as to the effects of excessive drinking on work performance, whatever the job. Time may be lost from work due to sickness or absenteeism; the individual may still be at work but may be functioning inefficiently or leaving his work to others; he may be an actual danger to himself or other people because of the way in which he is managing machinery; drinking may have led to a block in promotion or to demotion; he may have drifted down the scale from his previous skilled employment; and finally he may be unemployed or unemployable. And this is the place again to emphasize that here, as in most other parts of this book, 'he' must be read as a shorthand for 'he or she'. In many societies women are at the same time moving towards a greater participation in the work-force and in management, a heavier level of drinking, and a greater incidence of drinking problems in employment.

Beyond the commonalities, each type of employment presents possibilities for particular types of problem to develop. In the senior positions in industry or the armed services, or the diplomatic service, drunken indiscretion, irascibility, or bad judgement at some crucial meeting may be the major problems set by excessive drinking. For the bus or train driver, the aeroplane pilot, the ship's officer drunk on the bridge, intoxication carries enormous dangers for the public. In some professions, such as the church or teaching, the hint of scandal may be specially damaging, though it is astonishing how tolerant or blind–eyed those in the individual's environment often appear to be, even when one would have thought his position particularly vulnerable. The seriousness with which excessive drinking is officially viewed by the medical profession is evidenced by the disciplinary procedures which in many countries may be called into action if a doctor's drinking comes to official notice, although the story is again often of complicity and cover-up until a late moment. The conclusion to be drawn from this paragraph must therefore be that, whoever the individual we are trying to assess and help, the analysis of his alcohol-related social problems requires a job-specific and person-specific enquiry.

HOUSING

Urban housing problems and urban drinking problems often go together (each exacerbating the other), and where there are great concentrations of substandard housing and social deprivation, drinking is simply one of many endemic disorders contributing to, and deriving from, the totality of social disorganization.

On the other hand, cases are frequently encountered where drinking is leading very directly to a housing problem. There may always be some element of circularity, but in this latter type of instance, the patient's claim that he is 'drinking because of his rotten surroundings' has a hollow ring – his is the only house in the street which is shabby and unpainted, and with an old sofa lying in the front garden. Housing problems of this kind are going to be more acute the more marginal the family's income, but even the initially prosperous middle-class family may eventually be forced to sell up as drinking eats into the mortgage repayments.

Bad relationships with neighbours, gross evidence of poor house maintenance, failure to meet the rent, eviction, the sojourn in 'temporary accommodation' or in some sort of shelter, and multiple changes of address are some of the familiar elements in the housing history as the drinking problems becomes more extreme.

FINANCIAL PROBLEMS

An awareness of the possible financial complications of drinking problems, and of the family's financial position, is necessary for any complete case assessment. To maintain a major drinking habit is expensive and large additional sums are often spent without the drinker quite knowing how the money has gone – drinks for his friends or drinks grandly offered to strangers, meals out and taxis home, a massive cigarette consumption, a bit of gambling, and so on. As with housing problems and many other social complications, the well-moneyed are going to be better protected for a longer time, but even the rich may finally be bankrupted.

The financial balance is determined not only by the cost of the drinking and associated spendings, but also by the inflow of cash. Demotion, sickness and unemployment add to the stringencies. Very complicated and devious stratagems may be engaged in to maintain the cash flow. 'Moonlighting' or the second job is common (often in a bar so as further to aid the drinking), loans are negotiated on preposterous terms, goods are pawned, houses re-mortgaged. The employee 'works a bit of a racket' and a load of bricks disappear from the builder's yard. It becomes vital to evade income tax and to defraud Social Security. The wife goes out to work. The rent is not paid, hire purchase payments fall behind, and the gas and electricity services being cut off becomes a familiar crisis.

The wife and family may have reached the stage where financial chaos has become the central and pressing pain. From the social work angle, sorting out that chaos may be the necessary first-aid, but it will be very temporary aid if the drinking problem is not radically met.

HOMELESSNESS AND VAGRANCY

As with housing difficulties, so with homelessness and vagrancy, there may be circular processes. The vagrant way of life offers many pressures towards drinking, and at the same time the man with a serious drinking problem may move towards vagrancy. Professionals with a special interest in alcoholism would do well also to remember that 'the homeless single person' may be homeless for many other reasons than his drinking. Economic hardship and unemployment vary in the contribution they make to vagrancy from decade to decade, while mental illness, physical incapacity, epilepsy, and personality disorders contribute continually to the genesis of a city problem which in many countries still seems to be intractable, come boom or slump.

With those provisos noted, it is still very evidently true that the man who is sleeping under the railway arch may be manifesting the social end-result of a drinking career – a 'social complication' of highly visible and dramatic nature, and the concern of the nineteenth-century social reformer. The elements of this 'complication' constitute a complex system of related problems: the homelessness itself, the difficulty in getting a wash, the lack of clothes, the lack of fixed employment, the breakdown in family contacts and lack of any kinship or friendship supports, the petty criminal involvement, the poor nutrition and the risks of illness and accident. Drinking is what particularly contributes to the ultimate core characteristic of this situation – its seeming inescapableness, the sense of the treadmill. It is easier to find a way into that degradation than a way out.

What is the likely background of the shabby man who is begging at the street corner and hoping to raise funds for the next bottle of cheap wine? There are many routes into alcoholic vagrancy, but the average story is often somewhat as follows. That individual is much more frequently a man than a woman, although some women do reach this plight. The parents were usually themselves hanging on to socio–economic survival rather tenuously – the father an unskilled worker living in poor urban conditions or rural poverty, and the childhood family often large and lacking in care. Gross disruption of the childhood home is a quite frequent finding; education is likely to have been meagre and job-training nil. The picture is therefore typically of someone who has started with few advantages and many handicaps. The vagrant alcoholic is with over-whelming frequency a casualty with origins in the most underprivileged working class, and the shopkeeper or skilled tradesman who becomes involved in drink and falls on hard times seldom goes in that direction. The geographical origins may be well-known and typical in a particular country: in Chicago the casualties may well have been bred in that city, while in London the casualties will usually not be London-reared but have come from Scotland or Ireland.

After leaving school the story tends to be of a few odd jobs in the home town (and perhaps some petty delinquency), a period perhaps in the armed forces or the merchant navy, a short-lived marriage and an unsuccessful attempt to settle down, and then very probably the mobility and root-lessness of the casual labourer who moves from town to town, who follows the big construction work and the big wages. Contacts with family and friends are lost. As the drinking becomes more incapacitating, there is a drift towards low-grade work, such as kitchen portering, periods of unemployment, spells in prison and mental hospitals, and the final arrival at that disorganized way of life which is often referred to as 'skid row'. That term was originally used in America to indicate the downtown tract of rooming houses, cheap hotels, blood banks, rescue missions, winos and bottle-gangs found in many North American cities. In the UK and other European countries such clearly segmented patches of Bowry-type social disorganization generally do not exist. 'Skid row' refers more to a way of life than to particular streets.

As for the involvement of drinking in this unfolding story, excessive drinking has often started at an early age and then followed a very accelerated course. Soon after the age of 30 drink has become a dominantly destructive influence, and this man is now beginning to stand apart even from other heavy-drinking members of the casual work-force, is beginning to be picked up for drunkenness with alarming frequency, is violently shaky every morning, and is finally drawn into companionship with the bottle-gang in the park and to sharing their cider, wine or industrial spirits. The skid row way of life may appear to be total chaos and disorder, but it has of course its own social organization and subculture; it becomes the individual's only support system and gives him his values and expectations as well as his drink.

The discussion of how the vagrant alcoholic is best helped is taken up in Chapter 19. Here we should note, though, that accurate and sympathetic understanding of this extreme social complication of drinking is very much needed if we are to be able to cope with such problems. Too often the person in this condition tends to be even further alienated and his pessimism further reinforced by responses which indicate that we do indeed regard him as alien, hopeless, beyond the pale. One of the certain lessons of close experience is in fact that this condition is recoverable, and that there are pathways off skid row, however difficult to find.

CRIME

The relationship between crime and excessive drinking is as complex as with any other social complications of alcoholism, and simple, direct and one-way causality is seldom a sufficient analysis. Personality, background and social circumstances which predispose to crime may as much and independently predispose to alcoholism. The alcoholism and the criminality are both then just symptoms of an underlying nexus of disorders. A drinking problem may also in passing affect a dedicated and professional criminal, perhaps at a late stage of his career. Alternatively, one may see the person who is primarily an alcoholic and who at a much later age than the usual 'first offender' falls foul of the law, or is caught up in a sudden flurry of recidivism. Sometimes the person is seen who suddenly shifted from a circulation around the prisons to a hospital and voluntary agency circuit; his drinking remains much the same, but he has learnt to present himself and his problems rather differently. Such analysis in terms of a set of common relationships between alcohol and offence may be a useful preliminary guide to identification of patterns of career, but there are dangers in any too tidy listing, and we need as ever to learn to look closely at the individual.

The offence may by definition involve the actual intoxication itself, and here one needs to examine the problems of 'the drunkenness offender' and 'the drunk driver'. The drunkenness offender considerably overlaps with the vagrant alcoholic population – most of these people parading each morning before the courts will have come to regard the magistrate as just another routine figure in the skid row play. Such offenders are likely to be heavily dependent on alcohol, and have perhaps been arrested as the police clear up a park, a railway station or a warm subway. But this is not the whole picture of the drunkenness offender population, and a proportion of these offenders will be settled citizens with job and home, whose mounting drink problems have led to public incapacity. A very small contribution is made by the casual reveller who has cheeked a policeman or otherwise gone too far, but who has no serious drinking problem.

The drunk driving offenders are also a mixed population, but a very different mixture. Drunk driving is in itself a serious social complication, and given the inherent danger to other people which is involved, it is a pity that social attitudes often seem to dismiss this behaviour as not quite 'real' crime. At lower blood alcohol levels it is likely that drunk driving is often an offence committed by someone who is not otherwise experiencing problems with his drinking. On the other hand, the drunk driving offence may be an early warning signal that someone is drinking heavily, allowing his drinking to interfere with his judgement, and showing a need to drink heedless of consequences. An important, smaller, but significant proportion of drunk drivers will be people with very serious drinking problems indeed. Suspicion should certainly be aroused if there is a high blood alcohol (say over 150mg per cent), or if this is a second or further offence.

The remaining variations on the alcohol–crime connection are legion. There is no type of offence which will not sometimes be related to drinking, and many types of offence which will often be so related. The problems load particularly at the 'petty' end of the spectrum: petty theft, minor assault, travelling on public transport without a ticket, failing to pay for the meal in the cheap café, urinating in the subway, begging. The person with a drinking problem may know that when he is drunk (and only when he is drunk), he is apt to engage in his own particular offence, for example, he takes cars and drives them away, 'goes burgling' in a clumsy sort of fashion, or passes dud cheques. Alcohol may be related to sexual crime, again in a predictable fashion – the patient is terrified that he will molest a small girl when drunk. Drinking may be the story behind an embezzlement. The relationship between alcohol and violence can be close (see pp. 75, 125), although again personality, circumstances and social set have always also to be taken into account, rather than alcohol being seen as the total and direct 'cause' of wife battering, affrays at the football match, or murder.

IMPACT ON EDUCATION AND TRAINING

An aspect of social complication which deserves greater note is the long-term handicap which results when an educational or training opportunity is partly wasted or totally lost. Being sent down from university, failing to complete a post-graduate degree, the abandonment of an apprenticeship, may all have serious long-term consequences. Drinking in secondary schools is spasmodically reported as a problem in the UK and more frequently seen as cause for local concern in North America, and the pupil who is drunk in the afternoon is not going to follow much of the lesson.

THE ESSENTIAL THEMES

Having started this chapter with a general discussion of the nature and genesis of social complications and having then worked through a listing of specific problem areas, it is useful finally again to emphasize certain essential themes. The individual's social being involves the interlocking of many different roles. His success or failure in these roles has many determinants. Excessive drinking can impair or destroy previous adjustments, but drink is always an element which *contributes* to causality and its impact can never be properly understood in simple-minded terms. Impairment of social well-being is as real and important as the physical and mental impairments with which it may interact. The ability to understand not only the *events* but also the *processes* of social impairment is a skill to be expanded with every case encounter.

REFERENCES

Aarens M, Cameron T, Roizen J *et al* (1977) *Alcohol, Casualties and Crime*. Report C-18. Berkeley: Social Research Group.

Berry RE and Boland JP (1977) *The Economic Cost of Alcohol Abuse.* New York: The Free Press.

Comptroller General (1979) *Report to the Congress of the United States. The drinking-driver problem—What can be done about it?* Publication CED-79-33. Washington: General Accounting Office.

Cook T (1975) *Vagrant Alcoholics.* Boston: Routledge and Kegan Paul.

Havard JDJ (1977) Alcohol and road accidents. In: Edwards G and Grant M (eds) *Alcoholism: New Knowledge and New Responses,* pp 251–263. London: Groom Helm.

Department of the Environment (1976) *Drinking and Driving. Report of the Departmental Committee.* London: HMSO.

Hore BD (1977) Alcohol and alcoholism: the impact on work. In: Edwards G and Grant M (eds) *Alcoholism: New Knowledge and New Responses,* pp 244–250. London: Croom Helm.

Kissin B and Begleiter H (eds) (1976) The Biology of Alcoholism, Vol. 4: *Social Aspects of Alcoholism.* New York: Plenum Press.

Pernanen K (1976) Alcohol and crimes of violence. In: Kissin B and Begleiter H (eds) The Biology of Alcoholism, Vol. 4: *Social Aspects of Alcoholism,* pp 351–444. New York: Plenum.

Rada RT (1976) Alcoholism and the child molester. *Annals of the New York Academy of Sciences,* **273,** 492–496.

Robinson D (1976) *From Drinking to Alcoholism.* London: Wiley.

Saad ESN and Madden JS (1976) Certificated incapacity and unemployment in alcoholics. *British Journal of Psychiatry,* **128,** 340–345.

World Health Organisation (1976) *The Epidemiology of Road Traffic Accidents.* Copenhagen: WHO Regional Office for Europe.

Chapter 5
Alcoholism and Psychiatric Illness

Anyone who works with alcoholism must cultivate an awareness of the range of mental illnesses that may result from, or lie behind, the drinking, otherwise very serious problems are going to be overlooked. Part of the coincidence of alcohol problems and mental disorder lies in the fact that both are common, and they are bound therefore in any population to overlap. More important is the fact that alcohol is a readily available medication for many types of mental distress, and in such cases the drinking is a complication of the underlying and primary pathology. Some spects of the relationship between personality, mental illness and alcoholism have already been touched on briefly in Chapter 1 when discussing the causes of excessive drinking. Yet another facet of the relationship is that in some instances the drinking actually causes the mental illness. Although in this section of the book it would be inappropriate to divert into any detailed consideration of treatment issues, some note must occasionally be given here of treatment implications.

To insist that an awareness of the possibility of coexistent psychiatric illness is essential, is not to suggest that *all* patients with a drinking problem have such an underlying illness. Such a statement would be far from true. To put a percentage on the matter is impossible, and the answer will depend on the setting within which patients are being seen; the probation service, the social work office, the general practice, the general or psychiatric hospital, will all draw a different type of case-load.

This chapter considers the range of mental disorders which may coexist with alcoholism, and the workaday problems which may result. We will look firstly at alcohol–related hallucinatory states as exemplifying conditions where drinking or withdrawal of alcohol are of undoubted and central causality, and then go on to discuss the relationship between alcoholism and types of general psychiatric disorder. Alcoholic brain damage and the Wernicke–Korsakoff syndrome are discussed in Chapter 6.

TRANSIENT HALLUCINATORY EXPERIENCE

There is still a debate as to how alcohol–related hallucinatory states should best be classified, and that question will be touched on again both when discussing delirium tremens and alcoholic hallucinosis.

Transient hallucinatory experience deserves note for two reasons. Firstly, it may herald the onset of delirium tremens or alcoholic hallucinosis, and can often give early warning of the likelihood of these much more serious illnesses. It may therefore be viewed as *continuous* with those states, rather than an altogether discreet clinical entity. But secondly, it is important to be aware that transient hallucinations may occur without the illness progressing to either of the major presentations. The diagnostician who is unfamiliar with these transient phenomena may be tempted to record incorrectly that the patient has 'suffered from DTs' when this was not the case.

The essence of this condition is that the patient fleetingly and suddenly experiences any one of a variety of perceptual disturbances, often very much to his surprise and consternation, and with the episode then immediately over. These occurrences may be experienced during periods of continued, heavy and chaotic dependent drinking, or during withdrawal. There is no delirium or evidence of severe physiological disturbance as seen in DTs. Here are some examples of how patients described such experiences:

> 'I would be driving along the road and suddenly something would run across in front of the car – a dog, a cat, I couldn't be sure – and I'd slam on the brakes. A real fright. And then I'd realize there was nothing there.'

> 'I'd be walking down the road and, ZOOM, a car would come up behind me and I'd jump up on the pavement. Frightened out of my life. But it was all imagination.'

> 'What used to happen was that I would turn around thinking someone had called my name.'

The degree of insight is often characteristic; the patient immediately disconfirms the reality of the hallucination. A relatively stereotyped and limited kind of hallucinatory experience is also typical; for one patient it is nearly always the car coming up from behind, for another a pigeon flying into the room.

It is important to realize that some patients can experience such discomforting happenings for many months without progressing to a major disturbance. But the meaning and significance of 'continuity' will immediately become clear as we go on below to discuss delirium tremens and alcoholic hallucinosis.

DELIRIUM TREMENS

THE CLINICAL PICTURE

Delirium tremens (DTs) can produce varied clinical pictures, so much so that there have been attempts to split the syndrome into categories. It is more useful to view the condition as unitary, with a continuum of severities, and a variation in symptom clustering. Delirium, hallucinatory experience and tremor provide the essential diagnostic triad, but other elements are frequently also present. The disturbance is often rather fluctuating, with the patient's condition worsening in the evening or when the room is unlit and shadowy. The total range of possible elements within the syndrome may then be listed as follows:

(i) Delirium

The patient is more or less out of contact with reality, and potentially disoriented as to person, place and time. For instance, he may believe that he is cruising on a liner, mistake the male nurse for a steward and order a drink, but five minutes later he again knows he is in hospital and correctly identifies the people around him.

(ii) Hallucinations

The hallucinatory experiences are characteristically vivid, chaotic and bizarre, and they may affect any sensory modality – the patient may see visions, hear things, smell gases, or feel animals crawling over him. The classical visual hallucinations are of horrifying nature, such as snakes or rats attacking the patient as he lies in bed, or they may take a 'microscopic' form (small furry men dancing on the floor), but any type of visual hallucination can in fact be encountered. These visions are often vividly coloured. Hallucinatory voices or bursts of music may be heard, or the screams of animals. Hallucinations are often based on a ready tendency to illusional misrepresentation: the wrinkles in the bedclothes become snakes, patterns in the wallpaper become faces.

(iii) Tremor

At worst the patient may be shaking so severely that the bed is rattling, but as with other symptoms there can be a continuum of severity and the tremor may not be very noticeable unless the patient is asked to stretch out his hands.

(iv) Fear

The patient may be experiencing extremes of horror in reaction, for instance, to the snakes which writhe all over his bed, but on other occasions the hallucinations appear to be enjoyable or entertaining, and the patient is perhaps happily watching a private cinema show.

(v) Paranoid delusions

The illness often has a degree of paranoid colouring: enemies are blowing poison gas into the room, assassins lurk at the window and there is some sort of nameless conspiracy afoot. The *mood* can in fact be paranoid, with every happening and stimulus being misrepresented as it comes along, but the patient's mental state is far too muddled for the delusional ideas to become systematized.

(vi) Occupational delusions or hallucinations

The barman, for instance, may believe that he is serving in his cocktail bar and pour out imaginary drinks, or the bricklayer may be building an imaginary wall.

(vii) Restlessness and agitation

Partly as a consequence of the fearfulness of the hallucinatory experiences, the patient is often highly restless, clutching and pulling at the bedclothes, starting at any sound, or attempting to jump out of bed and run down the ward. This over-activity, when combined with a degree of weakness and unsteadiness, can put the patient seriously at risk of falls and accidents.

(viii) Heightened suggestibility

The patient who is suffering from delirium tremens can show a heightened susceptibility to suggestion, which occasionally becomes evident spontaneously but may only come out on testing. The older textbooks often mention such stories as the patient agreeing to deal from an imaginary pack of cards or his 'drinking' from a proffered but empty glass.

(ix) Physical disturbances

Heavy sweating is typical, with risk therefore of dehydration. Appetite is usually lacking, the pulse is rapid and the blood pressure likely to be raised, and the patient is feverish. If the illness continues over many days the picture gradually becomes that of dehydration, exhaustion and collapse, with the possibility of a sudden and disastrously steep rise in temperature (see p. 195).

AETIOLOGY AND COURSE

Delirium tremens is today generally viewed as essentially an alcohol withdrawal state, although it is conceded that other factors such as infection or trauma sometimes play an ancillary part. The withdrawal which actually precipitates the attack may have been occasioned by admission to hospital, arrest and incarceration, or a self-determined effort to give up drinking. Often, though, there is no history of abrupt withdrawal and the illness starts while the patient is still drinking. (Those who believe that DTs is always and simply a withdrawal state would hypothesize that there has been at least 'partial withdrawal', and that this can be sufficient to precipitate an attack.) In some instances the patient seems to have hovered on the brink of delirium tremens for many preceding weeks, with much evidence of transient hallucinatory experience, whereas in other instances the illness has a more explosive onset. It is unusual for a patient to experience delirium tremens without a history of at least several years of severe alcohol dependence and many years of excessive drinking, but an attack may occur even after one or two weeks if a previously abstinent patient rapidly reinstates dependence. Recurrent attacks are common once a patient has had one such episode.

The condition usually lasts for three to five days, with gradual resolution. On rare occasions the illness seems to drag on for some weeks, fluctuating between recovery and relapse. The possibility of severe physical complications has already been mentioned; and before the advent of antibiotics intercurrent chest infestion or pneumonia constituted serious risks. Reported mortality rates have varied from centre to centre and even with skilled care a degree of risk remains, with death occurring among perhaps one to five per cent of admissions.

POSSIBILITIES OF DIAGNOSTIC CONFUSION

It might be supposed that delirium tremens woud give a picture so vivid and distinct as to make diagnostic mistakes unlikely. Confusions do, though, occur, and they may be in either of two directions. The first direction relates to the possibility of some underlying condition which is contributing to the picture being overlooked, with liver failure, pneumonia, head injury, or barbiturate withdrawal providing the most important examples. These possibilities should always be borne in mind.

The second way in which confusion may occur is when the possibility of delirium tremens is entirely overlooked, although in retrospect the diagnosis was plainly evident. Despite the seemingly obvious nature of the classical presentation, it is not at all 'obvious' if at the time it is on no one's check-list. For instance, the diagnosis is frequently overlooked in the setting of a general hospital ward. The patient is noted to be suffering from 'confusion', to be 'rambling a bit', or to be trying to get out of bed at night, but the condition is put down to the non-specific effects of infection, trauma or operation. The diagnosis is certainly also at times overlooked in the psychiatric hospital setting, with such a label as 'acute schizophrenic reaction' then perhaps being attached. The emergency admission where the patient's immediate presentation is in terms of floridly paranoid ideas and a lot of wild acting-out, and where the police have been called by neighbours because a starkly disturbed woman has been running up the street with a knife in her hand, is exactly the type of situation where in the anxiety of the moment the possibility of DTs presenting in this way will be forgotten.

Treatment of delirium tremens is discussed on p. 193.

WITHDRAWAL FITS

In a heavily alcohol–dependent person, withdrawal of alcohol (or partial withdrawal) may cause fits. About one third of patients who experience a fit will shortly afterwards go into an attack of delirium tremens; fits typically first occur within 12 to 24 hours of withdrawal and thus precede the onset of delirium tremens by one or two days. These attacks are of the *grand mal* variety (generalized epileptic convulsions involving a loss of consciousness followed by convulsive movements in all four limbs). During a particular withdrawal experience the patient may have only one fit but more commonly there will be three or four convulsions over a couple of days. Very rarely *status epilepticus* will supervene – a continuous run of attacks with one fit merging into another, and with risk to life. Alcohol withdrawal convulsions have sometimes been termed 'rum fits', but there is no reason to believe that they are associated more with one type of beverage than another.

A patient who has experienced attacks during one withdrawal episode may never have any further convulsions during subsequent withdrawals, or he can discover that withdrawal is for him now always associated with risk of convulsions.

The clinical significances are several. There is firstly the problem of diagnostic confusion and oversight; not every physician seems to be aware of the existence of a condition which is far from being a rarity. Any previous history of withdrawal fits must be seen as a pointer to the possibility of a further attack or risk of delirium tremens during an ensuing withdrawal experience, and such a history thus firmly indicates the need to provide in–patient cover for any projected detoxification. Prevention and treatment of withdrawal epilepsy is discussed on p. 195.

Tragedies have sometimes occurred when a severely dependent patient has stopped drinking on his own initiative and sustained a withdrawal fit which has led to an accident. For example, the driver of a heavy truck had after a long period of sobriety relapsed into dependent drinking, but after two to three months he determined abruptly to put a stop to this drinking. He had a fit, his truck went out of control and mounted a pavement, and killed a woman who was standing by a bus stop. There are thus a number of cogent reasons for taking withdrawal fits and the risk of such fits very seriously.

Other possible reasons for epilepsy in alcoholics are discussed on p. 105, under consideration of physical complications of excessive drinking.

ALCOHOLIC HALLUCINOSIS

As has already been mentioned, the patient who is suffering from delirium tremens may be experiencing auditory hallucinations, and on occasions auditory hallucinations may dominate the picture of what is still fundamentally a delirious illness. The term *alcoholic hallucinosis* should, though, be restricted to a very different type of presentation, and the following essential diagnostic points both delineate the condition which we are now talking about and serve to differentiate this state from delirium tremens.

(i) The patient experiences auditory hallucinations but no other types of hallucination. He may hear unformed noises or snatches of music, but most typically he is hearing voices. These voices may be talking to him directly, but are more often talking about him in terms of a sort of running commentary. Sometimes there is only one voice but often several engage in discussion, and the same voices may come back again on different occasions. The commentary may be favourable and friendly, or accusatory and threatening. On occasions the voices may seek to dictate to the patient, and result in acting-out behaviour or an attempt at suicide. There is a lack of insight and the voices are regarded as real, but the patient will seldom elaborate any complex explanation as to the supposed mechanism by which such voices are reaching him. The voices may come and go, or haunt the patient more or less incessantly.

(ii) The patient is not delirious and does not show the physical disturbances typical of delirium tremens.

(iii) The relationship with alcohol withdrawal is often not so obvious as with delirium tremens, and the patient frequently experiences alcoholic hallucinosis while continuing to drink in unabated fashion.

(iv) Delirium tremens is a very manifest disturbance, whereas the patient with alcoholic hallucinosis may not mention his 'voices' unless sympathetically questioned.

(v) Recovery from delirium tremens usually takes place within a few days or a week, while alcoholic hallucinosis can on occasion persist for weeks or months.

The usual diagnostic problem is to differentiate between alcoholic hallucinosis and paranoid schizophrenia. With alcoholic hallucinosis a complicated delusional system is unlikely to be seen, and such delusions as occur are usually just attempts to explain the hallucinations. A family history of schizophenia is unlikely, and schizophrenic thought-disorder is absent. But although such guidelines provide useful indications, it can still in practice sometimes be very difficult to make the differentiation, and in such circumstances the sensible course of action is to get the patient into hospital, withdraw him from alcohol, and see what evolves. Recovery may take place rather abruptly, but more often there is a slow fading of the symptoms. The voices become less persistent, they do not make such an urgent demand on attention, and their reality begins to be doubted. The possibility that the illness will indeed finally declare itself to be schizophrenia has of course to be borne in mind, and if symptoms have not cleared within, say, a couple of months, the latter diagnosis becomes more likely, although it has been reported that alcoholic hallucinosis may sometimes require even six months for complete recovery. Some drug intoxications including most notably amphetamine psychosis, can also result in a picture mimicking alcoholic hallucinosis, and with a presentation of this sort it is always wise to carry out urine testing for drug substances.

When a patient has experienced one attack of alcoholic hallucinosis he is at risk of recurrence of this condition if he drinks again, although such reinstatement is not inevitable. He may, for instance, discover that if he starts to drink seemingly quite moderate quantities of alcohol by his previous standards (perhaps no more than four to eight pints of beer in an evening), he 'begins to hear voices'.

Alcoholic hallucinosis is often stated to be a rare condition, but that assertion is incorrect. Once the therapist is alerted to the reality of this disorder and patients are asked the right questions, cases begin to be seen. Terminology continues to set difficulties and there are transatlantic differences in usage – in America the term is sometimes used more embracingly to include the acute delirious illness where auditory hallucinations predominate – but much confusion will be dispelled and an important clinical entity brought into proper focus if the term is given only the restricted meaning which we have employed here.

'PATHOLOGICAL INTOXICATION'

Such a condition is recorded in the literature (sometimes under the name of *'mania á potu'*) and its supposed bearing on criminal responsibility some-times forms the basis of a defence plea in the courts. The story is then of a man or woman who commits murder or some other crime of violence without premeditation and after ingesting a relatively small amount of alcohol. There is classically an amnesia for the event, and it is alleged that the aggressor was in a trance state or displaying automatism. It is often argued that the behaviour may have had an epileptic basis and the diagnosis is thought to be strengthened if an EEG (electroencephalogram) abnormality can be demonstrated.

In fact, it is doubtful whether such a distinct entity deserves recogni-tion. A relationship between alcoholism and violent crime certainly exists (see p. 64), the aggressor in such circumstances does indeed often display an alcohol–induced amnesia if he has sustained a very high blood alcohol level at the time of the offence, and a non–specific EEG abnormality may sometimes be picked up. But careful questioning will usually reveal that the amount of alcohol ingested was very much more than 'a relatively small amount' and that there has been previous evidence of propensity to violence. If the defence is to plead automatism or 'diminished responsi-bility', it is best to argue in terms of the general effect of very high alcohol levels on brain functioning, with the amnesia put forward as ancillary evidence for the likelihood of impaired cerebral functioning at the time of the offence, rather than argue specifically for 'pathological intoxication'. The relevance of the EEG findings is usually rather dubious.

Dangerous and perhaps fatal drunken assault may also be committed by the acutely intoxicated person who is not alcohol–dependent, as well as by the dependent subject, and again amnesia may or may not be present. Here is an account of the type of case which frequently comes before the courts:

> A young man aged 23 had a pattern of frequent but intermittent heavy drinking. At his brother's wedding he became very drunk and argumentative. The best man tried to quieten him down but a quarrel ensued, and without warning this young drinker picked up a knife and stabbed a bystander, narrowly missing the victim's heart. The assailant said that he had 'only taken a drink or two', but

this was clearly untrue. He displayed a patchy amnesia for the surrounding events. Enquiry revealed that he had on several previous occasions been involved in dangerous fights, both when drunk and when sober.

It can hardly be doubted that this young man's intoxication contributed to his loss of impulse control, and it was probably the crucial additional factor which sparked off his violence, given also the background importance of predisposition and circumstance. The position taken here is not that intoxication is irrelevant to undrstanding of such events, but rather that it is unproductive to segment cases into those due to 'intoxication', as opposed to instances where 'pathological intoxication' is deemed to be the cause. This false distinction is encouraged by legal systems which give simple drunkenness no standing, and which therefore lead defence lawyers to search for a medical basis on which to argue that their client's intoxication was a disease manifestation. On occasion some loss of tolerance to alcohol may be part of the story.

We are obviously here giving only a brief note on what can in the individual case constitute a very complicated forensic presentation, and the way in which the matter is argued will depend on the law and the legal traditions of the particular country. But from the strictly medical point of view 'pathological drunkenness' is a very uncertain concept.

ALCOHOLIC BLACKOUTS (AMNESIAS)

This widely used lay term refers to transient amnesias which may be induced by intoxication. Although such occurrences are frequently experienced by people with serious drinking problems or dependence, they can also occur among social drinkers after incidents of heavy indulgence. It is therefore incorrect to regard blackouts as proof-positive of alcoholism, although anyone who is consuming alcohol in such a way as thus to insult the brain is clearly drinking very unwisely.

PHENOMENOLOGY

Blackouts have been described as being of two types. The *en bloc* variety is characterized by a dense and total amnesia with abrupt points of onset and recovery, and with no subsequent recall of events for the amnesic period, either spontaneously or with prompting. This period may extend from say 30 to 60 minutes up to as long perhaps as two or three days. In contrast *patchy* amnesias or 'greyouts' have indistinct boundaries, with islands of memory within those boundaries, are often characterized by partial or complete subsequent recall, and usually extend over a much shorter period than the previous type. In reality blackouts can occur with every degree of gradation, and although it is useful to recognize the two kinds of blackouts described above as constituting prototypes, the experience of each patient has to be separately described.

Blackouts may begin to occur early in a career of excessive drinking, at a late stage, or never at all. Once they start to be experienced with any frequency, they tend then to continue to occur, and a patient may often be able to identify the phase at which he 'began to get bad blackouts'. The reason why alcoholics show such varied susceptibility to this disorder is unknown, although it is speculated that onset of severe and frequent blackouts may be related to onset of alcoholic brain damage. Concurrent use of sedatives and hypnotics may increase the likelihood of amnesia.

The person who subsequently claims amnesia for a stated period may during that blackout be engaging in any type of activity, and to the observer he will not obviously be in an abnormal state of mind (other than his being intoxicated), although a wife or someone else who knows the patient very well may claim to be able to recognize subtle changes which indicate that amnesia is going to be experienced – for instance, 'he gets that glazed look'. The underlying disturbance of memory does not involve *registration* of events but their *recall*.

THE JOURNEY SYNDROME

Patients will sometimes report that during an amnesic period they wander away from home, later 'waking up' in a strange place, an event which in psychiatric terms is described as a 'fugue state'. Here is an example:

> When I came round I was sitting in a barber's chair having a shave. Hadn't a clue where I'd got to this time, terribly embarrassed, didn't like to ask. I had to go outside and look at the shop signs until I found the answer, and then to my amazement I discovered I was in this town, 150 miles from home. To this day I don't know how I got there. That was the worst experience of that kind, but time

after time I woke up in strange places or found myself sitting on a train going to the coast.

AMNESIA, AUTOMATISM AND CRIME

The occasional concurrence of alcoholic amnesia with criminal acts and the problem of whether 'automatism' may then be relevant to a defence plea is discussed on p. 75.

BLACKOUTS AND THEIR SIGNIFICANCE TO THE PATIENT

One patient may mention his blackouts only on direct questioning and appear not to be at all worried about such experiences, while another patient may be very worried indeed about these experiences and see them as a leading reason for seeking help. Blackouts for that type of patient are often a matter of dread with, for instance, recurrent anguished fear that he may have hurt or killed someone while driving home; he does not remember getting his car into the garage the previous night, and he goes out in the morning fearfully to check the paintwork.

This discussion of alcohol-related hallucinatory states, withdrawal fits and alcoholic blackhouts, when taken together with the account given in Chapter 6 of alcohol-related brain damage (p. 102), covers the spectrum of conditions making up the classical list of mental disorders which can result from drinking. We now go on to look at the very many practical ways in which alcoholism and syndromes of general psychiatry can interlock. The classical list is certainly important and it is relatively well-known. It is the practical significance for diagnosis and therapy of the entries in this second and general list that today requires wider recognition.

DEPRESSION

An understanding of the possible relationships between alcoholism and depression is of much clinical importance, but the problems here are a not infrequent cause of muddle. Before going further it is necessary first to decide what meanings are to be given to the word depression itself. Distinction has to be made between the experience of being depressed, and depressive illness.

THE EXPERIENCE OF BEING DEPRESSED

(i) The ordinary range of experience

Sometimes to be low in mood, frankly miserable, or even despairing is part of ordinary life. People vary greatly in temperament in this as in all other respects. Within the spectrum of what may be called normality, there are some people who as a lifelong trait have a frequent tendency to feel unhappy or overthrown.

(ii) Depressive experience and personality disorder

Fluctuating experience of depression which may transiently seem over-whelmingly difficult to cope with may often be seen as part of the presentation of personality disorder. The person himslf may sometimes make this a leading complaint, although closer knowledge soon shows that the feelings fluctuate and are much embedded in wider problems of emotional control and life adjustment.

(iii) Depression colouring the presentation of other psychiatric syndromes

Whatever the psychiatric syndrome, there is always the possibility that the picture will in addition show some depressive colouring; schizophrenia, dementia or obsessional illness can provide examples.

DEPRESSIVE ILLNESS

Depression as a psychiatric illness which exists in its own right has to be distinguished from any of those normal or abnormal states listed above, where a person may feel depressed. The core symptoms of depressive illness include mood disturbance – depression, anxiety, absence of pleasure. These symptoms are often worse at a particular time of day, most usually the morning. Accompanying the mood disturbance there may be a sense of worthlessness, and self-accusation. But the symptoms of depressive illness frequently go beyond the mood disturbance itself. The patient may complain of poor sleep, bad dreams and early waking. There is often a loss of weight and lack of appetite. Sexual interest is lost. Concentration is impaired. The patient may be agitated, or greatly slowed down. Constipation is a typical feature. The patient may become convinced that he is physically ill and develop hypochondriacal symptoms. With a severe depressive illness the patient may become deluded or hallucinated – he is going to be punished because of his sins, the police are waiting outside his house, voices accuse him.

Depressive illness exists in degrees, and there are many variations in the way symptoms cluster and present. The picture will be influenced by culture, by the patient's age and by his personality. No one description can do justice to the true variety of presentations. There have been many attempts to typologize this disorder – endogenous versus reactive depression, for instance, or 'neurotic depression' versus true depressive illness. A distinction is today usually made between *unipolar* affective illness, and *bipolar* illness where the patient suffers from attacks of hypomania (elation of mood) as well as attacks of depression.

The approach to depression which is being taken here rests centrally therefore on a distinction between the general experience of being depressed, on the one hand, and the specific *illness* of depression on the other. In trying to aid people who are unhappy, this distinction is of crucial practical importance in deciding how best to help.

So much for the basic concepts. Deciding whether a person is just miserable or on the contrary dangerously ill with depression can, though, be extraordinarily difficult when he is drinking, and there is the ever-looming possibility of suicide as the price of a mistake. Depressive illness is often over-diagnosed in alcoholics, with consequent needless prescribing of drugs or pointless administration of ECT (electroconvulsive therapy), while on other occasions the diagnosis may be overlooked. This is an instance where correct diagnosis will speak very importantly to correct management. If the patient is suffering from non-specific unhappiness rather than a depressive illness, that aspect of his situation may still require skilled help, but not the same type of help as would be indicated for the undoubted illness (see p. 83). A picture of alcoholism together with complaint of depression, is illustrated by the following case extract.

> A married woman aged 35 had been drinking excessively for three or four years. Visited at home by a social worker, the house was in a terrible state and the children much neglected. The patient herself was dishevelled, obviously rather drunk, and declaring in a

maudlin fashion that she was no good and that the family might as well be rid of her.

How should the social worker respond to this situation? Quite certainly an entirely inadequate course of action would be simply to arrange for a prescription of anti-depressant drugs, and let the patient mix these drugs with the drinking. Treatment cannot be intelligently and usefully started until it is known what there is to treat. The obverse approach, and one as misguided as the ill thought out use of drugs, is to assume that all alcoholics can be a bit maudlin at times, and to dismiss this woman's complaint as 'just the alcoholic miseries' – later perhaps to hear that she killed herself.

How is the question as to whether such a patient as this is suffering from a depressive illness in practice to be decided? Assessment of the history is very important – a previous history of depressive illness, an event such as childbirth or bereavement which might have precipitated the illness, a sense of some more or less demarcated point where 'things changed' and the patient knew that whatever the previous ups and downs of mood, something was now being experienced which was fixed and of different degree. A family history of depression can also be an important indicator. With the history has to be integrated what details can be observed of present behaviour and mental state. But it is also quite true that many alcoholics will when drinking show emotional lability, will cry easily, will talk of the hopelessness of their lives. Immediately in all such instances to leap to a diagnosis of depressive illness would result in a great deal of over-diagnosis. The dilemma can be very real, and even ex-perienced clinical judgement may be unable to resolve this diagnostic question while that patient is drunk. The patient's account may be inconstant, it may seem to be overdramatized, drinking certainly makes people miserable, the immediate life situation may be distressingly fraught and chaotic, but it is still unclear whether or not behind this drinking lies a depressive illness.

In such circumstances the sensible rule is indeed to admit that diagnosis cannot be made in the presence of drinking, and to see the patient's stopping drinking as the prerequisite to the resolution of the diagnostic difficulty. After a week of sobriety it may be obvious that the misery has almost miraculously faded away – such often happens. Alternatively, it may become very apparent that a classical depressive illness now stands out as certainly as a rock left by the tide. Sometimes, though, even after a few weeks of in-patient observation and continued sobriety, it may be difficult to know whether what is emerging is a depressive illness, or a personality chronically prone to unhappy feelings and explosive declarations of misery. The ultimate resolution of the diagnostic problem might, for instance, be that the woman described above had always been a rather unhappy and insecure person, that in this setting and to relieve these feelings she had gradually started to drink and had been drinking heavily for five or more years, but that against all this background she had undoubtedly a year previously and following childbirth developed a true and severe depressive illness which had been untreated. The unravelling of such a story may require a lot of time, but arriving at a proper understanding is no optional extra if the depressed alcoholic is effectively to be helped.

The initial diagnostic question is whether a depressive illness is or is not present, but the coincidence of this illness and alcoholism may then have different meanings.

(i) A depressive illness has recently and almost fortuitously developed against the background of a long-standing alcoholic history. Life stresses associated with the drinking may have contributed to the precipitation of the depression.

(ii) The depressive illness has made a contribution to the genesis of the drinking problem. Sometimes the advent of a depression seems to accelerate the development of what was already a serious and developing alcohol problem. On other occasions the relationship seems to be even more direct – the drinking problem has arisen as a result of the patient's self-medicating a depressive illness with alcohol, and before the onset of the depression there has been no question of there being a drinking problem at all. This latter type of story is a not uncommon reason for development of alcoholism in middle-age, with a rapid worsening in the drinking over a surprisingly short period of time – perhaps over six months or a year.

THE PRACTICAL IMPORTANCE

Reasons for it being of practical importance to determine whether an alcoholic patient is suffering from a depressive illness are several. If such an illness exists it of course deserves treatment (as well as whatever psychological or social help may be necessary) – the illness may respond to an anti-depressant drug, or ECT may still sometimes be indicated if the patient does not respond to drug treatment. The second important reason for believing that every effort must be made not to miss this diagnosis is that if depression is untreated, any attempt to treat the alcoholism will be grossly handicapped. A depressed patient may find it extremely difficult to stop drinking, and untreated depression can on occasion run on for two or three years or even longer, perhaps then with partial remissions and further relapses making the time course even more blurred and extended.

A further important reason for taking the diagnostic question extremely seriously is the influence which the answer must have on assessment of suicidal risk. Alcoholics who are not suffering from depressive illness may kill themselves, but the risk is certainly enhanced if this illness is present.

For the long-term management, knowledge that there has been a depressive illness has a bearing which must be openly discussed with the patient. Once someone has suffered from one such illness he is at some risk of later again developing depression, after a longer or shorter interval, and if he can recognize early signs and seek appropriate help, a lot of trouble may be averted. A depressive illness is a not uncommon cause of relapse into drinking after a longish period of sobriety. Paradoxically, the development of an underlying depression may be the reason after many years for the alcoholic's eventually seeking help. It may be an expression of his depressive illness when he says that he 'can't carry on any more', starts to blame himself rather than others for his drinking, or makes the suicidal gesture which gets him into hospital.

Summing the matter up, it can fairly be said that an awareness of the significance of depressive illness is so essential to working with alcoholics that anyone who is going to take a close interest in alcoholism will also need to develop a very good understanding of depression. If in relation to this question there exists a golden rule, it is that if an alcoholic is suffering from depressive illness, the therapeutic priority is to aid and persuade that patient first to stop drinking (offering perhaps immediate admission to achieve this purpose). Treating the depression is then the second phase of help and the immediate follow-through. It is generally messy and ineffective to try to treat a depressive illness when the patient is still drinking.

HYPOMANIA

Pathological elevation of mood is not so common a condition as pathological depression, and when it occurs does not carry a particularly high risk of being associated with drinking. Occasionally the hypomanic patient may, though, find that alcohol relieves unpleasant elements in his feelings – accompanying the basic elevation of mood the hypomanic state may be characterized by a considerable admixture of anxiety, irritability and suspiciousness. Mixed affective illnesses exist where the patient is both excited and tearful, with a confusing presentation that moves within minutes from elation to depression. A patient with repeated hypomanic bouts may give the appearance of 'bout drinking'. In an attack he is likely to lose his social judgement, and to spend large sums of money and live things up, and this general disinhibition, as well as the more specific seeking of relief from unpleasant feelings, may contribute to the drinking. The treatment is primarily that of the underlying illness.

A more difficult diagnostic problem arises when there is just a suspicion that the patient's mood may phasically be becoming slightly elevated but with the condition in no way approaching a hypomanic illness in severity. This slight elevation and disinhibition may appear to be sufficient to spark off some weeks of drinking, and on occasion this is a plausible explanation of 'periodic drinking', although there are many other explanations for such a drinking pattern (p. 41). What is being talked about here is a mood disturbance which would usually be seen as a character trait (cyclothymic personality), rather than as an illness, but clearly there is no absolute demarcation between this sort of state and hypomania. In turn, hypomania merges with mania, with the latter term indicating a state of appalling overexcitement, or the traditional picture of 'raving madness'. A patient with fully developed mania is far too disordered to be other than rapidly admitted to hospital, and drinking as a complication of this illness is not a question which arises other than in the very short term.

PHOBIC ANXIETY STATES

The phobic anxiety syndrome is a common psychiatric condition. It is characterized by acute anxiety in certain situations, with consequent avoidance of those situations. Fear may be of open spaces, or even of going outside the house at all – the problem of 'the house-bound housewife'. There may be a fear of closed spaces, of getting into a lift or of travelling in the underground or subway, or in trains or buses. Quite often a fear of public places is coupled with an acute distaste for being observed – eating in a café is quite impossible. There may be a fear of heights. Sudden overwhelming attacks of anxiety may occur, with the patient convinced that he is going to collapse, or even die. There may be an elevated background anxiety level, or the patient may only experience abnormal anxiety in specific situations. The symptoms can vary over time, or be relatively unremitting. There may be a rather narrow and easily identi-fiable range of situations which are anxiety provoking, or such a wide range of situations may be held responsible that it is a difficult task to list them. The syndrome which is being described here is very different in degree from a monosymptomatic phobia, such as a fear of spiders.

The majority of patients who find themselves developing phobic anxiety will not use alcohol for relief, and some will soon realize that alcohol poses a tempting danger and will avoid drink. For others alcohol is, however, used for self-medication, and particularly perhaps by the person who has willy-nilly to get out of the house and continue work. Alcohol may in the short term provide highly effective relief, and because the drink gives such immediate and large reward, dependence is then apt to develop rapidly. It is as if there were symptoms *ab initio* to be relieved, which were in many ways equivalent to withdrawal symptoms, without there being any need for the patient first to drink for years and develop withdrawal. This is precisely an example of the sort of condition which a therapist may believe to be uncommon until properly alerted, when he will begin to discover many such problems among his case load.

A woman aged 50 was admitted to hospital with a long history of drinking. Her immediate presentation was that of a working woman who earned her living by getting up early and going out to do office cleaning. She would have a drink at six o'clock before leaving the house, and then put a couple of bottles of wine into her bag. What was to be found in the old notes was that many years previously her first presentation to the hosptial was as someone with a phobic state who found great difficulty in leaving her house. Careful questioning revealed that phobic anxiety symptoms still

very much persisted, although alcohol dependence had by now
certainly been contracted as a problem in its own right.

Very often, though, there is a catch, for rather than the drinking being
consequent on the underlying phobic anxiety, phobic symptoms seem to
develop as a consequence of the drinking. In such latter instances the
mechanism may be that the drinking and the repeated withdrawal
ultimately lead to the building-up of a high background state of anxiety,
and this type of mood disturbance can bring out any latent capacity to
develop situational phobias.

The practical clinical approach when an alcoholic appears to be suffering from a phobic anxiety state is usually to arrange hospital admission,
both for purposes of diagnosis and of treatment. It is difficult to assess the
true severity and fixedness of the phobic symptoms until the patient has
been completely off alcohol for some weeks, and sometimes a longer
period of observation is required. What may then happen is that seemingly
rather severe phobic symptoms fade away, and that in the event there is no
phobic anxiety to be treated. The symptoms were part of general alcoholic
'bad nerves'.

If, however, phobic symptoms persist in severe degree, an effort then
has to be made to treat them, with treatment started while the patient is in
hospital. Treatment of the underlying condition requires sobriety, and an
attempt to treat these symptoms when the patient is still drinking is a
hopeless undertaking. Treatment will today usually involve the planned
application of specialized behaviour therapy techniques, and the response
is often excellent provided that the patient can co-operate, that there is not
too high a background level of anxiety, and that the phobic situations are
not too universal. It would, though, be optimistic to suppose that behaviour therapy is a panacea, for those favourable conditions are not
always fulfilled.

The use of minor tranquillizers or hypnotics with such patients has to
be approached with extreme caution. To treat the phobic alcoholic, while
he is still drinking, by giving him a minor tranquillizer is likely to be both
dangerous and ineffective. Drugs and alcohol will be haphazardly mixed,
with risk of superadded drug dependence. Indeed, by the time the severely
phobic alcoholic presents for treatment, it is not uncommon to find that he
has a medically-induced drug problem, as well as his alcohol dependence.

SCHIZOPHRENIA

Schizophrenia is not a frequent concomitant of alcoholism, although the association occurs sufficiently often to deserve its place in any diagnostic check-list. This statement depends on the strictness with which the diagnosis of schizophrenia is being made, and the word is given a habitually more circumscribed clinical meaning in Britain than in the USA. It is not appropriate here comprehensively to tackle such a major and classically complex aspect of general psychiatry as what counts as schizophrenia. For present purposes the assumption will be made that this diagnosis is properly restricted to a progressive psychotic illness with many variations on the central themes of fixed delusions which may or may not be paranoid, auditory or other hallucinations, strange feelings of being influenced or having one's thoughts interferred with or of being able to influence other people, jumbling of thought processes, flattened or inappropriate emotion and diminution or lack of drive.

The reason for schizophrenia not more often leading to seconday alcoholism is presumably that alcohol is largely not sensed as a useful drug for relieving the schizophrenic's unpleasant feelings. An additional reason may be that the person who is developing schizophrenia is often attempting to mobilize psychological defences which will enable him somehow to hold his being together in the face of a frightening threat. In such a position, alcohol might be dysfunctional, with intoxication bringing too great an upsurge of dangerous feelings at a time when it is in any case extremely difficult to integrate surging psychic material. Such an explanation is, though, speculative.

Those few schizophrenics who do run into difficulties with drink appear to do so for one of a number of reasons. The illness is sometimes associated at a certain stage with much experience of anxiety, and such a patient may sedate himself with alcohol. A patient who has socially deteriorated as a result of his schizophrenia, and become involved in a skid row way of life, may in that environment drift into drink. It is, though, not uncommon to find in the most disabled skid row population a few schizophrenics who are keeping themselves rather apart from the drinkers, and who certainly do not want the companionship of the drinking gang.

The differential diagnosis between alcoholic hallucinosis and schizophrenia is discussed elsewhere (p. 74). If an alcoholic patient appears to have schizophrenia, this is certainly another strong indication for a hospital admission so that in a sober setting diagnosis can be made and treatment initiated. Treatment of schizophrenia is likely to involve the use of major tranquillizers, the follow-through of continued out-patient care and social help. Schizophrenic symptoms may often but not always be brought under control wih drug treatment, and the drug will usually have to be continued in maintenance doses. A long-acting drug will perhaps have to be given by injection once a month. Special problems arise when the patient's continued drinking results in a chaotic life, and failure to keep in contact with after-care services.

The general aim should therefore be both to treat the schizophrenia and the alcoholism as effectively as possible. Untreated, each condition works against the other but, equally, success in one sphere makes treatment of the other problem more possible. The alcoholic schizophrenic is certainly someone who is going to need very long-term help, and all the integrated skills of a treatment team.

DAMAGE TO THE TISSUE OF THE BRAIN

The question often arises as to whether an alcoholic is suffering from brain damage. If the damage is gross there will be no diagnostic difficulty, but the diagnosis (and significance) of lesser degrees of damage commonly sets problems.

The most familiar picture is that of an associated alcoholic dementia, and this condition is discussed more fully on p. 103 in relation to physical damages which can result from drinking. Much the same sort of picture is to be seen when the patient is developing a dementia for any other reason (pre-senile dementia, for instance, or senile or arterio-sclerotic dementia). The patient with alcoholic dementia will typically give a history of many years heavy drinking with ultimate development of brain damage. With non-alcoholic dementia the sequence of events is the other way round: the patient develops dementia and, as a result of the ensuing disinhibition and personality deterioration, becomes involved in drinking.

The fact that brain damage can be cause as well as consequence of drinking needs to be written into any diagnostic check-list. Besides brain damage due to degenerative processes such as those already mentioned, the significance of a history of brain injury should be specially borne in mind. Instances certainly occur where personality change as a sequel to head injury is disproportionate to any fall-off in intellectual functioning, and this type of personality change may result in alcoholism as a late sequel of a road accident. The following brief case extracts show some of the many possible organic relationships which should be on that check-list:

A young man aged 23, of previously stable pesonality, sustained a severe head injury in a car crash, and was unconscious for several days. He appeared to make a good recovery and there was no paralysis. However, his concentration seemed rather impaired, his wife complained about his irritability, and although he went back to clerical work his performance had fallen off. Five years later he was drinking very heavily.

A woman civil servant aged 50, of previously unblemished record, suffered a subarachnoid haemorrhage (a bleed into the space around the brain). The leaking blood vessel was operated on, and she 'recovered completely'. But she had in fact sustained a degree of brain damage. Work habits which had for a lifetime been almost over-meticulous now deteriorated, and she was suddenly found to be drinking secretly in the office.

A boy aged 16 developed a severe viral brain infection (encephalitis) and was for a time desperately ill. Within a few years he was dramatically involved in crime and continued a career as a burglar even after losing one arm in an accident. Drinking became a superadded problem. He came from a stable home, and his two brothers and his sister grew up to lead settled and happy lives.

A man aged 40 suffered from crippling obsessional symptoms, and a leucotomy was performed. His obsessional symptoms were relieved, but although up to the time of his operation he had been a very moderate drinker, he now rapidly developed alcohol dependence.

A woman of 60 presented with alcoholism, seemingly of recent onset. She was found to have a brain tumour.

Some of these case histories certainly illustrate only rather rare associations, and the precise part that brain damage played in the aetiology of the drinking is in some isntances difficult to establish. But the general picture which is built up by listing these diverse cases is valid and important. Some associations between brain damage and alcoholism are relatively common (dementia or post traumatic personality deterioration, for example), while others, such as tumour, are rare, but the general message that no diagnostic assessment is complete without thinking about the possible significance of brain involvement has to be stressed. Alcoholism can also supervene as a complication of mental subnormality of any origin.

Whatever the underlying brain syndrome associated with alcoholism, the clinical features can be grouped under a number of headings. There are of course firstly the primary symptoms of the brain damage itself. Features of the drinking problem will also stand in their own right, but it is the interaction of the underlying brain damage and the drinking which gives these cases their colouring. Personal and social deterioration may seem to be disproportionate to the drinking, or suddenly to have accelerated. Drunken behaviour where there is underlying brain damage appears to be particularly heedless of consequences, antisocial, or plain careless. There are increasing episodes of violence, or the patient sets his lodgings on fire. There is also an increased sensitivity to alcohol; the patient gets drunk on less drink, and with relatively little alcohol becomes disinhibited or begins to fall about.

Given proper alertness to the possibility of such underlying problems, what are then the practical implications? If brain involvement is in any way suspected, this usually constitutes an indication for hospital admission, so that appropriate neurological and psychological investigations can be carried out with a sober patient. The sad fact is that most of the possibly relevant brain conditions are going to prove more diagnosable than treatable, but even so an accurate diagnostic formulation is the necessary basis for working out what best is to be done. If, for instance, an alcoholic is severely brain damaged, the only kind and safe policy may be to propose long-term hospital care, or care in some tolerant but controlling residential community. If there is milder damage, the patient will be able to keep going outside an institution, but brain damage adversely affects the course of alcoholism, and relapse and further troubles are probably to be expected. The continuing treatment policy must be so set up as to be able to meet these sorts of eventuality, and be designed in particular to protect the family in what may well be a miserable and worsening situation. The emphasis may sometimes have to be on rather directive intervention, on 'management' rather than the subtleties, on ensuring that money is properly handled or that the local publicans will not serve drinks. But even here there is no cause for absolute pessimism, for sometimes a patient with brain damage will be able to stop drinking, the progression of alcoholic dementia will be arrested, and the patient's behaviour will improve.

PATHOLOGICAL JEALOUSY

Jealousy is a normal human emotion, and it is not easy to set a cutting point between the normal and pathological. At one end of the spectrum there are, though, a group of people whose lives are plagued and corrupted by their jealous feelings, and who make life miserable for the objects of their jealousy. For reasons which will be discussed below (p. 92) this condition is likely to be met quite frequently in the treatment of drinking problems, and one should know how to recognize its features.

> A 34-year-old garage owner said that he had been painfully jealous ever since adolescence. His jealousy was now threatening to break up his marraige. He would repeatedly charge his wife with infidelity, taunting her and threatening her, as well as accusing her. His mental state when he made these charges was one of extreme distress – an overwhelming sense of being betrayed, of not being loved, of having a secret kept from him. There would then be explosive rows, and sometimes violence resulted. Later he would be desperately sorry, and transiently realize the falseness and cruelty of his accusations. But very shortly worrying doubts would again return. He would come home secretly and keep watch on the house, and sometimes he would follow his wife down the road. He would cross-question his children as to whether any other man had been into the house. He went through the ashtrays to see whether an unfamiliar brand of stub end was to be found in the litter. His wife's handbag was regularly searched, and he checked on her underclothes for seminal stains. Recently he had thought of hiring a detective. He remained sexually potent, and wanted to keep his wife pregnant so as to make her uninteresting to other men. His drinking appeared to be inextricably mixed with the

whole story, but his jealousy only came to light when his wife was interviewed.

The essential characteristics of this syndrome suggest that it may sometimes parallel an obsessional disorder, although this is not a view of the condition which finds approval in the standard psychiatric texts. The constant rumination, the fact that there is frequent (if only short-lived and partial) realization of the falseness of the belief, the unpleasantness of the associated feelings, the compulsive need to check, and the transient relief from the act of checking, are features very reminiscent of obsession. But it seems certain that pathological jealousy cannot be related to any one all-embracing psychiatric diagnosis, and underlying the common present-, ing features of pathological jealousy may be any one of several psychiatric disorders, including paranoid schizophrenia. 'Alcoholism' is then given its place in the conventional check-list, with pathological drinking being seen as one of several possible underlying causes for the common picture.

The usual view is therefore that alcoholism may be a cause of jealousy (rather than jealousy a cause of alcoholism). The psychodynamic explanations offered for this chain of events is complex, but can be sketched out in very abbreviated terms as the individual's doubting his own masculinity and therefore drinking, his drinking leading to impotence, and the reaction to impotence being jealousy. Impotence and pathological jealousy are thus alleged frequently to coexist. Pathological jealousy is also sometimes vaguely subsumed (if not explained) under the general heading of 'alcoholic paranoia'.

There is much still to be found out about this condition, but it may be questioned whether the conventional view that alcoholism causes pathological jealousy is too simple. The story which the patient gives more often suggests that jealousy has been in some degree a lifelong feature, perhaps even with manifestations in childhood, and very early family dynamics are rather obviously related to the genesis of the problem. The distress which is associated with the experience of jealousy may be appalling, and the patient in adulthood discovers that this distress is at least temporarily relieved by drinking. Rather, therefore, than there always being a specific relationship between jealousy and alcoholism, it may sometimes provide just another illustration of the fact that anyone for whom drink is available, and who suffers from any sort of chronic psychological distress, may be led into excessive drinking as a result of self-medication. The general level of heightened anxiety so often associated with alcohol dependence may then make the jealousy more intractable, and the situation becomes circular.

However, by the time the patient comes for help both jealousy and drinking have probably been going on for many years, and it can be extremely difficult to untangle the true historical relationship of the two elements. In the here-and-now they are usually best seen as mutually interacting, as exacerbating each other, than as either taking precedence. The practical approach is to try somehow to persuade the patient to stop drinking, and then assess the seriousness of the jealousy. What happened to the garage owner is fairly typical, and shows that pessimism is by no means always well-founded if drinking can be got out of the way.

> He 'realized that something had to be done about it', and as an act of faith he stopped drinking. He immediately needed to talk about his jealousy, which was at first very painful for him. But the terrible scenes of destructive accusation forthwith ceased. He was able to realize that drinking had certainly in this sense been making matters worse, and been leading to drunken acting-out of his anxieties. He and his wife were for the first time able safely to discuss his jealousy, both admitting its irrationality, but agreeing that his feelings were a serious and painful problem for both of them. Over the next few months he then reported that 'my nerves are much better, not all jumpy the way I used to be when I was drinking'. As his mood lifted, the intensity of his jealousy considerably faded, and to his surprise he and his wife settled on a rather joking way of dealing with the problem, and one which helped them both. 'Come on, love, I say to him, none of that old nonsesne, you're my one and only and you know it.' Seen a year later he still on occasion had a surge of jealous feelings (he would not take his wife to a party), but these feelings were less severe than they had been for many years, and he and his wife could live with the situation.

One might guess that the degree of recovery in this man's jealousy was related to the generally much happier and more mutually supportive marriage which evolved when he stopped drinking. If the condition is in any true sense similar to obsessional illness, obsessional disorder tends to improve when mood disturbance improves, and this too had probably contributed to the amelioration. The destructiveness which results from a jealous man being drunk is perhaps just an example of the general truth that when someone is intoxicated every conflict tends to be acted out, to achieve frenzied proportions, and thus a vicious circle is set up.

The extracts from this case story illustrate an approach which focused initially on the drinking, in the hope that the jealousy would then become more manageable. This is almost inevitably the best approach, for unless one is dealing with an underlying psychotic illness (which is seldom the case), there is no specific treatment available for the jealousy. Drugs have no part to play, and behavioural treatments are largely untried. But talking the matter through in sympathetic and common-sense fashion, bringing husband and wife together to work on the problem, encouraging a sense of optimism, may if the patient stays off drink often bring good results. Sometimes, though, the condition is intractable. The patient simply cannot stop drinking, and the result is break-up of the marriage (with the husband still haunting the doorstep), or even a tragic drunken murder. The condition does not, however, generally deserve the pessimistic reputation with which it has been stigmatized.

The reasons for giving this space to what has often been termed a rare syndrome are several. It may be doubted whether the condition is in fact all that rare; with an open eye and alert questioning, many more cases will come to light. Although the basic description of the syndrome is to be found in the textbooks, the clinical handling of this problem seldom receives due attention. It is a condition easily missed, but very real once recognized, and it needs to be given a definite place on the check-lists of anyone working with alcoholism.

ANOREXIA NERVOSA

Very rarely a case may be encountered where a patient who is primarily suffering from anorexia nervosa is found to be drinking excessively. Despite the unlikelihood of any of us ever encountering such a presentation, a brief note is worthwhile and awareness of the possibility of such a picture may help to resolve an otherwise baffling diagnostic problem. There are of course many more common reasons for weight loss among alcoholic patients including malnutrition and self-neglect, but here is an example of anorexia concealed within the drinking presentation.

A young woman aged 22 was admitted to a psychiatric hospital because of her excessive drinking, which to the perplexity of her close and controlling family had been of serious but intermittent severity over the previous two years. On admission she was evidently rather underweight. She showed no withdrawal symptoms, but within a few days the nurses were commenting on her lack of appetite. The possibility of depression was considered. The patient then complained of 'inability to keep anything down', and was often going off to her room and being sick immediately after a meal. A wide variety of investigation was then made and a gastro–enterologist called in for an opinion. The weight loss became very worrying indeed and there was mounting concern as to the patient's survival. At this late state the correct diagnosis was at last made when a nurse discovered the patient secretly making herself vomit.

Anorexia nervosa usually affects young women, but men can also be affected. The primary picture is of weight loss, refusal of food or self–induced vomiting or purgation, together with a constant worry over possible weight gain and frequent reference to the mirror. Amenorrhoea is a common accompanying symptom among women. Patients with this condition seem to work by every trick and strategem against attempts to restore their weight, while insisting that nothing is wrong There may, though, be occasional short-lived eating binges. Why a very small minority of patients with this puzzling condition should engage in excessive drinking at the same time as starving themselves is quite obscure. There are various schools of thought on the treatment of anorexia nervosa but good nursing is probably the most essential ingredient.

MENTAL ILLNESS: THE GENERAL IMPLICATIONS

The account which has been given in this chapter of the many types of mental illness which may be associated with excessive drinking, and of the complex nature of those possible relationships, must not be interpreted as meaning that only the psychiatrist can treat the alcoholic. Neither does the fact that psychiatric treatment or admission to a psychiatric hospital may be indicated for some of these patients mean that treatment of alcoholism is a psychiatric preserve. However, what must be evident is that psychiatry may quite often have a part to play, and that a working liason with psychiatric services should be available to anyone helping with drinking problems. An awareness of this psychiatric dimension must, moreover, be important, whatever the therapist's professional discipline.

REFERENCES

Cutting J (1978) A reappraisal of alcohol psychosis. *Psychological Medicine*, **8**, 285–295.

Freed EX (1973) Drug abuse by alcoholics: a review. *International Journal of Addictions*, **8**, 451–473.

Freed EX (1975) Alcoholism and schizophrenia: the search for perspectives. *Journal of Studies on Alcohol*, **36**, 853–881.

Goodwin DW (1977) The alcoholic blackout and how to prevent it. In: Birnbaum IM and Lawrence ES (eds) *Alcohol and Human Memory*, pp 177–184. Hillsdale NJ: Erlbaum.

Goodwin DW, Crane JB and Guze SB (1969) Alcoholic blackouts. *American Journal of Psychiatry*, **126**, 77–84.

Goodwin DW and Erickson CK (eds) (1979) *Alcoholism and Affective Disorders*. Jamaica NY: Spectrum.

Gross MM (ed.) (1973) *Alcohol Intoxification and Withdrawal*. New York: Plenum.

Gross MM (ed) (1975) *Alcohol Intoxification and Withdrawal. Experimental studies II*. New York: Plenum.

Gross MM, Lewis E and Hastey J (1974) Acute alcohol withdrawal syndrome. In: Kissin B and Begleiter H (eds) Biology of Alcoholism, Vol. 3: *Clinical Pathology*, pp 191–263. New York: Plenum.

Keeler HM, Taylor CI and Miller WC (1979) Are all recently detoxified alcoholics depressed? *American Journal of Psychiatry*, **136**, 586–588.

Kendell RE (1976) The classification of depression: a review of contemporary confusion. *British Journal of Psychiatry*, **129**, 15–28.

Merry J, Reynolds CM and Bailey J *et al* (1976) Prophylactic treatment of alcoholism by lithium carbonate. *Lancet*, **2**, 481–482.

Pottenger M, McKernon J, Patrie LE *et al* (1978) The frequency and persistence of depressive symptoms in the alcohol abuser. *Journal of Nervous and Mental Diseases*, **166**, 562–570.

Ritson B (1977) Alcoholism and suicide. In: Edwards C and Grant M (eds) *Alcoholism: New Knowledge and New Responses*, pp 271–278. London: Croom Helm.

Schukit MA (1973) Alcoholism and sociopathy: a diagnostic confusion. *Quarterly Journal of Studies on Alcohol*, **34**, 157–164.

Shepherd M (1961) Morbid Jealousy: some clinical and social aspects of a psychiatric symptom. *Journal of Mental Science*, **107**, 687–704.

Stockwell T, Hodgson R and Ranklin H (1982) Tension reduction and the effects of prolonged alcohol consumption. *British Journal of Addiction*, **77**, 65–73.

Victor M and Hope JM (1955) The phenomenon of auditory hallucination in chronic alcoholism: a critical evaluation of the status of alcoholic hallucinosis. *Archives of General Psychiatry*, **126**, 451–481.

Weissman MM and Myers JK (1980) Clinical depression in alcoholism, *American Journal of Psychiatry*, **137**, 372–373.

Chapter 6
Physical Complications of
Excessive Drinking

This chapter deals with medical matters but every care has been taken to avoid the mystification of medical language. Within a total and balanced approach to alcoholism the physical element must be seen as often very important. Helping services must be so organized as to cope effectively with diagnosis and treatment in the physical domain, and whatever the particular professional affiliation of the person who is working with the alcoholic, there is need for an alertness towards possible physical pathologies. For instance, the voluntary worker in a lay counselling centre is, of course, practising his own special types of skill, and no one would suggest that he should also cultivate a highly specialized knowledge of liver pathology. It is, though, a reasonable expectation that he should know enough about the liver to understand the significance to his client of a diagnosis of cirrhosis, rather than himself being mystified by this term and consequently deflecting that client from talking about something of vital importance. A polite conspiracy can be set up which pretends that the body does not exist.

WHY PHYSICAL COMPLICATIONS MATTER

Firstly, it should be stressed that we are not talking about 'small print', and a range of unlikely happenings. Many of these physical complications are common in any alcoholic population. That they are frequently recoverable if detected early and will regress if the patient stops drinking is another fact that needs to be underlined. If, on the other hand, drinking continues, many of these conditions can be crippling or will seriously threaten life. Yet another reason why physical complications must be important to everyone working in this area (whatever his professional role) is that absolute segmentation between mental, social and physical disability is unreal. As has already been stressed (p. 56) the real-life experience of the patient knows no such divisions.

This leads to the most fundamental and compelling reason for believing that physical complications matter: *understanding of their significance has to be integrated by the patient himself into an appraisal of his position.* Such understanding must frequently bear on his decision as to what he does about his drinking problem. As ever, the therapist is the informant, the person who brings up the issue, and who shares and reflects the patient's feelings and concerns, rather than the disembodied pronouncer of facts. The way in which information on physical problems is presented to the patient can be part of therapy, and the substance of therapy is often the proper handling of the realities of the patient's situation. Here are two dialogues which illustrate different ways in which the patient's concern over his physical health can be met at interview. Firstly, and very briefly, a dialogue which is not to be dismissed as caricature.

> *Patient* What did the doctor mean when he said my liver had been hit by the drinking?
> *Counsellor* You will have to ask the doctor to explain.
> *Patient* But he never explains anything.
> *Counsellor* Well, he's the person to ask.

Secondly, and more constructively:

> *Patient* What did the doctor mean when he said my liver had been hit by the drinking?
> *Counsellor* That's something pretty important to talk about. What did you think he meant?
> *Patient* I suppose I was dead scared. Not sure I believe him, though. He may just be trying to put the frighteners under me. But if what he's really saying is that I'm going to die of cirrhosis, I'll go out on the crest of the all-time greatest booze-up.
> *Counsellor* I don't think anyone is wanting to scare you in a horror-story sort of way, but it's your own liver and you've a right to know about it.
> *Patient* So what's the score?
> *Counsellor* I spoke to your doctor on the phone. You've undoubtedly done your liver some harm and if you go on drinking, you would be risking cirrhosis, and that's a miserable way to die. If you stop drinking, your liver's going to heal. You've a right to

know all the facts, it's reasonable to be anxious, but at least there's
something very positive you can do towards repairing the damage
– just stop drinking.
Patient When I was getting that pain, I guessed it must be my liver,
but I suppose I've just been shutting my eyes, doing the 'it can't
happen to me' trick.

The vital question is indeed what any information on physical consequences means to the patient. Too often the results of the physical
examination and laboratory tests are left in the case-notes, and no one
thinks even to ask whether these findings have been shared with the person
most intimately affected. It is material which is labelled 'not to be handled
by the patient'. The patient deserves to be given the facts, but for this
information to have meaning it has to be talked through, thought about,
and felt about. This is an occasion for the therapist further to establish the
quality of a warm and open relationship.

There can be no doubt that some patients who have continued up to
that moment to drink in the face of every other type of catastrophe stop
drinking abruptly when persuaded that alcohol is posing a tangible threat
to their physical health. One may suspect, though, that even if the news of
physical damage constitutes the turning point, in reality this is only the
final event to tip a decision where the moment for change has been set up
by many previous happenings. But using the results of the physical
examination or the laboratory tests for crude scare-tactics is likely to be
counter-productive. The patient may dismiss what he is being told simply
because the information is too frightening to be accepted, or he may
indeed decide that all is lost and that he may as well drink himself to death.

CAUSES OF PHYSICAL COMPLICATIONS

Alcoholism causes physical damage by many direct and indirect effects on
the body. For instance, alcohol has a direct toxic effect on the liver, and a
good diet and vitamin supplements will not protect the person who is
continuing to drink heavily from developing cirrhosis. On the other hand,
certain varieties of brain damage are due to associated vitamin deficiency,
and vitamins can protect against likelihood of damage even when the
person continues to drink. Deficiencies seldom involve only one vitamin
or nutritional element, and more often there are multiple deficiencies. In

some conditions, both the toxic element and disturbance of nutritional status may be implicated as a cause of damage at the same time.

What level of alcohol intake constitutes the threshold for physical dangers? The answer must vary according to the particular condition, but in general the evidence points to the probability that risk for many varieties of damage increases in proportion to alcohol intake, even within the range of what passes as 'social drinking'. This is probably true, for instance, in relation to brain damage, cirrhosis, the foetal alcohol syndrome, and certain other alcohol-related problems. Paradoxically, at very modest levels of alcohol intake, there is a suggestion that the drinker has an advantage over the teetotaler in longevity, but it is unclear whether this association exemplifies true cause-and-effect. But whatever the risks at the relatively lower ranges of intake, by the time someone is drinking in the fashion dictated by the dependence syndrome, the question of whether his level of intake carries dangers hardly needs to be asked. The answer is resoundingly 'yes' for nearly every tissue of the body. And quite apart from any specific tissue damage discussed in this chapter, it should be remembered that as a consequence of heavy drinking and dietary neglect, almost every aspect of the body's chemistry may in some circumstances be put out of balance; even such seemingly obscure aspects as serum zinc or magnesium levels may be disturbed.

CHECK-LIST OF PHYSICAL COMPLICATIONS

In the ensuing sections of this chapter, a range of physical complications which can result from excessive drinking will be described. As far as possible, non-technical language will be used, and tissue pathology and laboratory investigations will not be discussed in any detail. The medical reader should refer to a standard textbook for more technical information, but even the person with a specialized knowledge of medicine might with profit check through this list to be reminded of the variety of complications which can occur.

Rather than trying to arrange the list in order of importance (an almost impossible task), the headings have been arranged alphabetically for convenience of reference. But under those headings some indication is usually given of whether one is dealing with common or less common disorders.

ACCIDENTS

There are many well-recognized physical consequences of alcoholism which rightly receive textbook attention, but the fact that excessive drinking often leads to involvement in accidents goes relatively unnoticed. And yet the contribution of alcohol and alcoholism to minor accidents at home, at work and on the roads is enormous. Reports from the USA suggest that in that country drinking is involved in one-third of the injuries resulting from motor vehicle accidents and in one-half of deaths in such context, in over 40 per cent of industrial accidents, in perhaps 70 per cent of accidental drownings, and in 60 to 70 per cent of injuries or fatalities resulting from a fall. What proportion of all these casualties is to be attributed in any sense to 'alcoholism', as opposed to casual drinking is still largely unclear and must in any case vary from setting to setting. But practical experience confirms that people with serious drinking problems are very prone to accidents, and particularly nasty mishaps occur on account of ordinary attention and protective reflexes being impaired.

BLOOD DISORDERS

Alcoholism can be associated with almost any variety of anaemia. Bleeding, liver disease, malnutrition, malabsorption, chronic infections and the direct toxic effect of alcohol on bone marrow can all play a part. A lowered white cell count or, in certain conditions, a raised count may occur. Various mechanisms may affect clotting or cause a tendency to bruising or bleeding. An enlargement of the actual size of red blood cells (macrocytosis) can occur, and has been found of use as a screening test to detect otherwise undeclared excessive drinking.

BONES AND JOINTS

(i) Gout

A painful and intermittent swelling of the joints, particularly of fingers and toes, is fundamentally a constitutional metabolic abnormality, giving rise to high blood uric acid levels (the uric acid is deposited in the joints). An otherwise latent tendency towards gout may be brought out by heavy drinking, or established gout may be made worse.

(ii) Bones

Research has recently shown that alcoholics can develop degeneration in their bones. At present little is known about the incidence of this condition, but there is a problem here to which we should be alert. The patient who has broken his leg as a result of minor trauma may need his drinking history checked on.

BRAIN DAMAGE

(i) The Wernicke-Korsakoff Syndrome

Although Wernicke's and Korsakoff's syndromes were originally described as different entities, it has gradually become clear that they are intimately related consequences of the same pathology: a deficiency of thiamine (vitamin B1), giving rise to damage in a particular part of the brain (the periventricular area). The Wernicke element can be thought of as the acute presentation, while the Korsakoff element is the residual defect which is left after the acute illness, although sometimes a Korsakoff disorder develops insidiously and without a clear prior history of the Wernicke type of illness. These rather strange-sounding eponyms should not deflect the non-specialist from trying to understand what is being talked about and the following case abstract illustrates both how the acute element can present very suddenly and the type of chronic disorder which may occur when the Korsakoff state supervenes.

> A woman aged 48 who had been drinking a bottle of whisky each day for 10 or more years was admitted to a psychiatric hospital for detoxification. It was noted that she was suffering from severe peripheral neuropathy (weakness, tingling, and pain in the legs). On the evening of admission, she was found to be rather confused, to be complaining of double vision, and to be staggering. By the next evening, she was stuporose, and her eye movements were unco-ordinated (external ocular palsies). At this stage, and very much too late, she was started on massive doses of thiamine – the classical picture of confusion, neuritis, staggering gait, and ocular palsies should have alerted the staff to the dangerous onset of a Wernicke syndrome. After five days of acute illness, the confusion

cleared and the patient was then found to have a grossly impaired memory for recent events, a tendency to make things up to fill her gaps in memory (confabulation), and very little ability to remember new information, as witnessed by her difficulty in finding her way around the ward. This amnesic syndrome (Korsakoff's psychosis), showed very little recovery over the ensuing months, and arrangements had to be made for the patient's transfer to long-term residential care.

That is a story of a tragedy which might have been averted, and there is a good argument for giving thiamine prophylactically to any patient who is in danger of this sort of complication. The acute phase has a 15 to 20 per cent fatal outcome.

Perhaps 5 to 10 per cent of patients who continue with an unabated alcoholic career will experience Wernicke–Korsakoff type of damage, but given that in different parts of the world the nutrition of patients varies greatly, any precise statement on likely incidence rates would be misleading.

(ii) Alcoholic dementia

The classical picture of the Wernicke–Korsakoff syndrome has attracted most of the textbook attention in the past, but more recently it has become evident that an insidious and non-specific type of alcohol-related brain damage of varying degree of severity is a more common problem. It is a reasonable guess that among alcoholics attending any ordinary type of treatment facility, upwards of 50 per cent of cases aged over, say, 45 years, and with a protracted drinking history, will be found on careful assessment to show some degree of brain impairment.

At one end of the spectrum the picture tends to be so subtle as not easily to be picked up unless one is specially alert – some impairment of judgement, loss of perseverance and concentration, some minor interference with memory. At the other extreme is the fully developed picture of major dementia.

The introduction over the last few years of new X-ray technology (computerized axial tomography, or CAT scan), means that it is now much easier to determine the presence and extent of brain damage. The full clinical significance of what these pictures reveal only becomes evident over time, for in some patients the seeming 'atrophy' (brain shrinkage) corrects itself after a few months of abstinence. One immediate message is that psychological testing may be misleadingly pessimistic if carried out too soon after withdrawal and interpreted as evidence of irreversible brain damage.

(iii) Cerebellar degeneration

The cerebellum is a part of the brain concerned with balance and integration of movement, and it is sometimes the primary focus for alcohol-related brain damage. The patient then shows an unsteady gait (and difficulties in co-ordination). Cessation of drinking will halt the progress of the disorder, but the patient may still be left with a disabling condition. This syndrome is not very common, but deserves to be better known.

(iv) Alcoholic amblyopia

This uncommon condition presents as a gradual blurring of vision, accompanied perhaps by difficulty in distinguishing red from green. Testing reveals a central blind spot (scotoma), with the peripheral field of vision intact. The cause is probably a mixed nutritional deficiency. The same picture sometimes occurs as 'tobacco amblyopia'.

(v) Very rare organic brain syndromes

To complete the list of alcohol-related brain syndromes, brief mention must be made of two conditions which are of great rarity and which in any case are only likely to be diagnosed post-mortem. Central pontine myelenolysis is a quickly fatal condition characterized by lesions in the lower part of the brain (brainstem). Marchiafava–Bignami disease is an atrophy of a deep structure in the brain (corpus callorum), resulting in dementia.

CANCERS

Because heavy drinkers are frequently also heavy smokers, it has been difficult to partition the relative contribution of either factor in the genesis of certain cancers. There is now, though, persuasive evidence that alcoholics experience a heightened incidence of cancers of the mouth, tongue, pharynx, larynx, oesophagus (gullet) and liver. The relationship with cancer of the stomach is more uncertain.

CHEST CONDITIONS

Alcoholism is the occasional cause of a variety of chest illnesses. Before the days of antibiotics, alcoholics used rather often to die of pneumonia. In an era when tuberculosis is becoming a rare disease, alcoholics still show a special susceptibility to this disease. Alcohol may led to chest infection by suppression of the body's immune responses, but self-neglect and the associated way of life must also be important, specially in the skid row alcoholic population. Because alcoholics may both vomit and become stuperose, they are prone to inhale material into their lungs and hence develop lung abscesses or bronchiectasis (dilation and infection of the smaller bronchi).

That many alcoholics are heavy cigarette smokers should again be remembered. A carcinoma of the lung is not, therefore, an uncommon coincidental finding, sometimes confusing the diagnostic picture. What is thought to be an alcoholic dementia turns out, for instance, to be a secondary cancer in the brain, or a severe 'alcoholic' peripheral neuropathy is found to be a cancer-related (carcinomatous) neuropathy.

The simple message is that if an alcoholic who presents for assessment has not had a recent chest X-ray, such an examination should be arranged.

EPILEPSY

Withdrawal fits have been fully discussed on p. 72, but a number of other possible reasons for epilepsy among alcoholics must also be borne in mind, as well as the fact that epilepsy may be entirely coincidental. Heavy drinking may, for example, lower the threshold of convulsions in a person with an underlying epileptic tendency of any origin.

Alcoholics are often heavy cigarette smokers and a fit may on occasion be the first and tragic signal of the secondary spread to the brain (metastasis), from a cancer of the lung. Alcoholics are prone to accident and a fit may be symptomatic of old or more recent head injury. Alcoholic dementia may sometimes be accompanied by fits. A rather common cause of convulsion is coincidental withdrawal of sedative or hypnotic drugs, particularly barbiturates. Much rarer causes include alcohol–related hypoglycaemia (lowered blood sugar, p. 108), and fatty emboli lodging in the brain (see p. 110).

FOETAL ALCOHOL SYNDROME

That the mother's drinking can cause foetal damage was widely believed in the nineteenth century, but was later to be forgotten or dismissed as temperance scaremongering. It is only over the last few years that firm evidence has accumulated for the reality of the danger, and even so there are questions remaining as to the level of maternal drinking which carries risk. The evidence of a distinctive syndrome is much more widely accepted in the USA than in the UK, and it is unclear whether this reflects differing levels of awareness or a real difference in prevalence rates.

As it is now being described, the fully developed picture of the foetal alcohol syndrome (FAS) includes, among other features, a small head (microcephalus), certain facial deformities, deformities in the limbs, and often also an associated congenital heart disease. During infancy there is subsequent retardation in growth, co-ordination and mental development. As well as the occurrence of this major and typical syndrome, there are reports of increased rates of more non-specific congenital abnormalities and of stillbirth among babies of women who drink heavily. The greatest risk to the foetus is probably during the first few weeks of conception.

The crucial public health question relates of course to what is meant by 'heavy drinking' in this context. To start on solid ground, there can be no doubt that a woman who is drinking at a level which implies her having developed alcohol dependence is at risk of damaging her baby. For any alcoholism treatment service the practical message must be that a woman of child-bearing age who has a serious drinking problem requires very special counselling, and should be discouraged from having a baby until the drinking has been dealt with successfully. One has to think not only of the potential damage to an unborn child, but also of the lifetime guilt of the mother should a deformed child be born.

When one is seeking to advise as to what is the safe upper limit of drinking, the ground on which one can stand is less defined, and the evidence from different studies is conflicting. The most worrying interpretation is that any drinking during pregnancy may carry some increased risk of foetal abnormality. It seems best at present to advise the woman who is pregnant or contemplating pregnancy not to drink.

HEART AND BLOOD PRESSURE

The toxic effects of alcohol on heart and circulation do not often produce gross or obvious damage, but nonetheless they deserve note. Serious damage to the heart muscle is, for instance, exactly the sort of not very common but not very rare condition which is likely to be missed unless it is on one's check-list.

(i) Cardiac arrhythmias

Disorders of the heart's rhythm may occur as a result of acute intoxication or during withdrawal. The mildest presentation is that of palpitation caused by a few extra and irregular beats (extrasystoles). The induced irritability of the heart muscle may also give rise to atrial fibrillation, or more seriously, ventricular fibrillation (rapid and uncontrolled contractions of the chambers of the heart). In the USA, alcohol-induced fibrillation of the atrial chambers has been termed 'the holiday heart syndrome'.

(ii) Alcoholic cardiopathy (degeneration of the heart muscle)

This may be due to nutritional deficiency (beriberi heart disease), to the direct toxic effect of alcohol or of some impurity in the drink, or to a combination of such factors. This condition has been known as 'beer-drinker's heart', but can occur with excessive drinking of any other type of alcoholic beverage. The presenting signs and symptoms are an enlarged heart, heart failure, and arrythmia. This is again a condition where cessation of drinking is of paramount importance to survival.

(iii) Hypertension

There is epidemiological evidence to suggest that heavy alcohol intake may be associated with a raised blood pressure. Statistically, even quite moderate alcohol intake is associated with raised blood pressure. A rise in blood pressure is often seen during the first week or more of withdrawal, later settling completely.

(iv) Coronary artery disease

Here the position is rather obscure. There are some reports to suggest that a moderate intake of alcohol may actually protect against heart disease, but heavier long-term exposure is probably a risk-factor for coronary disorder.

LIPAEMIA

For a variety of complex reasons, alcoholics may show a rise in circulating blood fats (serum triglycerides). This will only be picked up by laboratory tests, but probably carries implications for enhanced risk of arteriosclerosis.

HYPOGLYCAEMIA

Heavy drinking can cause a serious lowering of blood sugar level (hypoglycaemia). The condition is similar to that experienced by the diabetic who takes too much insulin, or who after his insulin goes too long without food. The mechanism involved may include the inhibitory effect of alcohol on glucose formation in the liver (fasting hypoglycaemia), or a complex disturbance in hormonal regulation (reactive hypoglycaemia).

Clinically, the patient may present as flushed and sweaty with a rapid pulse, and with the appearance of being 'drunk' and unco-ordinated. Alternatively, the patient may already be in coma when his hypoglycaemia first comes to notice. There are dangers of hypoglycaemia being overlooked and mistaken for simple alcoholic intoxication, or head injury. The condition carries about a 10 per cent risk of death.

Hypoglycaemia sometimes also occurs when a child takes a large dose of alcohol – the six-year-old who, for example, finds some cherry brandy left around in the kitchen and who is attracted by the taste. Such a happening can result in tragedy, and the condition is much more dangerous than in the adult.

LIVER DISEASES

A variety of different liver conditions can result from excessive drinking.

(i) Cirrhosis of the liver

Cirrhosis can be due to causes other than drinking, but in many Western countries alcoholism is an important or indeed the major cause of this disease. In the USA, cirrhosis now ranks as the fifth most common cause of death among adults aged between 25 and 65 years. And although excessive drinking has for long been recognized as carrying a frightening risk of cirrhosis (about 25 per cent of a clinical population of alcoholics will develop cirrhosis over, say, 20 years of heavy drinking), lesser degrees of drinking also enhance risk. The person who is drinking a regular four pints of beer per day somewhat enhances his risk of contracting cirrhosis, and women appear to be more vulnerable to liver damage than men, given equal alcohol exposure.

Cirrhosis results directly from the toxic effect of alcohol on the liver, rather than its being caused indirectly by nutritional deficiency. Essentially what happens is that the liver tissue becomes scarred and its architecture disorganized. The consequences are twofold. Firstly, the actual loss of functioning liver tissue will cause a range of metabolic disturbances, and ultimately liver failure may occur as a fatal termination. But secondly (and very importantly), the scarring and disorganization lead to blood vessels being squeezed and blocked off, with this physical damming causing a build-up of pressure in the portal venous system (the veins which carry blood from the alimentary tract to the liver). This can, in turn, cause bleeding from veins at the lower end of the gullet (oesophageal varices), and this bleeding may be massive and fatal.

Cirrhosis can exist in degrees. There is persuasive data that if the condition is not too advanced, the alcoholic cirrhotic who stops drinking greatly enhances his life expectancy, and at best the condition will completely cease to progress. From the patient's point of view, he may know nothing of this insidious condition until he suddenly becomes jaundiced, finds his abdomen swelling up with fluid (ascites), or has a massive bleed. More often, the diagnosis is picked up by a routine physical examination at an earlier stage, with confirmation coming from various special investigations.

That the alcoholic is at risk of this potentially devastating condition, which is, however, often recoverable if early diagnosis is made, is by itself a very strong reason for pleading that physical assessment of the patient with a drinking problem should never be neglected.

(ii) Alcoholic hepatitis

By this is meant an alcohol–induced *inflammation* rather than a *scarring* of the liver. The liver tissue is inflamed, but fixed structural damage has not occurred. The condition may, though, be 'pre–cirrhotic' and lead to a later scarring. Minor degrees of this inflammatory condition are common among alcoholics, but a major inflammatory state can also occur. The patient with a severe acute alcoholic hepatitis will be feverish, jaundiced, nauseated, lacking in appetite, and very ill. This picture usually develops in a patient who has had a fairly prolonged history of heavy drinking, but the onset may then be sudden and dramatic. About 10 per cent of patients with acute alcoholic hepatitis die in the attack.

(iii) Fatty liver

Not every enlarged painful liver is a cirrhotic liver. Interference with ordinary metabolic breakdown can lead to accumulation of fat in the liver, but the condition does not cause scarring, and is reversible. Careful assessment and full laboratory investigations may be needed for the differential diagnosis, and from the patient's point of view the fact that the liver problem has progressed even thus far should be taken as serious warning. Fatty infiltration can sometimes cause jaundice (obstructive jaundice), and may very occasionally result in liver failure, or death due to a fatty embolism (globules of fat getting into the circulation and obstructing arteries in the brain).

(iv) Carcinoma of the liver

The liver which is affected by alcoholic cirrhosis is particularly prone to the development of liver cancer. A cirrhotic patient who has seemingly been doing well rather suddenly begins rapidly to deteriorate.

MYOPATHY

Degeneration of the muscles (myopathy) is again one of those complications of alcoholism of which the public seems unaware and the medical profession not well–informed, and it is therefore a presentation which is easily overlooked. Here is a case abstract which illustrates a fairly typical picture.

A 45-year-old storekeeper who was severely alcohol dependent but who had succeeded in fragmenting his drinking into irregular bouts came along to complain that after his most recent drinking episode he had developed 'terrible rheumatics'. There was severe pain and some tenderness and swelling of both upper arms, and he could no longer lift his stock down from the shelves. It took about two months for him to make a reasonable recovery.

Myopathy can occur with all degrees of severity from the subclinical presentation, which is detected only on careful investigation and which is common, to the explosively acute condition, which is rare. Myopathy is often accompanied by a more or less severe peripheral neuritis (see p. 113), and it is the large muscle masses at the top of the legs or arms which are most typically affected. Rarely, the sudden breakdown of muscle tissue leads to metabolic disturbance, kidney failure and death. It is technically correct to distinguish between myopathy (muscle degeneration) and myositis (muscle inflammation), but in reality the conditions often merge.

OESOPHAGUS (GULLET) AND STOMACH

Here one is probably dealing largely with the direct corrosive effect of alcohol on the linings of these organs. Oesophageal cancer is discussed elsewhere (see p. 104).

(i) Oesophagitis

Inflammation of the oesophagus may occur and give a picture similar to gastritis.

(ii) Malory–Weiss syndrome

This is a tear of the lower end of the oesophagus caused by severe retching, with a consequent vomiting of blood.

(iii) Gastritis

Inflammation of the stomach lining gives rise to symptoms of dyspepsia.

The nausea and vomiting of acute alcoholic gastritis, occurring during or after a drinking binge, must not be confused with the gastric element in the withdrawal syndrome, which has its origin in the reactivity of the central nervous system rather than in any inflammation of the stomach lining. A couple of drinks will 'cure' the withdrawal retching, but make gastritis worse.

(iv) Peptic ulceration

There is an association between alcoholism and the occurrence of duodenal and gastric ulceration. This is due largely to the direct effect of alcohol, but a link in terms of common personality predisposition has been suggested. The surgeon who forgets to enquire into the drinking habits of his ulcer patient before operation may find himself dealing with DTs post-operatively, or a year later be confronted with a recurrence of ulceration.

Certain types of operation for ulcer (with partial removal of the stomach) may subsequently result in a much increased rate of alcohol absorption, so that the patient finds himself drunk and incapable after a quantity of alcohol which he could previously tolerate easily.

PANCREATITIS

Here is a brief description of a case of acute pancreatitis which emphasizes the potential seriousness of this unpleasant and by no means uncommon condition.

> A 50-year-old man turned up at a hospital emergency room, complaining of 'terrible pain in the guts'. With his history of frequently pestering this department, it was at first thought there was nothing much wrong. His groaning and the mounting intensity of pain then led to a diagnosis of perforated peptic ulcer. He was operated on that night and there was no perforated ulcer but a grossly inflamed pancreas. He went into a state of irrecoverable shock and died 12 hours post-operatively.

Pancreatitis is a highly dangerous condition, and because a mistaken diagnosis and ill-chosen operation much increase the risk of death, it is important to get the diagnosis right.

Most people have at least some idea as to where their liver is situated and are aware that liver damage can occur with heavy drinking. On the other hand, the majority of the population still seem uncertain as to where the pancreas is located or what it does, and are quite unaware of the nature and threat of pancreatitis.

An acute attack of pancreatitis is typically marked by sudden and very severe upper abdominal pain (often radiating to the back), vomiting, and every appearance of an emergency. A mortality rate of 10 to 40 per cent has been reported in various case series. As with cirrhosis of the liver, there are causes other than drinking, but if the condition is alcohol-related, there is usually a well-established history of alcoholism, although pancreatitis sometimes occurs after an isolated Saturday night binge in a relatively young person. As well as the acute form, relapsing or chronic pancreatitis may develop, with a repeated or continuing experience of low-grade pain and a gradual destruction of the pancreas leading to malnutrition (failure in secretion of digestive enzymes), or diabetes (failure of insulin secretion). Severe and chronic pain may lead to a dependence on opiates. Acute pancreatitis can allegedly induce a transient psychotic illness.

PERIPHERAL NEUROPATHY (OR NEURITIS)

A degeneration in sensory and motor nerves supplying the limbs can occur in alcoholics as a result of an associated deficiency of B group vitamins. The legs are more usually affected than the arms. The common picture is simply of absent ankle reflexes, some diminution in sensation, and perhaps a complaint of pins and needles or of burning feet. The much rarer and florid presentation is that of a patient supporting himself on crutches, and complaining of numbness and burning, together with great pain and weakness of the lower limbs. The neuropathy improves with adequate vitamin treatment, but even after one or two years recovery may not be complete.

TESTICULAR FUNCTION AND IMPOTENCE

Male alcoholics may show a considerable reduction in levels of circulating male hormone, and this may contribute to the high incidence of sexual problems among men with drinking problems, although physical and emotional factors are interrelated. The complaint may be both of impotence and loss of sexual drive. The extent to which recovery takes place when drinking is stopped is variable and not always complete.

THE NEED FOR TWO KINDS OF ALERTNESS

This chapter started with the plea that everyone working with alcoholics should be more aware of the importance of the physical element within the assessment and treatment plan. It should similarly be pleaded that everyone who works in the medical field should be vigilant as to the possibility of undeclared alcoholism being behind any one of a host of clinical presentations.

REFERENCES

Akhtar MJ (1977) Sexual disorders in male alcoholics. In: Madden JS, Walker R and Kenyon WH (eds) *Alcoholism and Drug Dependence: A Multidisciplinary Approach*. New York: Plenum.

Ashley MJ, Olin JS, Le Riche WH *et al* (1981) The physical disease characteristics of inpatient alcoholics. *Journal of Studies on Alcohol*, **42**, 1–14.

Benjamin IS, Imrie CW and Blumgart LH (1977) Alcohol and the pancreas. In: Edwards G and Grant M (eds) *Alcoholism: New Knowledge and New Responses*, pp 198–207. London: Croom Helm.

Birnbaum IM and Parker ES (eds) (1977) *Alcohol and Human Memory* Hillsdale NJ: Erlbaum.

Burch GE and Giles TD (1974) Alcoholic cardiomyopathy. In: Kissin B and Begleiter H (eds) The Biology of Alcoholism, Vol. 3: *Clinical Pathology*, pp 435–460. New York: Plenum.

Chanarin I (1977) Blood disorders due to alcohol. In: Edwards G and Grant M (eds) *Alcoholism: New Knowledge and New Responses*, pp 218–221. London: Croom Helm.

Isbell H, Fraser HF and Wikler A *et al* (1955) An experimental study of rum fits. *Quarterly Journal of Studies on Alcohol*, **16**, 1–33.

Kissin B (1974) Interactions of ethyl alcohol and other drugs. In: Kissin B and Begleiter H (eds) The Biology of Alcoholism, Vol. 3: *Clinical Pathology*, pp 109–161. New York: Plenum.

Kissin B and Begleiter H (1974) The Biology of Alcoholism, Vol. 3: *Clinical Pathology*, New York: Plenum.

Kissin B and Kaley MM (1974) Alcohol and cancer. In: Kissin B and Begleiter H (eds) The Biology of Alcoholism, Vol. 3: *Clinical Pathology*, pp 481–511. New York: Plenum.

Korsten NA and Lieber CS (1979) Hepatic and gastro-intestinal complications of alcoholism. In: Mendelson JH and Mello NK (eds) *The Diagnosis and Treatment of Alcoholism*, pp 19–58 New York: McGraw Hill.

Lundy J, Raaf JH and Deakins S (1975) The acute and chronic effects of alcohol on the human immune system. *Surgery, Gynaecology and Obstetrics*, **141**, 212–218.

Lyons HA and Saltzman A (1974) Diseases of the respiratory tract in alcoholics. In: Kissin B and Begleiter H (eds) The Biology of Alcoholism, Vol. 3: *Clinical Pathology*, pp 403–434. New York: Plenum.

Marks V. (1977) Alcohol-induced hypoglycaemia and endicrinopathy. In: Edwards G and Grant M (eds) *Alcoholism: New Knowledge and New Responses*, pp 208–219. London: Croom Helm.

Marsden CD (1977) Neurological disorders induced by alcohol. In: Edwards G and Grant M (eds) *Alcoholism: New Knowledge and New Responses*, pp 189–197. London: Croom Helm.

Richter D (ed) (1980) *Addiction and Brain Damage*. London: Croom Helm.

Rosett HL (1980) The effects of alcohol on the fetus and offspring. In: Israel Y, Glaser FB, Kalant H *et al* (eds) *Research Advances in Alcohol and Drug Problems*, Vol. 5, pp 595–653.

Parsons V and Cundy T (1981) Alcohol and bone disease. *British Journal of Addiction*, **76,** 379–382.

Pratt O (1981) Alcohol and the woman of childbearing age: a public health problem. *British Journal of Addiction*, **76,** 383–390.

Schmidt W and De Lint J (1972) Causes of death in alcoholics. *Quarterly Journal of Studies on Alcohol*, **33,** 171–185.

Victor M, Adams RD and Mancall EL (1959) Alcoholic cerebellar degeneration. *Archives of Neurology*, **1,** 579–688.

Victor M, Adams R and Collins G (1971) *The Wernicke-Korsakoff Syndrome* Philadelphia: Davis.

Chapter 7
Women with Drinking Problems

There are three basically important things to be said about women with alcoholism. The first is that a lumber of misperceptions has to be got out of the way before the subject can be seen accurately. The second is that the psycho-biology and social position of the woman are inevitably brought with her to her alcoholism, and to this extent female alcoholism has features which are special and sex-related, and to which the therapist has to be specially alert. Premenstrual tension, pregnancy, unwanted pregnancy, abortion, the menopause, are obviously specifically female concerns, and women must also cope with society's definitions of the roles of mother, wife and daughter, as well as increasingly often competing in the job market. And thirdly, although there are special features to female alcoholism, there is also much in common between the problems of men and women. This chapter will look at each of those three questions in turn.

THE LUMBER OF MISPERCEPTIONS *of Women Alcoholics*

Here is an extract from a discharge letter written by a hospital to a patient's general practitioner:

> 'As is usual with these women alcoholics, the degree of personality disturbance made treatment very difficult and I think we have to accept a bad prognosis. Mrs Green got little out of the groups and was unwilling to lower her defences and discuss her neurotic tendencies. We see her as an inadequate personality with depressive features. With her children grown up, she now has too much time on her hands and instead of helping her husband in his very busy career she seems willing to risk his public position. He is a very supportive and long-suffering chap but has clearly almost had enough, and one must sympathize. We have discharged her on amitryptyline [an antidepressant drug], 25mg three times per day.'

116

That letter enshrines some of the more usual misperceptions which affect the response to the woman patient. A look at the unguarded testimony of letters, case records and the casual remarks of professional discussions will confirm that these ideas really are in common circulation.

THE ALCOHOLIC WOMAN AS SPECIALLY DEVIANT PERSONALITY

The literature on alcoholism at its simplest proposes that the origin of the problem is determined by the interaction between personality and the invitation to excessive drinking which circumstances provide. If the social circumstances strongly invite drinking, then not much personality weighting is required in the two–factor equation, and that is supposed often to be the male case. If there are social prohibitions against excessive drinking, then a heavy weighting of personality disorder will be required, and that is supposed to be the typical female equation; QED, the woman alcoholic is more or much more disordered than her male counterpart. On the basis of this oversimplified piece of logic the stereotype of the woman alcoholic as someone who is specially disordered receives its under-pinning.

Where the logic goes wrong is that although in general most societies have stricter prohibitions against women than men drinking too much, the woman who develops a drinking problem is not necessarily in the position of 'women in general'. The circumstances of the woman described in that letter included the setting of a middle–class household with a lot of entertaining, and a social world where many of the old prohibitions on women drinking have slackened. She was as much expected to pour the gin as her husband. Furthermore, an element in the total circumstances which led to her drinking undoubtedly included the loneliness and loss of role which came with her children going away and her being left only as an appendage to her husband's career. If a man had been left at a lonely posting with drink freely available, we would see with ready sympathy the degree to which his drinking was circumstantial. Mrs Green is, though, 'an inadequate personality with depressive features' – the fault lies in her rather than with the circumstances.

Another argument which is used to bolster the two–factor analysis is the alleged disparity between male and female alcoholism rates. Until recently in many Western countries there might have been six diagnosed male alcoholics for every female. The gap is, however, steadily narrowing. The older evidence that the woman was statistically odd has been interpreted as in tune with the belief that only the odd personality will ride through the social barriers to excessive drinking and become an alcoholic. Leaving aside the basic fallacy in the 'women in general' step of the argument, it must also be noted that the statistics inevitably deal with *diagnosed* alcoholism. The woman with a drinking problem may or may not have had her problem as readily diagnosed as the man; she may not have sought help as readily; 'depression' or other substitute diagnosis may more often have been employed, and her problem may not have looked like the male and expected diagnostic picture. The argument is in any case rapidly losing its credibility as the disparity between female and male alcoholism rates begins to close.

None of this is to deny the ultimate possibility of differences between male and female personality correlates of alcoholism being demonstrated in this or that population or sub-population. Such differences may well exist in degree, kind, and constellation, but they are likely to be far more subtle than proposed by the old formulation. Very little research has been done in this area, and a fixed view has been accepted which is supported neither by logic nor data. Every case is different, whether male or female, and every case should be approached without blinding and potentially damaging preconceptions.

THE WOMAN ALCOHOLIC AS PECULIARLY UNTREATABLE

Given that the idea of the woman alcoholic as a specially deviant personality is abandoned, the traditional reason for believing her to be relatively untreatable must at the same time fall away. There is in fact no convincing research evidence that women alcoholics have in general a worse prognosis than men.

Difficulties with female patients which the individual therapist or treatment centre may anecdotely report should therefore be looked at anew in terms perhaps of the aptness of the treatment approach rather than the relcalcitrance of the patient. For instance, if Mrs Green had difficulty in discussing her problems in a predominantly male ward group, it is possible that the group failed to meet her needs, made her feel the odd one out, shaped the discussion in terms which she did not see as 'her' problem, and generally frightened and alienated her.

And if Mrs Green does indeed prove to have a 'bad prognosis', this could be a self-fulfilling prophecy which has been inflicted on her. She has been given open or covert indication that she has not done well in treatment, she has been discouraged rather than encouraged by the treatment experience, and the essential problems in her feelings and her realities have not been met or worked through. She has been fobbed off quite inappropriately with an antidepressant rather than any attempt having been made to deal with what is depressing in her life.

Problem of diagnosed Alcoholism – depression Antidepressants etc

THE MALE VIEW

Despite every effort, it is easy for men dealing with this problem to slip unconsciously into a set of male prejudices and preconceptions. This need not necessarily be the case, and to set up a stereotype of the male therapist as crass and unsympathetic is as uninformed as any conventional views on the woman alcoholic. But if the dangers are to be avoided they must first be admitted.

A man may have to overcome some atavistic and deeply embedded attitudes towards the woman alcoholic before he can see her accurately. In our culture the woman is conventionally expected by her men to be 'good'. The standards expected of her are subtly but pervasively different from those which are expected of the male. Attitudes towards drinking and drunkenness are only one expression of these basic culturally determined and sex-linked values. *→ drunkenness part of this*

The way in which these deeper assumptions affect attitudes to drinking can, for instance, be seen in the likely reactions towards drinking in a student group. A young man who gets drunk at the football club dance is a bit of a lad, and loses no friends or prestige. If a girl gets drunk, she will damage her reputation. The drunken woman is not funny but embarrassing. Attitudes here also have their sexual overtones; a woman who drinks too much is 'an easy lay', is suspected of being promiscuous.

It all ends up with Mrs Green being disdained (the disdain dressed up in professional language), with Mr Green being a good fellow, long-suffering, someone with whom one must have sympathy. The subconscious attitudes come through dangerously to affect reactions to the individual patient and family, with a very practical impact on treatment. *— a -ve one*

Another result of cultural prejudice is that a belief that 'women don't drink' leads rather easily to female alcoholism being undetected. The symptoms are before the doctor's eyes but his eyes are averted; he prefers the diagnosis of 'neurosis' or 'depression' so far as the woman is concerned.

SOME SPECIAL FEATURES OF FEMALE ALCOHOLISM

Given the paucity of research on these problems, what is said in this section is inevitably fed more by clinical experience than by data.

FEMALE DRINKING PATTERNS

A woman is likely to have her drinking pattern *shaped* by a different context than usually affects a man. If she is a housewife, she is more likely to be drinking in the home than in the pub or bar. A common story is of the day's supply bought at the off-license or liquor store and carried home. Her expendable budget is often limited, so she may seek value for money – cheap wine or cheap sherry rather than expensive spirits. Because of the stigma attached to her drinking, her habit may for a long time be secret or furtive. Rather than the drinking being scheduled around pub opening times or business engagements, it is timed by the opening of the off-license, her husband's absences from home, the children rushing back from school, or perhaps a resolution to get some of the housework done before the day's drinking gets under way. It may then be a matter of slow solitary drinking to a level of mild, plateau intoxication, rather than the peaky drinking which the man's schedule may invite. It must, though, be emphasized that the picture described here is largely that of the alcoholic housewife. The businesswoman may show a drinking picture not very different from that of the businessman, and today female alcoholism is very much more than a stay-at-home business.

Because of current medical prescribing habits, which show a bias towards prescription of tranquillizers for women, there is a likelihood of the drinking problem being compounded by the use of minor tranquillizers. These drugs may have been prescribed for non-specific 'nervous' complaints, with a hasty writing of a prescription the substitute for a full enquiry.

The constraints on a woman's drinking tend to mean that the average age at which women come to notice with a well-established problem is later than with men. If the onset of the excessive drinking is thus delayed, once the drinking is under way the course of development is often accelerated.

As for the adverse consequences which result from the woman's drinking, differences between the lives that men and women lead mean rather different problems. The check-lists designed to score 'drinking problem experience' tend to be male-oriented. The woman will not be late for work or lose a job through drinking if she does not go out to work; she is unlikely to be arrested for public drunkenness if her drinking is confined to her home; and she will not be prone to drink-related crime. Rather than being violent when drunk (though this may happen), it is more probable that she will present with consequences of her enraged husband's violence.

The typical cluster of symptoms as it affects the alcoholic housewife is therefore rather undramatic. The children are neglected, the evening meal is not cooked, the housekeeping money has run short. As the drinking escalates and becomes more uncontrolled, her husband may find her drunk and collapsed when he comes home, and the rows and recrimina-tions get under way. Accidents in the home are not uncommon though these 'accidents' may be a cover-story for marital violence. Where the woman is doing a job outside the home, she may still be carrying home responsibilities and experiencing symptoms of the sort just described, but in addition she may be experiencing alcohol-related problems at work which are not very different from those encountered by the man who is doing the same type of job. It seems probably that biological differences make the woman prone to liver damage at lower levels of sustained intake than are on average needed for liver impairment in the man, as was mentioned in the previous chapter.

Given the shame which often surrounds a woman's drinking, the baffled and hostile reception with which the family often responds, the woman's fear of losing her children, and, too, the sense of being trapped and the difficulties in reaching for aid, it is not surprising that a suicidal gesture may be the woman's first effective cry for help.

ALCOHOLISM AND THE TENSIONS OF THE FEMALE ROLE

This is not the place to enter into a protracted analysis of the role of woman in a society which offers her partly traditional, partly changing, and often confused expectations. However, the various roles of any woman patient *role of women* ↓ [handwritten annotation]

have to be individually examined, to assess what problems or conflicts she may be experiencing in her role as daughter, mother, wife, single woman, widow, housewife or career woman. Such a plea should hardly be necessary – parallel questions should be asked of any man – but given that the traditional male view is still often a reflex (even among women in the helping professions), a reminder is still required of the need for greater sensitivity to the woman's position as woman. Role strains may be closely related to the genesis of the drinking problem, and the exploration of these issues may be an essential part of treatment.

Causes or factors toward drinking [handwritten annotation]

DEPRESSION

Given that the relationship between depression and excessive drinking is complex, it is still necessary specially to stress these connections where the female patient is concerned. Untreated depression in the woman seems rather easily to be self-treated with alcohol, while the erosion of happiness and the 'disgrace' which come from the drinking contribute to the possibility of a depressive presentation. Puerperal depression requires special note under this heading. The atypical and fluctuating depressive states which are not well described in the textbooks but which may be the chronic residuum of an unrecovered puerperal depression sometimes present with a confusing picture of drinking, a muddle of irresolute medication, and uncertainty as to whether 'depression', 'neurotic depression', or 'personality disorder' is the label to apply. Typically, the case-notes reveal that these diagnoses have been applied in random order, while the true intricacies of the case have not been unravelled.

PREMENSTRUAL TENSION

Premenstrual tension no doubt has its psychological and social, as well as its biological determinants. Whatever underlies the symptoms in a particular case, a woman may find that the anxiety, irritability or depression which she experiences is relieved by drinking. Alcohol may even have been advised as an accepted folk-remedy. It is unlikely that premenstrual tension is ever a satisfactory, single and mechanical explanation of why excessive drinking develops, and it may be a cover-story for wider anxiety symptoms or a projection of more fundamental unease in the female role.

OVERT SEXUAL DIFFICULTIES

Occasionally drinking is found to be directly related to unsatisfactory sexual experience. A woman may have found sexual intercourse emotionally or physically frightening, or have doubted her sexual capability, and discovered that 'a few drinks first' made sex more tolerable or even enjoyable. Again the oversimple acceptance of such a direct and unitary causal link is unwise; we are dealing with difficulties in sexuality rather than in sex.

THE EMPTY NEST

The Mrs Green with whom we started this chapter provides an example of what has been called the 'empty nest' syndrome – the woman who loses her investment in life when her children leave home, and who in that setting starts to drink. If the marriage is fundamentally unfulfilling, the problems in the marriage become more acute once the children have gone away. It is of course not the physical emptiness but the empty feelings which are the root of the trouble, and the children going away only serves to reveal an emotional problem with a longer history than the day of the last departure. To suggest a remedy in terms of a part-time job 'to give her something to do' is seldom the answer, with its implications that this woman needs to be given something to fill idle time and distract her from her indulgence. A job which has meaning in terms of conferment of worth and a different balance in the marital relationship, and which offers new social contacts and horizons, may, though, be a useful step forward within a more general and needed rethinking of worth, roles, expectations and balances.

FUNDAMENTAL COMMONALITIES

Whatever the differences that men and women bring to the origins and presentations of their drinking problems, whatever the special sensitivities needed to analyze and appreciate the position of the woman with a drinking problem, and whatever the special issues which the treatment of the woman alcoholic may raise, there is fundamentally much in common between the man and woman patient. There is no merit in making a fetish of 'the woman alcoholic' and forgetting the fundamentals of the individual approach to each and every patient. One side-benefit of the interest in female alcoholism which has been emerging over recent years, and of the casting aside of myths about women may indeed be a general attack on stereotypes and a consequent overthrow of male as well as female stereotypes.

REFERENCES

Annis HM (1980) Treatment of alcoholic women. In: Edwards G and Grant M (eds) *Alcoholism Treatment in Transition*, pp 128–140. London: Croom Helm.

Beckman LJ (1975) Women alcoholics: a review of social and psychological studies. *Journal of Studies on Alcohol*, **36**, 797–824.

Belfer ML and Shader RI (1976) Premenstrual factors as determinants of alcoholism in women. In: Greenblatt M and Schuckit MA (eds) *Alcoholism Problems in Women and Children*, pp 97–102. New York: Grune and Stratton.

Camberwell Council on Alcoholism (1980) *Women and Alcohol*. London: Tavistock.

Corrigan EM (1980) *Alcoholic Women in Treatment*. London: Oxford University Press.

Curlee J (1969) Alcoholism and the 'empty nest'. *Bulletin of the Menninger Clinic*, **33**, 165–171.

Kalant OJ (ed) (1980) *Alcohol and Drug Problems in Women: Research Advances in Alcohol and Drug Problems*, Vol. 5. New York: Plenum.

Chapter 8
Some Special Presentations

This chapter gives five special clinical presentations: the patient who is drunk and violent; the younger person with a drinking problem; alcoholism in later life; the patient who comes from a culture other than the therapist's; and, finally, what may be called 'the very important patient'. These five pictures are selected arbitrarily from a much wider gallery, and anyone who practises in this field will soon himself begin to identify additional headings. To see types in this way and keep as it were a mental card index which allows one to see patterns and use the last such case to illuminate understanding of the next, can add greatly to the reward and interest of therapeutic work. The only proviso to be borne in mind is the latent danger of forcing people into pigeon-holes; management of the next elderly alcoholic will be helped by thinking through one's previous case experience with patients in this age group, but each new patient is at the same time different.

THE PATIENT WHO IS DRUNK AND VIOLENT

Every now and then a therapist will be faced by the worrying problem set by the patient who repeatedly turns up drunk and violent, and demanding to be seen. The safety of staff and other patients may be at risk, and an enormous amount of anxiety can be engendered. If an alcoholism treatment service is co-existing closely with other facilities, alcoholism will get a bad name if disruption is allowed to get out of hand.

> The patient is a 40-year-old man who after a long drinking history had been thrown out of his own home, and was now drifting around reception centres and hostels. He had over the previous six months twice been admitted to hospital but had on each occasion got drunk on the ward, assaulted the nurses, and smashed up the furniture. A few days after his last discharge he came up to the hospital late at night and got into a fight with a porter. He has now

turned up at out-patients very drunk and demanding admission,
with threats of further violence if admission is not granted.

In such circumstances there are two courses of action which are anti-
therapeutic and should not be followed. The first of these is to tolerate
further violence or threat of violence. The patient will not be helped, the
morale of the treatment service will be torn apart, and staff may indeed be
seriously hurt. The second non-answer is simply to ban the patient from
the hospital. Even if the banning is successful, it will only land the problem
of violence on someone else's doorstep, and things will not look too good
if a week later the man is on an assault charge with the court told that a
hospital has seemingly abrogated its responsibilities.

Such a problem is certainly dealt with more easily by a treatment team
than by anyone working in isolation. A hospital, for instance, ought to be
able to meet this type of problem and the general practitioner and other
local services will not be grateful if the hospital seeks to pass the buck.
What is needed is a firm treatment policy drawn up for this individual, and
one which sets very explicit limits but which is nonetheless a treatment
rather than a mere containment policy. It must reward constructive
behaviour and in no way reinforce unacceptable behaviour, and it must be
communicated fairly and openly to the patient himself, put at the front of
the case-notes, and a copy given to all staff who may be involved. It is
useful to hold a staff meeting for formulation of the plan so that things go
forward by agreement, and with everyone fully in the picture. It may be
wise to ensure that the hospital's administrative staff are consulted, with a
legal opinion obtained if necessary.

On the basis of such consultation a note such as the following might
be put into the case-notes of the man whose story has just been sketched.

Mr Smith: *agreed treatment plan*

So that we can go on helping this patient the following guidelines have
been agreed by the treatment team, and we would be grateful if everyone
will give this plan support.

1   Mr Smith will only be seen by appointment, and if he comes up
without an appointment he should be asked to leave.

2   He will then only be seen at appointment if he is not intoxicated. If
there is any suspicion of intoxication he will be asked to leave without
being seen further.

3   If Mr Smith refuses to leave when asked, or if he threatens or offers violence, emergency help should be summoned through the hospital's usual emergency system and the police should immediately be telephoned. The number is .... and the police station has been alerted. On no account should an individual staff member attempt to argue with this patient.

4   Mr Smith has been told that if he commits any chargeable offence on the hospital premises, the hospital will not hesitate to press charges.

5   These ground rules hae been explained to Mr Smith personally, and they have been set up not only to protect the staff but also so as to make it possible for us to go on working with this patient on an active treatment plan.

Contained within those seemingly harsh guidelines is indeed a plan designed to enable the team to go on offering help to a man who would probably be rejected by many centres as unhelpable. In practice this drawing of limits is often reassuring to the patient himself. A disorganized and inconsistent response, which may even involve a sort of complicity with his violence, is likely to exacerbate anxiety and violence, whereas a firm policy often results in the patient showing a capacity to go along with constructive expectations. He is able to come to appointments sober, and makes a new and positive therapeutic engagement. Things do not, however, always run smoothly, and if the patient does turn up drunk and tries to hit someone, a charge must be brought, for otherwise no learning can take place. To be able to use the police as therapeutic ally in such a situation requires careful liaison with the local police station. With prior discussion full co-operation is usually obtained. Things go wrong, though, if the police are not forewarned, and are called only in a sudden panic, with no groundwork of preparation.

With the immediate threat of violence contained, it should be possible to get down to an individually planned and constructive treatment programme. Violence is then no longer the central issue, and it is very necessary that the patient's reputation as 'a violent man' should not be allowed to overshadow therapeutic dealings. There will, though, be some need to talk about the violence, and the patient has to come to terms with the full implications of the fact that alcohol from him releases violent feelings.

The problem has also to be met as to how flexibly the stated rules are to be interpreted in certain difficult circumstances, for instance, if there is anxiety about the possibility of head injury, a deterioration in the patient's physical condition, or concern as to whether a depressive illness is now hidden within the picture. There has therefore to be an understanding that individual clinical judgement allows a flexible response to emergency, but the team should whenever possible be brought into the decision or at least very promptly informed as to what has been done.

THE YOUNG ALCOHOLIC

In many countries a common experience over recent years has been the increasingly frequent presentation of young people (including young women) with drinking problems. 'Young' may in extreme instances mean the early teens, but the particular focus of this discussion will be on patients in their late teens or early twenties. However, more important than the exact boundaries of chronological age is the fact that these are people who in some important sense see themselves as *not adult,* and who have not made the social transition from adolescent to adult self-image. The therapist is encountering someone who is still fighting a way through adolescent conflicts, and who has not resolved fundamental questions about the balance between dependence on others and independence. For the anxiety, anger and despair which may be generated by these frustrations, alcohol can be a panacea. It temporarily relieves the painful confusion of feelings, provides at the same time a 'high' of optimism and excitement, while intoxication and the chaos of drunken behaviour act out the aggression, and the natural energy and physicality of this age guarantees intensity to all this chaos. Moreover, drinking can also give companionship and the badly needed approbation of peers.

As for the pattern of alcohol use itself, in most instances the young patient will not have had a drinking history of sufficient duration to establish the dependence syndrome. The picture is that of repeated drinking to the point of intoxication, often with a repeated experience of amnesias. When the money runs out, the drinking stops, or much decreases until the next pay-day. But even among patients of this age careful questioning may reveal early signs and symptoms of dependence, and sometimes even a fully developed picture.

POSSIBILITIES FOR GROWTH

There is a common belief that severe personality disorder is always associated with a drinking problem of such early onset, and a diagnosis of underlying psychopathy is very readily pinned on to the patient. But it is important to realize that the immaturity of the behaviour often speaks of the *possibility* of change. There is the paradox with this type of disturbance that the very unformedness of personality can itself bear witness to potential for growth. A uniformly pessimistic attitude towards the prognosis of the young alcoholic is therefore unjustified, even when his behaviour is flagrantly disturbed. Here is a brief case history on one such young patient whose story typifies this kind of presentation.

> A 22-year-old man from the West Indies was referred to a counselling centre by the court. He had been charged with assault after a pub fight, and he had also broken his landlady's front windows. There had been several suicide gestures. He had been working as a bus conductor, but had just been sacked. His drinking involved getting explosively and obstreperously drunk whenever he had money in his pocket. He had been thrown out of his parental home because of his rowdy drunkenness at the age of 19, and his respectable parents certainly did not want him back in Barbados. Five years after being seen at this centre he had a steady job in the Post Office and was happily married. He now drank occasionally and moderately. He looked back on his past as very distant, and saw it in terms of 'I was all messed up at that time'.

By no means every story of this type has such a happy outcome, but what needs to be emphasized is that while pessimism is often self-fulfilling, a treatment approach which responds hopefully to the needs for growth may catch a moment of great possibility. There is no one recipe for treatment in this type of case, and the basic approach will have much in common with what is done to help the patient of any age. The young man from Barbados discovered a capacity to talk about his problems and was helped by a social worker who was able to arrange her schedule so that she had time to see him whenever he dropped in for an hour's talk – he needed to do a lot of talking. He also benefited from a six-month residence in a therapeutic hostel and from a set of friendships which developed from that stay. Later, he was lucky to meet the right girl at the right time. In essence what these various relationships offered, each in their own way, was a series of experiments in facets of growing up. If there are any common ingredients in such stories of therapeutic success they lie particularly in the qualities of the therapist – someone who is specially and evidently warm, who will be able to tolerate raw projection of unworked out feelings towards parents, but who will not be manoeuvred into treating the patient as a child. There is also often a need to find some way of helping this type of young person pull out of a pattern of living (or pattern of drifting) which is a series of makeshifts rather than one which offers either real demands or real rewards.

SOME SPECIAL DIFFICULTIES

Having taken as an illustration a case with a happy outcome, it is necessary also to look at some of the reasons why the story may on other occasions be more turbulent or marked by nothing but defeat. One reason may be that the personal handicaps are already much more fixed, a matter of psychological damage rather than of frustrated growth. The young man or woman who is profoundly anxious, restless and irritable, who cannot easily use or tolerate a relationship of any sort, who will not stay in any job and who is likely to disappear to another town or go off to sea, is going to be very difficult to help. Even so, it is worthwhile holding out the availability of friendship, with the modest expectation of working for only small immediate gains and taking a very long-term view.

Another reason for special difficulty, which may be grossly evident or only revealed by very careful assessment, is when excessive drinking in someone of this age is symptomatic of brain damage (see p. 89). A further common diagnostic perplexity is the interpretation to be made when a young patient reports 'being depressed'. Most often this complaint is to be understood in terms of a general lability of mood which so often accompanies problems in development. It is a mistake to over-diagnose depressive illness with such patterns, or inappropriately to prescribe antidepressant drugs. On the other hand, there are cases where recurrent depressive illness may first declare itself at this age, and where this distress leads to use of alcohol as self-medication.

Yet another type of story is that of the young man or woman who is referred to an alcoholic clinic because drinking has been seen as the problem. It then becomes apparent that one is dealing with a major psychiatric illness, the exact nature of which is perplexingly difficult to diagnose. The picture shifts perhaps from that of depression to a presentation that looks worryingly like schizophrenia, and then later there seems to be an admixture of obsessional symptoms. The only thing which is clear is that the excessive use of alcohol is no more than a confounding factor in a very complex disturbance.

Drinking problems at this age may be accompanied by drug problems, with alcohol one substance in a pattern of multiple drug use. The story may, for instance, be of the boy who was drinking heavily at 14 and who later turned to injected drugs, returning once more to heavy alcohol use after giving up injected barbiturates and heroin. Enquiry into the history of drug taking is therefore particularly important in this age group.

TAKING THE PROBLEMS OF THE YOUNG DRINKER VERY SERIOUSLY

With these young patients there are a number of compelling reasons for arguing with special force the general case that earlier rather than later intervention is much to be preferred. The patient is relatively unlikely at this age to be suffering from the dependence syndrome, and he should be helped before dependence supervenes. The risks are also social. The young drinker who is left to run deeper into trouble is at risk of becoming caught up in all manner of deviance, and his friends will incresingly be only other people who are in trouble. And, finally, it must also be remembered that it is particularly among young alcoholics that mortality rates are elevated, often as a consequence of accident or violence. There are therefore good reasons for taking the problems of the young drinker very seriously.

ALCOHOLISM IN LATER LIFE

There is no absolute division but in broad terms an important diagnostic question when assessing an elderly patient with a drink problem is whether the excessive drinking is of long-standing, or alternatively of comparatively recent onset.

(i) Alcoholism continued into old age

The story here is of the man or woman who perhaps first developed a serious drinking problem many decades ago, and who has survived to continue this problem into old age. Brain damage and other physical complications are likely concomitants. The drinking pattern may well have become rather fragmented compared with previous years, and severe loss of tolerance to alcohol is a frequent manifestation.

(ii) Alcoholism of late onset

Here the patient has taken to excessive drinking as a response to a problem or cluster of problems which he or she has encountered in this epoch of life. Widowhood, retirement and a general loss of role and purpose in life are frequently important factors. The possible significance of underlying brain disease or of depressive illness of old age should not be overlooked.

GENERAL FEATURES OF THE CLINICAL PRESENTATION

Many of the basic features of alcoholism will be the same whatever the age of the patient, and it is as ever important to make an assessment of the degree of alcohol dependence and of the full range of alcohol–related complications. But in addition one should be particularly aware of some elements which frequently colour the presentation at this age. For instance, there is often the likelihood of isolation and retreat, a general 'letting things go', a neglect of physical health and diet, and a run of accidents which may end disastrously. The psychiatric picture may well give rise to diagnostic muddle. Delirious states are common in the elderly and the possible contributions of alcohol or alcohol withdrawal are easily left off the check-list. At this time of life depression and a degree of dementia often go together, and to sort out their relative contribution in any presentation sets a classical dilemma. Alcoholism may add yet further confusion to the picture. Paranoid symptoms may raise suspicion of a paranoid illness of late onset. So far as physical illness is concerned, excessive drinking at this age is often just one contributory factor to multiple pathologies of multiple origin.

HELP FOR THE ALCOHOLISM

Basic principles again have to be borne in mind, whatever the patient's age. There is as ever the need to see the drinking in a personal context, and to plan treatment accordingly, but with this type of patient very special skills may be needed to design a treatment plan which effectively responds to his situation in life. This implies a good knowledge of the local resources which are available to help the elderly – clubs, day centres, home helps, community nurses, and so on. Mobilizing whatever family support is available can also be very important. The patient may be ambivalent about surrendering independence and 'afraid of being a burden', but living with relatives may turn out to be a rewarding possibility, or an old people's home may provide companionship and enable better adjustment than continued isolation. Initial hospital admission is often needed for diagnosis, but it should not be too prolonged. The sensitivity of the ageing nervous system to drugs should be borne in mind, and tranquillizers or sedatives used only in the short-term and with caution. Disulfiram is too dangerous at this age. Some old people will join Alcoholics Anonymous, but that kind of group experience may be difficult for others to accept at that age.

But whatever the specifics of therapy, the non-specifics are again very important – the warmth, the hopefulness, the shared understanding, the goal-setting. An old person will probably need things explained slowly, positions explored slowly, solutions negotiated slowly. Abrupt and clumsy interference will be met deservedly with tetchiness, and there will be no therapeutic gain.

NOT DISCARDING THE PATIENT AS HOPELESS

The approach of many people to geriatric problems still tends to be pessimistic and negatively influenced by a gulf in understanding. Those attitudes all too easily compound the response to geriatric alcoholism – 'Well, drink is all she's got, and if she drinks herself to death. . . .' Such attitudes are unjustified. Elderly people with drinking problems can be helped, wth large rewards in terms of health, enjoyment of life, and dignity.

THE PATIENT FROM A CULTURAL BACKGROUND
OTHER THAN THE THERAPIST'S

'I don't understand him at all,' said the social worker who was
reporting on a visit to her patient's home. 'He is a Pakistani who
owns a fruit shop, aged about 60, very much the head of the family,
two grown-up sons who help in the business and take orders from
their father. He only speaks poor English, and his wife doesn't speak
one word of our language. He has a bottle of whisky at the back of
the shop, and swigs at it steadily throughout the day. When I went
round there I was treated with deference, loaded with presents of
fruit, and met with massive denial. He says that he uses a little
whisky for medicine.'

The social worker had the openness to admit that she did not
understand this patient, and no doubt the Pakistani shopkeeper and his
family were equally puzzled as to the role, credentials and purpose of this
person whom their doctor had asked to call on them. To admit bafflement
can be the necessary preliminary to any forward movement.

The cultural meaning of the drinking itself may of course be very
puzzling. What does 'normal' drinking mean within a particular culture,
and how are any religious prohibitions in practice interpreted? What are
the legitimate functions of alcohol and its symbolism? What are the
culturally determined ideas which define 'drinking too much', and if there
is a concept equivalent to 'alcoholism', with what adverse connotations is
that idea loaded? These questions relate to difficulties in understanding the
drinking itself and deal with only a very small part of the total puzzle. The
essential background problems relate to such issues as understanding of
personality, family and family roles, religion, social class and status, and
who has a right to say what to whom. The way that a culture perceives the
therapist also requires consideration: the very idea of a 'social worker'
may, for instance, be untranslatable both linguistically and in terms of any
connections with cultural expectation. Different cultures will carry
different assumptions as to what constitutes 'treatment', the primacy
given to the prescription of medicines, or the degree of directiveness
which is expected.

The case of the Pakistani just used is only one example of the many and
varied cross-cultural problems in understanding which may be met

whatever the country in which one is practising. The immediate presentation may be the recently immigrated family, the post-graduate student from Africa, the immigrant labourer who is today part of the work-force in many parts of the world, the long-settled Polish or Italian-American family which still has a very distinct cultural identity, or the patient of the therapist's own culture but with regional or social class identity very different from the therapist's. The problems set by the extreme cases of cultural difference can in fact serve as a useful reminder of the need for a much more general awareness of nuances of culture-clash which are often present in the ordinary therapeutic encounter.

There can be no one formula for dealing with such situations. It is certainly important to be alert to the need for understanding, and hence to avoid those clumsy errors which come from assuming that everyone else is like us, or that there is something funny about others if they do not comply with our own, parochial expectation. Over time, and with continued work in a particular locality, there will probably be a growing familiarity with cultures other than one's own, with the last case teaching something about the next.

But in essence every such case has to be seen as an exercise in building bridges, with thought given as to how in the present instance this is to be accomplished. For example, it may be possible to find a second-generation member of the family who can be a broker in understanding, and whose life experience may offer many insights relating to the meeting between cultures. The Pakistani's son may be subservient to his father and unable to talk in the shop, but eager to talk and a very helpful informant when he comes to the social worker's office; he may identify the key figures within the extended family network who have a right to advise and intervene. It may also be possible to find someone within the local agencies or hospitals who speaks the language and understands the culture, and who can help with an assessment interview.

THE 'VERY IMPORTANT' PATIENT

Frequently, and despite every supposed personal advantage, the man or woman with a large public reputation is the person whose alcoholism is likely to be sadly mishandled. Because of the aura of prestige no one quite dare make the diagnosis or take a firm line. Phone calls are made in the middle of the night, a quick visit is demanded to a hotel room, and instead of a full history there is a superficial and interrupted conversation, and everything is a whispering game. The therapist may need considerable confidence to stand his ground when dealing with the demands and expectations of the tycoon, the politician, the famous actress, the judge or the distinguished surgeon, but unless he is willing to hold to a therapeutic position his patient will not be well served. Paradoxically, the rich and famous may be as much at hazard of receiving inadequate treatment as the alcoholic on skid row.

The key to dealing with such problems is to act with an awareness that this person, as much as the vagrant alcoholic or any other patient who comes one's way, is indeed to an extent a 'special case'. But at the same time one has to hold to the commonalities and the basic working rules of the therapeutic approach. These two ideas need to be discussed briefly and separately.

Firstly, as regards the 'specialness' of this type of patient, the situation may be clouded by a very real fear of the consequences of any public revelation. For instance, the aspiring politician will be concerned about the damage to his reputation and his career from any rumour that he is 'an alcoholic'. Advice that he should attend Alcoholics Anonymous, where his face will almost certainly be recognized, may in these circumstances be impractical, and anxiety about the dangers of 'the newspapers getting hold of things' may consequently so dominate his thinking as to block every effort to help him. The truth of the matter can, though, be that his drinking habits are already public knowledge and a well-known embarrassment to his party – a rumour that he is getting help can only do good, not harm. He may find a surprising degree of sympathy and support if he talks to one or two of his senior colleagues, rather than trying to deceive them with an unconvincing cover-story about 'overwork'. The extent to which it is then possible for someone in this position to announce publically that he has had to deal with a drinking problem must vary from country to country. In the USA, for example, such openness is becoming increasingly and beneficially possible, but in Britain public admission would often still carry dangers.

There are certain other rather typical features. The pressure under which such patients are living and working can be extreme and engender a great deal of tension, with alcohol and tranquillizers used as self-medication. Fear of failure may be potently linked to this sense of stress. The life-style may involve frequent entertaining and thus pressures to drink. Marriages are often under strain, with an uncertain personal sense of worth and security despite every public success. But at the same time it must be realized that many men and women engaging in these kinds of career are coping with the stresses effectively, and ordering their personal lives happily.

So much then for a brief consideration of what may be 'special'. It must, however, be immediately obvious that what has been instanced as special could be turned around and argued the other way. There is nothing unique about fear of public exposure, and it may affect the driver of the company car as well as the company president, while stress and fear of failure are very common themes whatever the sector from which patients are drawn. Although it is necessary to be alert to the particular intensity and clustering of certain factors that affect the 'special' patient, one is soon brought back to the need to hold to the basics of the therapeutic approach. A full assessment must, for instance, be carried out, rather than the argument accepted that the patient is too busy for proper time to be given this task. The formulation has to be discussed, the diagnosis agreed, and goals appropriately set. And, as always, the quality of the relationships is fundamental. At one level the encounter may be between public figure and physician or psychiatrist, but more fundamentally it is between a patient with a drinking problem and a person seeking to offer help. Mystique cannot be allowed to get in the way.

REFERENCES

Bourne PG and Light E (1979) Alcohol problems in blacks and women. In: Mendelson JH and Mello NK (eds) *The Diagnosis and Treatment of Alcoholism*, pp 83–123. New York: McGraw Hill.

Edwards G (1975) The alcoholic doctor: a case of neglect. *Lancet*, **2**, 1297–1298.

Harper FD (1976) *Alcohol Abuse and Black America*. Alexandria, Virginia: Douglas.

Hawker A (1978) *Adolescents and Alcohol*. London: Edsall.

Levy JE and Kunitz SJ (1974) *Indian Drinking: Navajo Practices and Anglo-American Theories*. New York: Wiley-Interscience.

Mandell W and Ginzburg HM (1976) Youthful alcohol use, abuse and alcoholism. In: Kissin B and Begleiter H (eds) The Biology of Alcoholism, Vol. 5: *Treatment and Rehabilitation of the Chronic Alcoholic*, pp 167–204. New York: Plenum.

Mishara BL and Kastenbaum R (1980) *Alcohol and Old Age*. New York: Grune and Stratton.

Murray RM (1980) An epidemiological and clinical study of alcoholism in the medical profession. In: Madden JS, Walker R and Kenyon WH (eds) *Aspects of Alcohol and Drug Dependence*, pp 213–219. Tunbridge Wells: Pitman Medical.

O'Connor J (1978) *The Young Drinkers*. London: Tavistock.

Schukit MA and Miller PL (1976) Alcoholism in elderly men: a survey of a general medical ward. *Annals of the New York Academy of Science,* **273,** 558–571.

Schukit MA, Morrisey ER and Lewis NJ *et al* (1977) Adolescent problem drinkers. In: Seixas FA (ed) *Currents in Alcoholism,* Vol. 2, pp 325–355. New York: Grune and Stratton.

Shore JH and Von-Fumetti B (1972) Three alcohol programs for American Indians. *American Journal of Psychiatry,* **128,** 1450–1454.

Smart RG (1980) *The New Drinkers: Teenage Use and Abuse of Alcohol.* Toronto: Addiction Research Foundation.

Tinklenberg JR (1973) Alcohol and violence. In: Bourne PG and Fox R (eds) *Alcoholism: Progress in Research and Treatment,* pp 195–210. New York: Academic Press.

Zimberg H, Lipscomb H and Davis ER (1971) Sociopsychiatric treatment of alcoholism in an urban ghetto. *American Journal of Psychiatry,* **127,** 1670–1674.

PART II
ASSESSMENT

Chapter 9
Case History as
Initiation of Therapy

Taking a history from a patient should not be a matter only of obtaining facts to be written down in the case-notes. It is an interaction between two people, and ought to be as meaningful for the person who answers the questions as for the questioner. The patient should be invited to use the occasion as a personal opportunity to review his past and his present, and to make sense of what may previously have been a chaotic array of happenings. This self-examination should be conducted in a carefully created setting which should make open self-appraisal possible.

Assessment is therefore the beginning of therapy. The relationship between patient and therapist begins to be determined at this moment, and if the occasion is mishandled, the patient is quite likely not to attend for a second interview.

This chapter seeks to cover a great many practical issues related to the art and technique of history-taking. The earlier chapters have sought to lay out the general 'groundwork of understanding', and we now have to explore how that understanding is to be addressed to practical ends. The present chapter is largely cast in the form of a series of working guidelines. History-taking is an interesting and rewarding aspect of therapeutic work, and the reader should not be daunted by the details of this presentation. Anyone coming to this type of work for the first time should certainly not attempt to absorb everything that is being said here at one sitting. The full meaning of this discussion will only become alive as the therapist's experience of working with alcoholics feeds back and modifies the statements here. A seemingly small or theoretical point may then suddenly find its context in what a patient has just been saying. The table at the end of this chapter seeks to give a simple and intelligible summary of the key points in history-taking.

SETTING THE TONE

Handling the initial contact with a patient who has a drinking problem does not stand entirely apart from work with any other type of patient, but it may have been especially difficult for the alcoholic to get himself so far as to admit that he has any sort of need for help, and then to keep that first appointment. To admit that he is not fully in control of his drinking can be felt by the patient as tantamount to admitting disgrace, and he is probably highly ambivalent about walking into that office or consulting room.

It is therefore worthwhile for the therapist to ensure that he is not taking his own goodwill as self-evident, but is making his position overt. Special care must be put into showing ordinary courtesies; to walk up the corridor with the patient rather than five paces in front, to take his coat and hang it up, to show him towards a comfortable chair, are all small but telling gestures. It may be useful to say, 'I'm glad you've decided to come, and I hope that this afternoon can be useful for you.' The trick of imagining oneself in the patient's position is valuable.

Case-notes have, though, to be recorded, and a semi-structured approach is useful to follow. There is a way of handling this procedure which makes it informal and unthreatening. The first question should always be something like, 'Tell me what it is that we should talk about.' There should then be a great willingness to listen to the answer, while looking at the person who is talking. The answer may be discursive or brief, may bear on the drinking or deal with quite other issues, but the patient is setting the scene in the way that he himself finds useful.

The therapist then has to introduce the fact that he is going to take a history. A statement such as the following can be made:

> 'I've listened to what you are saying carefully. If you don't mind, it would help if I asked you some questions and made some notes. Tell me if any of the questions don't make sense. The purpose of the exercise is for both of us together to understand what's been going on. I'm going to assume that all your answers are honest and open. If there's anything too difficult to talk about, let me know, and I'll respect your feelings.'

This might seem to be emphasizing the ordinary assumption of the therapeutic position in a way which is overdrawn. But against this fear has to be placed the fact that the patient may be coming with the expectation that if he admits the reality of his behaviour he is putting himself very much at risk. The patient will have to face the painful consequences of admitting *to himself* that his behaviour really was his own behaviour. He is at the same time exposing himself to the reactions of a person he does not know, and he may be afraid that this stranger will demean him. There are therefore potentially good reasons for the patient adopting a defensive posture to protect himself from these risks. It can almost be guaranteed that if history-taking is clumsily handled and the initial relationship not sympathetically established, the interview will be interpreted as attack, and defences will rapidly be brought into play. The history obtained will then be filtered through these defences and be extremely inaccurate. The stereotype of the alcoholic as someone who 'never tells the truth' will have been confirmed.

Thus it cannot be overemphasized that the worth of the information obtained from a patient whose drinking is cause for self-blame will be highly dependent on the nature of the contact established between patient and therapist. The practical difference may lie in the patient insistently declaring either that he has no drinking problem at all, or its opposite that he is able boldly to confront his problems, perhaps for the first time in his life.

If the initial interview results in the patient taking a very defensive stand, it may later be difficult to repair the situation. Once the interaction between patient and therapist has been set in this form, the patient senses that it will now be even more dangerous to come out from behind his defences, for not only would he have to admit all the original problems but now also the fact that he has 'lied' to the therapist. To deal early with the cruder defences (by showing that they are unnecessary) is therefore better policy than to hope that the defences can be dealt with later, when they will in fact be further reinforced. Some of the commoner defences which may be encountered are discussed in the final chapter of this book. No doubt behind the immediate and rather primitive defences of denial and rationalization will often at a later stage be found many other problems about the ways in which the patient is distorting reality.

In summary, the disadvantages which stem from a neglect of the dynamic interactions of the initial interview are not only that the information obtained will be wrong and the assessment technically unsatisfactory, but also that damage will be done to what should have been the initiation of therapy. Rather than the patient having a good experience, he has a bad experience. His image of himself as someone who is untrusting and untrustworthy is reinforced, and his self-esteem is further lowered. There is no reason why this should be allowed to happen.

HOW MUCH TIME FOR HISTORY-TAKING?

The scheme which is to be described in this chapter envisages two parts to the historical reconstruction – the background history and the drinking history. To cover all the matters which lie in either area, and to conduct the interview at a pace which allows useful pauses and human interactions, clearly means that the process cannot be accomplished in a few minutes. For anyone working in, for instance, a busy social work office, time is very much at a premium. The busy general practitioner may know that five minutes is all the time which he can allow for a routine consultation. It might therefore seem impractical to lay out a basic scheme for history-taking which can often require several hours for completion.

The causes for believing that it is reasonable to set things out in this way are several. There need be no apologies for the *worthwhileness* of investing time in thorough initial history-taking (especially if this is also seen as the start of therapy, and therapeutic time well-spent). The only problem is how that time is to be found. In some settings it may, in fact, not be out of step with usual practices to expect that a lot of time can be found for the initial history – a hospital in-patient unit, for instance. In other settings it may be feasible to take part of the history and then ask the patient to come back so that the work can be completed. It is possible to find a point at which the history-taking can temporarily be interrupted, and the patient may return for the second session with some reflective working-through accomplished meanwhile, and an enhanced ability usefully to join in the work of historical review.

Another consideration is the usefulness of extended history-taking for training. The process of taking 10 such histories at full-length will mean the acquisition of very worthwhile skills. With trained practice an interview can then often be conducted more quickly than had previously seemed possible (and without undue sense of hurry), and it may be possible to abstract, as it were, a 'short form' which can subsequently be used for brief initial interviews or screening. To acquire skill in handling a full enquiry, and then to design for oneself a shorter approach based on what has been learnt and the needs of a particular setting, is better than to start out with a greatly abbreviated approach.

The essential framework of this scheme is moreover really not over-whelmingly complex, and on pp. 160–162 the basic structure of this approach is summarized and laid out in simple form.

BACKGROUND HISTORY

It is assumed that anyone coming to this work will already have developed his own general style of case-taking, or that the agency in which he works will have its own format. Whatever is useful in this section of the chapter will have therefore to be reordered and integrated with many different and already established ways of going about things. No attempt will be made here to lay out in detail all the basic aspects of constructing a general medico-social history. Emphasis will rather be placed on elucidating those aspects of background history which are likely to be especially relevant to the understanding of alcoholism.

In taking this history a habit that may be useful is to check what is coming in from the questioning by mentally pausing now and then to ask oneself whether one can really imagine what the patient was experiencing at the point in his life now reached by the history. What did his parents' house look like, and how would it have felt for a small boy to be walking in at the front door? In what sort of street did that house stand – and what kind of a street was it to play in? At school, would that child have been standing in a corner of the playground, or joining in a game? A striving to understand the culture and the social environment cannot be separated from the attempt to empathize with the individual.

Background history and drinking history are intimately related. In the *background* section many matters are touched on which will inevitably elicit information on drinking and drinking problems, and such information should be jotted down, rather than discarded or ignored because it does not come tidily at the right moment. The *drinking* section as well as eliciting further new information then gives opportunity to bring together relevant material which the patient has given earlier.

FAMILY HISTORY

1 *For both parents*. Age, health (and mental health), and occupation. Quality of relationships offered to patient in childhood, parents' drinking and drinking attitudes, present relationship with parents.
2 *Other significant figures in childhood*. Similar information.
3 *Siblings*. Basic information, social and personal adjustment or mal-adjustment (including drinking), present contacts with patient.
4 *Childhood environment*. Reconstruction of the home atmosphere during

childhood, and the social and cultural milieu to which this home related. Parental discord, separations.

The purpose of section A of this history is to obtain preliminary understanding of the crucial early relationships and experiences which have contributed to the shaping of the individual's most fundamental strengths or vulnerabilities, the manner in which he has continued to relate to his family, the possible dynamic meaning to him of alcohol (the meaning attached to alcohol because of parental drinking), and the cultural symbolization of alcohol.

PERSONAL HISTORY

1 *Birth.* Date of birth, any likely evidence of birth trauma which might result in brain injury.

2 *General adjustment in childhood.* Evidence of neurotic symptoms in childhood, difficulty in relating to other children, and childhood illnesses. Careful questioning around this area may help understanding as to whether the patient has exhibited lifelong traits of anxiety and difficulty in adjustment, and it is useful to go back to a period before the personality picture was overlaid by all the happenings related to drink.

3 *Schooling.* Basic information on schooling, with particular reference to social adjustment at school – how the patient got on with other children and with teachers, and school refusal or truancy.

4 *Occupational history and present occupation.* Basic information, the alcohol-exposed nature of any occupation, problems which drinking has caused.

5 *Sexual adjustment.* The satisfactoriness for the individual of normal sexuality must be assessed and the impact of drinking. Homosexuality must certainly be enquired into by direct questioning, and where there is any hint or indication, enquiry must be made into the range of less common forms of sexual maladjustment.

6 *Marriage.* This is a very important area of enquiry. (Marriage and the general implications of drinking for the family have already been discussed in Chapter 3.) Information must be gathered on the duration and quality of the marriage, on the impact of drinking on the marriage, and on attitudes of the spouse to the patient's drinking.

7 *Children.* Basic information, closeness of the patient to his children, awareness of any impact of drinking on the children.

8 *Finances and housing.* Information both on income and on extra sources

of income which help to support drinking, any debts and money worries, type and satisfactoriness of accommodation, rent arrears, eviction orders, and so on.

9 *Leisure*. Description of the way patient usually spends his leisure, the involvement of drinking in leisure pursuits, the degree to which other leisure activities have been curtailed by drinking.

PREVIOUS ILLNESSES

1 *Physical illness and accidents*
2 *Mental illnesses*

Information is needed under both subheadings, with particular emphasis on identification of any possible alcohol-related health problems. Under the heading of *mental health,* specific enquiry should always be made for any history suggesting experience of depressive illness or pronounced mood swings, phobic anxiety, or pathological jealousy, suicide attempts and drug taking.

BASIC PERSONALITY

A description of personality prior to drinking or in periods of sobriety – 'the real you'. Information is usefully elicited by open-ended questions such as:

What is the *real you* like?
Your good points?
Your bad points?
What do you want out of life?
What do you expect of friends?
What sort of things worry you or upset you?
What really makes you happy?
What would you do if you won a lot of money?

Prompts such as 'Go on. Tell me a bit more.' will often give revealing information at a point where the patient himself at first believes that he has nothing to add. For work with drinking problems, some impression should be obtained of at least the following aspects of personality: self-esteem; ability to experience warm feelings and relate to others; self-control, explosiveness, irritability; social conformity; habitual experience of anxiety; obsessionalism, rigidity; outgoingness, introversion; drive, ambition, passivity.

DRINKING HISTORY

EVOLUTION

For ordinary clinical purposes it is unnecessary to obtain a detailed history of everything that has happened over a lifetime's drinking. The major purpose of taking this history is that both patient and therapist should be able to sense the dynamic of an evolving story, and see how the present fits in to that story. It is necessary to identify important milestones, and to understand the phases of the drinking career and the broadly related influences on it. In general a picture of what has happened needs to be built up through exploring four different but closely related dimensions to the patient's life.

These dimensions are as follows:

(i) The evolution of drinking

Charting the major phases in drinking quantities and patterns, from first experiences of alcohol to the present. Useful questions may relate to such ideas as:

> first drinking other than the odd sip in childhood;
> first buying your own drink;
> first drinking most weekends;
> first drinking spirits;
> any periods right off drinking.
> first drinking every day;
> first drinking eight pints of beer at a sitting, or half a bottle of scotch;
> first drinking in your present pattern;

(ii) Evolution of dependence

Dating the onset of major symptoms of dependence, for instance:

> 1   When did you yourself first *realize drinking was a problem*? Why at that time? What sort of problem?
> 2   Looking back now with greater understanding, when in fact do you think drinking *really became a problem*? How long before you openly admitted it? What sort of a problem?

(iii) Evolution of drink-related problems

Apart from noting actual major adverse impacts on health and social functioning, there are two special questions which are often useful:

(1) When did you yourself first *realize drinking was a problem*?
Why at that time? What sort of problem?

(2) Looking back now with greater understanding, when in fact do you think drinking *really became a problem*? How long before you openly admitted it? What sort of a problem?

These two questions between them reveal that with hindsight patients will nearly always distinguish between the first self-admission of there being a problem (precipitated perhaps by some catastrophic event) and an earlier date now recognizable as the period when drinking was undramatically beginning to erode the happiness of a marriage, or interfere with work. This is an example of the sort of insight which may be given to the patient by history-taking and its processes of reflection.

(iv) Evolution of pressures and circumstances

The dimension which has to be charted out under this heading is concerned with an understanding of all those pressures and circumstances which have caused, contributed to, or shaped the evolving drinking patterns, dependence, and problem experience. Questioning has to sense out important influences which were already operating when the patient began to drink (parental example, peer group pressures, cultural influence), and then go forward to understand the subsequent impact of environment, personal relations, mental state, and so on. A few examples of questioning are these:

When you first started to drink:
where did you do your drinking?
what was drinking doing for you?

How did your drinking alter:
when you first left home?
when you were married?
after the children were born?
when you were promoted to manager?
when you worked abroad?
after your wife left you?

Did depression have anything to do with your drinking?

THE TYPICAL RECENT HEAVY DRINKING DAY

Review of the evolution of the drinking history seeks to build understanding which is *longitudinal* – the present is understood in its historical
perspective. Reconstruction of the typical drinking day, on the other
hand, focuses exclusively on the present – the cross-sectional rather than
the longitudinal view. The styles of enquiry are correspondingly different.
When reconstructing evolution of the problem it is the broad sweep which
is important, while analysis of the typical day requires in contrast very
detailed enquiry if full understanding is to be achieved. This understanding should be so exact that in the mind's eye it is possible to play out a
videotape of the patient's day – with no gaps and no occasions on which
there is a figure but no background. If necessary, the therapist should feed
back to the patient what the patient seems to be saying, until accurate
understanding is achieved. Some guidelines for this technique of enquiry
may be useful.

(i) Establishing the notion of 'typical'

Firstly, the concept which is involved has briefly to be conveyed to the
patient. He is asked to identify (i) a *recent period* when his drinking was, in
terms of his own definition, (ii) *heavy,* with the drinking then of a kind
which he would generally consider to be (iii) *typical* of his recent drinking.
The patient has to identify the exact period he has in mind – 'the way I was
drinking until two weeks ago when I lost my job and had to cut down'.
What has to be emphasized is the actuality, rather than any generalized
abstractions which have no real time base. Most patients find it possible to
identify such a period, but for others there is so much variability in their
drinking pattern that what is typical is difficult to define, and this in itself is
a reality which has to be described.

(ii) Waking and events around waking

Having explained the ground rules, it is necessary to establish at what time
the patient usually wakes. This first entry in the day's timetable may not be
8 am when he gets up, but 4 am when he wakes with experience of

withdrawal, has a drink, and goes back to sleep. Enquiry is then made as to the events immediately around the time of waking, for it is here that evidence will be gained of withdrawal symptoms, withdrawal relief drinking, and other signs and symptoms which help to elucidate the patient's degree of dependence.

(iii) Subsequent hour by hour timetabling

The patient is then taken through a reconstruction of the day, as follows.

The background structure of daily activities

For instance, what time he leaves the house in the morning, what train he catches, what time he gets to work, when he takes his lunch hour, and so on.

The timetable of drinking

What time the patient takes his first drink, how much he then drinks and over what duration, what beverage he chooses. This enquiry is then taken forward step by step, through the day. To a description of actual alcohol intake is in each instance added a note of where the drinking takes place, and with whom (if anyone) the patient is drinking. Note also has to be made of the patient's ideas as to the determinants of each drinking occasion – whether to relieve or avoid withdrawal symptoms, to relieve anxiety or other unpleasant inner feelings, whether in the setting of business or for the companionship of the pub, or for any other reason. A final aspect of drinking which has to be timetabled is the experience of intoxication, and whether at any point of the day the patient would consider that drink is interfering with ordinary functioning, for example, is he unable to work after lunch or falling about when he gets home, and so on.

Influence of drinking on personality

Some patients are not aware that drinking in any way alters their personality, while another patient will state that 'I'm an entirely different person when I've been drinking – Jekyll and Hyde'. The issue has to be examined, both in terms of positive and negative effects. Positively, someone may for instance see himself as more outgoing, confident, and assertive when drinking. On the negative side, the effect may be irritability and loss of control over temper (including violence), suspiciousness, moroseness, withdrawal, self-pity or lack of feeling for others.

Probing and checking

The following dialogue shows how an important aspect of the drinking history can be elucidated by careful probing:

> *Therapist* You say you don't usually take the first drink till opening time?
>
> *Patient* Yes, that's right.
>
> *Therapist* Well, you tell me you're really very badly wanting that first drink and are a bit shaky – why do you wait till opening time?
>
> *Patient* More often than not my opening time isn't the general public's opening time! I know the barman and he'll let me in the back way any time after 9.30 am. He's got a bit of a problem himself.
>
> *Therapist* So it isn't a matter of being able to hold out and wait patiently till 10.30 am?
>
> *Patient* No, I'm round there pretty regularly at 9.30 am – no hanging about, I can tell you. And of course I'm often staying in bed to 9 am, and then it's straight round to the pub as soon as I'm up and dressed.

Without probing, the patient's apparent lack of urgent need to relieve his withdrawal symptoms would be read as suggesting that he was not very dependent, a finding which would be inconsistent with the degree of withdrawal which he was reporting. Probing on such small details builds up a larger picture which is itself correct.

Another important area where probing is often needed is in relation to statements on the quantity drunk. Here is another piece of dialogue:

> *Therapist* All right, you say you have three pints of beer at lunchtime. How long do you spend in the pub at lunch-time?
>
> *Patient* Twelve noon till 2 pm, sometimes 3 pm.

Therapist More often 2 pm or 3 pm?

Patient Say, 2.30 pm.

Therapist Three pints in two and a half hours seems very slow drinking.

Patient Yes, you're right. If I'm there 12 to 2.30 I suppose it would be five or six pints. I was thinking of when I have a short lunch hour. It's more often a long lunch hour these days.

Therapist You say six pints – could it be eight?

Patient No, I'd get too bloated. I don't think I'd ever go above six pints.

Therapist Anything else besides beer at lunch-time?

Patient Probably have a couple of whiskies.

Therapist Why 'a couple' – could it be more?

Patient No, I'll have just a couple of whiskies to round things off when I've finished with the beer. Not more than a couple.

Therapist Double or single measures?

Patient Doubles.

Therapist Ever leave out the whisky?

Patient: No, its pretty regular.

Putting quantity consumed against time spent drinking, sometimes checking stated consumption against money usually spent, testing the stated upper limit by offering a higher or lower one, going through other alcoholic beverages than the one first named, relating the stated drinking to the company and other circumstances, all these provide useful methods for checking, which together help to build up a credible picture.

Totalling the daily intake

On the basis of information given of the quantity drunk throughout the day, the usual daily intake can be totalled. Almost invariably when daily quantity is determined in this way, it is found to exceed the figure obtained by a bald initial question of 'how much?'. As a very rough guide, different beverages may be taken to have the following alcohol content:

Medium strength beer	18g per pint
Cider	18g per pint
Spirits	10g per single pub measure
	(with 32 measures to a bottle)

Table wine	10g per usual wine glass
	(with 6 glasses to a standard
	bottle or 9 glasses to a litre)
Fortified wines (sherry, port)	10g per usual glass

On this basis, approximate conversions can be made, and the usual day's heavy drinking be expressed in grammes of absolute alcohol. To familiarize oneself with the implications of different levels of drinking it is useful to learn to think in terms of such totals.

BRINGING TOGETHER THE EVIDENCE FOR DEPENDENCE

Much information relevant to establishing the degree to which the patient is alcohol dependent will have been obtained from questioning in the areas of *evolution* and *typical drinking day*. It is, however, very necessary to have in the history a place where evidence on dependence is reviewed and brought together.

The picture of the dependence syndrome, and its degrees and variations has been fully discussed in Chapter 2 and the headings used in that chapter to describe the core elements of the syndrome provide the framework for this section of the history–taking. Brief notes are added below on the practical approach to questioning in each instance.

(i) Narrowing of the drinking repertoire (p. 24)

Useful questions relate particularly to the sameness or otherwise of drinking during weekdays as opposed to weekends, or during the working year as opposed to holidays. In determining the meaning to be given to the concept of the *typical* day (p. 150), relevant information will in passing have been collected on the degree of variability in recent drinking patterns.

(ii) Salience of drinking (p. 24)

Reconstructing the evolution of the patient's drinking will have implicitly provided an account of the progressive importance of alcohol in his life, and his progressive ability to discount other considerations. Some attempt should, though, also be made to sense out very directly with the patient how salient drinking has become in the here and now. Useful questions are, for instance:

Just how important has drinking become?
Is drinking more or less important for you than eating?
Is drinking more important than people?

Some particular phrase in the patient's answers may suddenly and empathetically convey the reality of his drink-centredness: 'When my wife said she would leave me if I went on drinking, I had the sly thought, well, if she leaves me, there will just be more money for drinking.'

Here it is often also useful to ask a question like, 'What are the good things that drinking does for you?' In this way one gains a sense of the functional significance of alcohol for that patient – whether, for example, he sees himself as drinking for company and the pleasures of the bar-room environment, or for the 'high' state and directly pleasurable effects of intoxication, or for relief of unpleasant feelings, or for a combination of these reasons. The highly dependent person may insist that he has ceased to get any pleasure out of drinking, or even say that he hates every drink – he is simply caught on a treadmill.

(iii) Increased tolerance (or evidence of decreased tolerance) (p. 25)

Nearly every patient with a drinking problem seems to say something along the lines that he can 'drink a lot without getting drunk', and the quantity which is habitually taken is itself evidence of degree of tolerance. If a severe *decline in tolerance* is being experienced, this is often reported as a very worrying happening.

(iv) Repeated withdrawal symptoms (p. 25)

Questioning has to deal with the frequency and intensity of any experience of the commoner withdrawal symptoms – tremor, nausea, sweating, mood disturbance. The possibility must be remembered of these symptoms being experienced not only on waking but also with partial alcohol withdrawal during the waking day. Any history of subacute hallucinatory experiences, delirium tremens or withdrawal fits should also be noted.

(v) Relief or avoidance of withdrawal symptoms by further drinking (p. 27)

Questioning must cover the frequency with which the patient drinks to relieve or avoid withdrawal, the perceived urgency for such a drink, and its perceived effectiveness.

(vi) Subjective awareness of compulsion to drink (p. 28)

Examples of what may bear on assessment of subjective experience have again been discussed in Chapter 2. A useful technique here is to focus on the actualities of some specific occasion and ask about the related feelings:

> When you were sitting in the pub last night, why didn't you leave after the third pint?
> Why couldn't you have walked out of the pub?
> Why couldn't you have had just one pint and gone for supper?
> Help me to understand what you were feeling.

(vii) Reinstatement after abstinence (p. 29)

Questioning should focus on the actualities of what happened on recent occasions when the patient was off drink, and went back to drinking again – when he came out of prison perhaps, or when he came out of hospital, or when after a period of involvement with Alcoholics Anonymous he 'had a slip'.

BRINGING TOGETHER THE EVIDENCE FOR ALCOHOL-RELATED DISABILITIES

Questioning in this section should be aimed at involving the patient himself in a sort of audit. He should be enabled to build a comprehensive picture of the way in which alcohol has adversely influenced his life. Each relevant fact is adduced with the patient's exploration of the significance of that fact and the degree to which alcohol was involved. The final listing of damages is therefore one in which each step has been included only with the patient's testing and agreement. It ends up as *his* list, *his* audit, rather than it just being the therapist's private clinical note.

(a) Testing each item: the 'agreed' audit

The introduction to this section of history-taking could be as follows:

'What we should do now is to try to bring together the ways in which alcohol may have been having any sort of bad effect on your life – on your physical health or your nerves or your job or your marriage or anything else. You've already told me quite a lot about this, but let's now try to make out the whole list.'

If, for example, the question of the impact of drinking on the patient's marriage were to arise in a particular case, discussion might then be as follows:

Therapist You told me that your wife walked out on you because of your drinking.
Patient Because of my drinking? That's what she said, yes. Not sure myself what the drinking had to do with it.
Therapist Well . . . ?
Patient Bit of one thing, bit of another. I'm not sure we were right for each other. Her mother got in the way, and I suppose the drinking didn't then make anything easier. I'm not taking all the blame.
Therapist But leaving blame aside . . . trying to understand . . .
Patient If it hadn't been for the drinking we might have made a go of it. I'm not saying we *would* have made a go of it. We *might* have made a go of the marriage.

There is obviously a question here which could be explored with this patient later at greater length, but for the purposes of this initial history it is sufficient to establish that the patient accepts as a fair assessment that without the drinking he 'might have made a go of the marriage'. A clumsy interrogation that faced him with no more than a sort of yes/no alternative would have given him no opportunity to convey and define a personally meaningful way of assessing the impact of drinking on marriage.

(b) Necessary areas to be covered

This section of questioning centres partly on further elucidating the meaning of information which has been given in reconstructing the evolution of the problem. But this will be supplemented by further questioning to make sure that all areas of possible damage are adequately covered. There is little to be gained by administering a formal check-list, but it must nonetheless be ensured that no important areas have been forgotten. The necessary background knowledge for this section of the work is an intimate awareness of the many ways in which alcohol can affect health or social functioning, and these are matters which have been discussed at length in Chapters 3, 4, 5 and 6. One important item which should always be enquired into under this heading is the experience of alcohol-induced amnesias or 'blackouts' (p. 76).

(c) Playing back the audit

What has been worked through is at this stage brought together and the patient is played back a summary of what seems to have been established – either fully established or accepted only with reservations. The summing-up has to be made with lots of room for interruptions.

HISTORY OF HELP-SEEKING FOR DRINKING PROBLEMS: MOTIVATION

Enquiry should be made both about help sought by the patient in the past, and help being given at present.

1 *Past*. Helping agencies with which the patient has been involved should be identified and listed, the duration and intensity of contact noted, and the patient's view of the usefulness of such contacts explored.

2 *Present*. All agencies or individuals must be identified with whom the patient is at present in contact about his drinking problem or an account of any other health, social or family matters. This information is needed for co-ordination.

It is then essential to understand the patient's reasons for coming to this present consultation – the pressure or compulsions he sees himself as experiencing (a court order, his wife's threats), what crisis may suddenly have precipitated the immediate help-seeking, what inner sense of need is motivating him. Once more, the process of history-taking is an experience for the patient as well as giving information for the therapist. The patient is exploring the question of why he is in this room, and himself trying to understand the ambiguous, confused or contradictory motivations which may have brought him there. Such knowledge is an important basis for later work. The history here has to be taken in awareness that motivation is always ambivalent: the patient both wants to go on drinking, and wants to stop drinking. It is these conflicting forces that have to be identified, rather than the reality of conflict being evaded.

PHYSICAL EXAMINATION AND INVESTIGATIONS

Physical examination and laboratory investigations (Chapter 6) must be part of the assessment routine in any medical setting. This needs to be stressed, for unless this procedure is firmly established it is all too easy in, for instance, the busy psychiatric out-patient clinic to become slack about it. In a social work or probation office this aspect of assessment is clearly not within expected practice, but there will be great advantage in such agencies ensuring that the patient receives a physical examination from his doctor, with the results fed back. This insistence on the importance of making a medical connection may go against the usual working methods of some non-medical agencies and be seen as burdensome – and indeed the difficulties in establishing the needed liaisons are not to be discounted. However, the likelihood of physical disorder in the patient with a drinking problem puts him in a different category from most social work clients, and medical assessment and help in this instance should be seen as a legitimate part of social-work responsibility.

HISTORY-TAKING: THE ESSENTIAL FRAMEWORK

On the following pages the essential structure for history-taking is layed out.
1   In the first column major areas of enquiry are tabulated, using the same headings employed previously.
2   The second column seeks to help the practical business of history-taking by providing a few important reminders as to what has specially to be kept in mind during the processes of interview – a series of working notes on technique.
3   The third column provides reminders as to the purpose of the whole exercise and of individual sections. These reminders are important: if the sense of purpose is lost, there is danger both of the history becoming inordinately long, and at the same time of its failing in its essential goals.

Area of enquiry	Matters specially to be kept in mind	Essential purposes
THE WHOLE EXERCISE	History-taking is conducted within a patient-therapist *interaction*. The quality of this interaction must purposively be developed so as to *invite the surrender of defences*.	
	A history must *serve the needs of both therapist and patient*.	FOR THE PATIENT: the *initiation of therapy*, in terms of (i) the accomplishment of a self-review which *factually arrays and interrelates a wide variety of experiences* (with drinking and its impact placed in context) and (ii) an *undefended exploration of the meaning of those facts*, together with (iii) laying the *foundations of a therapeutic relationship*.
		FOR THE THERAPIST: (i) the provision of initial factual and emotional understanding which will be the basis for *developing (with this patient), the patient's treatment goals and treatment programme*, and (ii) a basis for *therapeutic training* and the continued *growth of awareness and skills*.
BACKGROUND HISTORY		OVERALL: to provide (i) essential understanding of *the person in his own right*, of *his present* as continuous with *his past* (and endowed or constrained by his past) and (ii) the *context for understanding* the drinking history.
Family history. Both parents, other significant figures in childhood, siblings, childhood environment.	*To search after* what the home felt like and looked like and who was there: 'the street in which it stood'.	Preliminary understanding of crucial early relationships and experiences which may have contributed to the individual's fundamental strengths and vulnerabilities, the way he will relate to people, and the dynamic and cultural meaning he will give to alcohol.

Area of enquiry	Matters specially to be kept in mind	Essential purposes
Personal history. Birth, adjustment in childhood, schooling, occupational history, sexual adjustment, marriage, children, finances and housing, leisure, forensic history.	. . . what it feels like to have lived this life . . .	Serving the overall purpose, while in passing some information will be obtained on drinking and its consequences, which has later to be ordered.
Previous illnesses. Physical and mental.		Serves the overall purpose as above.
Personality	. . . and to be this person	Crucial exploration to serve the overall purpose.
DRINKING HISTORY	THROUGHOUT – the background history	
Evolution	Four strands of enquiry: 1, drinking pattern. 2, dependence. 3, drink-related problems. 4, pressures and circumstances.	To sense the broad dynamic of an evolving story: *the longitudinal perspective.*
Typical recent heavy drinking day. Waking and events around waking: the timetable of drinking, influence on personality, totalling the daily intake.	1, establish the *notion* of the typical day. 2, the need to focus down on small actualities. 3, the need to check and probe.	To understand the present in fine detail: *the cross-sectional view.*
Bringing together the evidence for dependence. 1, Narrowing of repertoire. 2, Salience of drinking.	To look for *coherence.*	An understanding as to whether dependence is *present*, and if so its *degree.*

Area of enquiry	Matters specially to be kept in mind	Essential purposes
3, Tolerance.		
4, Withdrawal symptoms.		
5, Relief or avoidance of withdrawal by drinking.		
6, Subjective awareness of compulsion.		
7, Reinstatement after abstinence.		
Bringing together the evidence for alcohol-related disabilities. Physical health, mental health, social functioning, and functioning within the family. 'Blackouts'.	Testing each item for the patient's agreement.	Building a broad and comprehensive picture of the way in which alcohol has adversely affected the patient's life – a *shared audit*.
History of help-seeking for drinking problems: motivation. Past and present.	Motivation is a matter of ambivalence.	To understand why the patient is in this room, and the work on motivation that has now to be done.

Chapter 10
Initial Assessment with the Spouse

In this chapter we will discuss why it is important to interview the spouse as part of the initial assessment procedures, how this interview is to be handled, and its content. It is often helpful if the patient can be interviewed by one member of the team, while the spouse is being seen by another, with the information and perspectives then later being brought together for joint appraisal and formulation.

That the patient is the man and the spouse the woman is still the likelier event, despite the narrowing gap between male and female alcoholism rates. This chapter will for convenience again largely be written in terms of 'he' as the patient, and 'she' as the spouse, with a short additional section then looking at the situation where the woman is the patient and the man the non-alcoholic spouse. But as ever the use of this convention should not be allowed to reinforce the assumption that it is only men who have drinking problems or only the drinking problems of men that really matter, with the alcoholism of women a mere afterthought.

That a special chapter is devoted to the interview with the spouse intentionally underlines the importance of this part of the assessment. An outline of the scheme is again given at the end of the chapter, and it should once more be emphasized that the detail should not be allowed to intimidate the reader who is working under extreme constraints of time. With practice, things are simpler than they first seem.

Although this chapter deals with the spouse, the value of at times also obtaining a story from other informants should be remembered – from another family member, from a friend, or from an employer. Permission has of course to be obtained from the patient, and confidentiality duly safeguarded in each direction.

MAKING CONTACT

The spouse who is asked to come for interview may be glad to attend or may come along only with reluctance. A wife may herself have formed the view that her husband's alcoholism is in some sense a 'family problem', while another woman may see the problem as being solely in her husband's behaviour and be resistant to seeing herself as other than passive victim. A wife may be needing not so much to talk about her husband but about herself and her perplexity as to her own behaviour, while another woman comes with an angry and determined need to use the occasion to complain about her husband's misdemeanours, and is wanting the therapist to take sides.

Before the therapist starts to guide the discussion into a loosely formal structure, he should therefore give the spouse time to talk freely and to feel assured that her real needs are going to be listened to attentively – that she herself has a right do define why she is here. The ordering of what is dealt with may be varied according to those needs.

The need to take a history from the spouse as person in her own right has already been emphasized in Chapter 3.

PERSONAL HISTORY OF THE SPOUSE

In many ways the basic format of this section will follow the same outline as was suggested for the patient's assessment in the previous chapter, and detailed discussion will therefore not be repeated unnecessarily.

FAMILY HISTORY

Information on parents, other significant figures in childhood, siblings, and childhood environments must be gathered. The worth of routinely making such enquiry (and the handicap which will result from not asking such questions), is illustrated by the following dialogue:

> *Therapist* How much did your parents drink?
> *Wife* I went through in childhood everything I'm going through
> now. How my mother put up with it none of us ever
> understood. I'd say for years my father never came home sober,
> and my mother put up with it. He'd come home blinding and
> swearing and just looking for a fight, and my mother took it year
> in and year out.

The extent to which this woman is acting out her mother's role is a question vital to any understanding of her (and her husband's) present position, and yet if no one bothers to ask about her parents, she may well feel that it is not relevant to tell anyone about her own childhood experience.

PERSONAL HISTORY

1 *General background.* Outline enquiry should be made as to general adjustment in childhood, schooling and occupational history, so as to build up some longitudinal sense of the woman's life adjustment.

2 *Sexual adjustment.* This is as important an area for enquiry with the wife as with the husband, and the two partners may give different accounts.

3 *Marriage and children.* In the initial assessment it is necessary to obtain from the wife firstly some picture of the history of the marriage – whether she knew that her husband was drinking before she married him, and whether there has ever been a period of good adjustment. A picture then has to be obtained of the present rewardingness of marriage – whether it is seen as a wasteland, or as still a potentially happy marriage, though overlain by the drinking.

4 *The reality situation.* Under this heading enquiry has to be made as to the family's financial situation, and the satisfactoriness of accommodation.

5 *Leisure and friendships.* Appraisal is needed of the extent to which the drinking problem may have forced progressive isolation. What contacts does the wife have with other people, to whom can she talk and from whom can she gain support?

6 *Health.* The wife's own health and that of the children must be asked about, and it is, for instance, important not to overlook the possibility of the wife being clinically depressed.

7 *Basic personality.* Thi should be assessed in much the same terms as with the husband (see p. 147).

8 *The wife's drinking.* Enquiry should be made into the wife's attitudes towards drinking, and the extent to which she herself drinks. It is also wise to ask about her use of tranquillizers and sedatives.

STATUS OF THE SPOUSE
AS INDEPENDENT INFORMANT

Before discussing a framework for the section of the interview which deals with the wife's account of the husband's drinking, attention must be given to the idea of the wife's status as 'independent informant'. In such a tangled and painful situation as a marriage complicated by alcoholism, it is un-realistic to suppose that either partner is able to convey entirely dis-passionate truth. Each is giving a perspective based partly on an attempt to be objective, but a perspective which is coloured also by self-justification, anger and many other influences. By assessing the coherence of either account and by looking sympathetically at the likely biases, the attempt must be made to arrive at the most accurate possible view of certain important objectivities – how damagingly, for instance, this man has *really* been drinking. To go ahead on the basis that the hard facts of the case do not matter can be disastrous. But the divergencies which indicate the different ways in which these two people feel about the situation are also important.

Having said that, it is useful to be alert to some of the commoner ways in which the wife's account may deviate from anything which could fairly be considered the independent and objective truth. Wives will, for instance, be found who will exaggerate their husband's drinking, and this either because of a conscious wish to blackguard a reputation, or because of a profound anxiety about drinking and drunkenness which at times may even lead to something approaching delusional misinterpretation. At the other extreme, a wife may in the face of her husband's appalling and long-continued drinking insist that all is well, either because she is frightened of her husband's anger if she divulges the truth, or again because of subconscious reasons. The more bizarre distortions are not common but they can give rise to a great deal of puzzlement when they occur, and it may be months before the treatment team tumbles to the fact that the husband's plaintive insistence on his sobriety is correct, and the wife's account based on a desire to obtain a divorce. But the importance of the issue which is being raised here is to be seen not in terms of the extreme case, but in the reminder that with every case (and each partner), one is presented not with abstract chronicles but with accounts coloured by the active involvement in the story of both people who are talking.

SPOUSE'S ACCOUNT OF THE DRINKING HISTORY

EVOLUTION

The wife's picture of the evolution of her husband's drinking problem may be the same as her husband's account, or she may be able to offer additional insights.

> 'He won't tell you this, but I've always felt that he's never liked the attention I've given to the children. I think it was soon after our first son was born that I noticed my husband's drinking. He didn't know how to fit back into the family. Sounds funny, but I've always thought *he* wanted to be the baby in the family.'

The wife may similarly pick up the significance of other influences which the husband has not talked about. The emphasis which she gives to a particular bereavement or to this or that disappointment or stress at work is not to be taken as necessarily either more or less valid than the husband's views, but as further help in understanding what has happened and how these two people construct meaning out of what has happened.

PRESENT PATTERN OF DRINKING

To suppose that the wife can be the independent informant who can give a print-out on the quantity and frequency of her husband's drinking is usually unrealistic, and questioning along that line only forces the wife into giving bogus estimates. What the wife can in fact very usefully describe is the frequency with which the husband behaves in a way which can be summarized as 'unacceptable'. She has probably developed a special eye for recognizing her husband's comportment, and will be able to integrate various cues of mood and behaviour which for her signal evidence of intoxication.

It is unlikely that the wife will be able to give a picture of the present drinking pattern in anything approaching the detail of the husband's account of his 'typical drinking day', but it may be worthwhile at least asking her something about the daily pattern of drinking. A wife may be able to identify withdrawal symptoms and know that her husband is shaky and retching in the morning, although in many instances she is not fully aware of these symptoms.

PROBLEMS AND HARDSHIPS

The wife may or may not be in a position to know what alcohol-related problems her husband has experienced, or be able to give information parallel to the heading of enquiry in the relevant section of the patient's own history (pp. 156–158). It is, though, worthwhile to ask her in outline about such matters as her husband's illnesses, accidents, lost jobs, forensic involvement, and so on.

There are, however, a range of other matters relating to the husband's drinking which the wife may be particularly well-equipped to speak about, and these concern the direct impact of his drinking on the family and herself – the *hardships* which she is experiencing.

Here are some indications as to the areas of questioning which may be useful.

(i) Has drinking made him 'unreliable'?

The word 'unreliable' may for the wife exactly catch the frustration of what she has been experiencing, and a question phrased in this manner then leads directly into matters she wants to talk about.

> 'Yes. That's it exactly. It's everything from you have the dinner ready and he's not there to eat it, to that dreadful time last year when we were all lined up for the summer holiday and he disappeared. You can never believe what he's telling you, never trust him to do what he says he is going to do.'

(ii) 'Rowing on and on'

Here the typical story is of the husband coming home after pub closing time, waking his wife up, and then embroiling her in a smouldering row which goes on for hours. She learns to expect these recurrent scenes in which he recapitulates all her faults and shortcomings, and with the wife knowing of no way to cut into or terminate these dreary replays. Jealous accusations are often part of the content.

(iii) 'Turning nasty'

The wife may come to recognize that at a predictable stage of intoxication *bonhomie* or self-congratulation suddenly passes over to a mood of anger or violence. She may know that in such moods he will start breaking up the furniture, or assault her or the children.

(iv) Money

A wife may report that whatever the course of the drinking problem 'he always gave me my money'. More commonly the financial hardships and uncertainties experienced by the wife are part of the chronic strain of living with a man with a drinking problem. It may be a matter of his taking money from her purse, of the housekeeping money not being provided, of the bills not being paid or of the gas meter being broken into. Possessions may have been sold or pawned.

(v) 'Useless in the evening'

The story here is of the man who gets home in the evening and who does not engage in rowing or violence, but who pushes aside his supper and then night after night slumps drunkenly asleep in an armchair. The wife finds him there in the morning.

(vi) Wetting the bed

Bed-wetting is a not uncommon feature of alcoholism, and in an advanced stage, the alcoholic may also soil himself. And in a state of drunken confusion he may get up and urinate in a corner of the bedroom.

COPING

The *coping mechanisms* which the spouse may employ have been discussed in Chapter 3. Some enquiry should be made into the ways in which the wife is dealing with her husband's drinking and the types of mechanism which she is deploying. It is useful to think in terms of different styles, such as circumvention, attack, manipulation, spoiling, constructive management and constructive help-seeking, although it is likely that in many instances some mixture of styles will be perceived. This type of understanding can provide a very useful basis for later therapeutic work. The wife begins to see patterns in her own behaviour, and to realize the degree to which she may be persevering in unproductive or counter-productive responses, and the possibilities of more constructive reaction.

ROUNDING OFF THE INTERVIEW

It must be stressed again that any assessment interview is properly a therapeutic encounter, whether that interview is with the person with the drinking problem or with the spouse. For the spouse, the interview should be an opportunity to bring some order and understanding to muddled and painful happenings, the chance to discover or express feelings and often a conflict in feelings, a confirmation of her worth as an individual, and a sensing of ways in which she may have compounded the problem. Part of the interview may have been abreactive and tearful, and what has happened may be difficult to carry outside the room.

When this interview is being rounded off, it is therefore very necessary to show some response to the feelings that may have been awakened.

WHEN THE HUSBAND IS THE NON-ALCOHOLIC SPOUSE

The problems of the woman alcoholic are covered in Chapter 8. To an extent the dynamics of the interaction which are brought to this interview are similar whichever partner is the alcoholic, but when the husband is the non-alcoholic spouse there must be a particular awareness of the need to meet and interpret the feelings of anger and disgrace which a man may experience when his conventional view of womanhood is betrayed. The degree of attack and denunciation which colours his account may drive the inexperienced interviewer either towards a very negative view indeed of the drinking woman, or more probably towards a very harsh view of the unsympathetic husband.

> 'I've given her everything any woman could want. Nice home, good neighbourhood. Holidays. Two lovely kids. You name it. And then she let's me down. She makes a Charlie of me, over and over again. If anyone in my business treated me like that, I'd just fire him.

Once more it is a matter of conducting an interview which is not only about the facts of the case but also about the feelings, with those feelings seen as material in their own right rather than dismissed as mere intrusion in the search for objective truth.

THE ESSENTIAL FRAMEWORK

The table which follows displays the essential framework for history-taking with the spouse, in a format parallel to that used for assessing the patient given at the end of the last chapter.

Area of enquiry	Matters especially to be kept in mind	Essential purposes
PERSONAL HISTORY OF THE SPOUSE	A history has to be taken of this person's background entirely in its own right: to know who this person is, where he or she is coming from, what is brought to the marriage.	Understanding how these heritages interact with current problems and determine present needs.
THE DRINKING PROBLEM	The objective facts are only to be sensed through the colouring which this witness must bring to a situation in which he or she is so much personally involved. The account given by the spouse of hardships experienced needs rather different headings than the patient's account of alcohol-related problems.	To sense the outlines and dynamics of the drinking story, the picture of the present drinking, and the extent of hardship. To enable the spouse to express grief and anger and ambivalence of feeling, and to know that it is safe to share these experiences.
COPING	The range and mixture of mechanisms which are being deployed.	Understanding the stage of development in the marital interaction and possibilities for more constructive response.
THE WHOLE EXERCISE	The interview must honour the spouse in his/her own right, and not just as 'independent informant'. Establishing the objective facts is important. Feelings and interactions also matter.	*For the spouse:* (i) the review of happenings and feelings in a way that begins to make sense and have shape. (ii) awareness of self as more than passive participant or victim. (iii) laying the foundations for future therapeutic work. *For the therapist:* (i) further understanding of the needs of the spouse. (ii) further understanding of the marital interactions. (iii) collateral information.

REFERENCE

Guze SB, Tuason VB, Stewart MA *et al* (1963) The drinking history: a comparison of reports by subjects and their relatives. *Quarterly Journal of Studies on Alcohol,* **24,** 249–260.

Chapter 11
Formulation and the
Setting of Goals

The initial diagnostic interview or interviews with the patient, interviews where possible with the spouse or additional informants, reports from other agencies, and any other enquiries are between them going to provide a mass of information. That information has to be synthesized into an initial case formulation. Lots of separate pieces may give many separate and partial insights, but it is crucial that the attempt should then be made to stand back and perceive the whole predicament. Formulation is the attempt to *understand,* and a well-constructed formulation is a creative act of empathy rather than just ordering of information under headings.

THE PURPOSES OF A FORMULATION

Why go to this trouble? Having gathered all the case material, the temptation is to sit back with a grateful sigh rather than to give time and energy to this added piece of work. There are in fact several reasons for believing that this additional investment is worth the demand. The therapist is directionless until the formulation is made. He does not know what to do or why he is to do it, has not properly thought out the options, is not yet in a proper position intelligently to get on with the helping business. Even if after data-gathering has been completed the therapist has a sense of understanding the patient, when the notes are put aside for a few weeks and the patient re-attends, the freshness of understanding has often faded unless the formulation has been written.

The original formulation will also be of great use if a case is reopened after a gap of a year or two, or if the case is eventually taken over by someone else. Construction of a detailed formulation is invaluable as a training exercise, and useful as the statement which brings everything together at a case presentation.

Besides these various ways in which the formulation is of use to the therapist or therapeutic team, it is equally to be conceived as a basis for discussion with the patient and spouse – as a basis for sharing and feedback on the assessment work which has been accomplished together.

A formulation should not be of inordinate length or it defeats its purpose. The format proposed here is to be taken only as a starting point, to be amended or scaled down according to individual professional needs and feasibilities. Obviously the busy probation officer with two clients in the waiting-room has not got the same amount of time as the psychiatrist in a teaching hospital, and it would be presumptuous to suppose that work can be conducted in exactly the same manner in widely different circumstances. But, however pressured one's working day, time will in the end be more economically and effectively utilized if even five minutes can at this stage be found to order one's thoughts on the case.

HEADINGS FOR A FORMULATION

DIAGNOSIS

It is preferable that this heading should be taken as an invitation to a *full listing* of diagnosis rather than just a statement of 'the' diagnosis. The necessary subheadings are as follows:
1   Alcohol dependence: its presence or absence, and if present its degree of development, with an outline of the supporting evidence.
2   All alcohol-related disabilities (medical, psychological, and social).
3   Ancillary diagnoses, including underlying or accompanying psychiatric conditions and physical disorders.

DESCRIPTION OF PERSONALITY

It is preferable to attempt a brief and very provisional description of personality, rather than to use such phrases as 'personality disorder' under the diagnostic listing. The aim here is to summarize provisional insights regarding both personal strengths and vulnerabilities.

PRESENT SOCIAL SITUATION

1   Marital status, marital interactions and rewardingness of the marriage, wife's coping, and role of children in the present situation.
2   Employment.

3 Accommodation.
4 Leisure.
5 Religious involvement.

DRINKING

1 *History of the drinking problem.* Synopsis of its evolution, with some appraisal of reasons as to why the problem has progressed more or less slowly, and its present rate of progress.
2 *Aetiology of the drinking,* in terms both of more distant determinants (cultural, parental conflict, etc.), and more recent pressures.
3 *The typical drinking day.* Summary description, and estimate of usual daily intake. Assessment of the degree to which drinking varies from day to day.
4 *The balance of present motivations.* Appraisal of patient's current losses and gains from drinking, with particular attention to the patient's own perceptions, as well as the therapist's interpretation.

THE FAMILY'S HEALTH AND WELL-BEING

Problems currently affecting spouse or children.

FURTHER INFOR..ATION NEEDED

A list, for instance, of what further information has to be sought from the patient or other informants, other agencies to be contacted, specialist opinion to be obtained, or specialized diagnostic procedures to be arranged.

GOALS

On the basis of what has already been laid out in the preceding sections of the formulation it should be possible to set up a series of specific treatment goals. As with diagnosis, what is required is a list rather than a single monolithic statement. Further discussion of goal-setting, which is a very important part of the formulation, is given in Chapter 14.

ACTION STEPS

Under this heading are set out in objective terms the steps which have to be taken to achieve the stated goals. The actualities should be listed, rather than any vague generalizations such as 'treat the alcoholism'. This is an aspect of the formulation which can certainly only be designed in co-operation with patient and family.

PROGNOSIS

Prognosis is a valuable exercise in trying to see round corners and get a jump ahead of events. It should again be written in very concrete terms – a statement such as 'patient will probably do moderately well' is too loose to be of any value.

THE FORMULATION AS SHARED EXERCISE

Reference has already been made to the necessity of the formulation serving the needs of the patient as well as the therapist. Before making final notes on the formulation there should have been an interchange in which the therapist says, 'What we have talked through is very valuable.... I see it this way.... What we ought to do is perhaps this.... How do you see it?... Can we agree then....' Such discussion ensures that not only is the therapist standing back from the data and trying to gain the whole view, but the patient is doing the same, and they are doing so together.

REFERENCE

Baekeland F (1977) Engaging the alcoholic in treatment and keeping him there. In: Kissin B and Begleiter H (eds) The Biology of Alcoholism, Vol. 5: *Treatment and Rehabilitation of the Chronic Alcoholic,* pp 161–196. New York: Plenum.

Chapter 12
Case identification
and Screening

Excessive drinking is frequently and in many settings overlooked. Only about 10 per cent of patients with serious alcoholism are likely routinely to be recognized by a general practitioner, and the level of detection is not much higher in the hospital setting. The detection rate in the social work setting has not been adequately investigated, but there can be little doubt that the contribution made by drinking to all manner of social presentations is passed by. We all, in fact, need to cultivate a more alert eye, and aim at earlier and more complete diagnosis. If the element of drinking is allowed to remain hidden, it will defeat our plans to help that patient. The 'depression' will not respond to the prescribed antidepressant, a stomach ulcer will fail to heal, a family's situation will deteriorate, and we will be left puzzled and frustrated. Treatment which is blind to the drinking problem may indeed do actual harm rather than simply fail in its goal, while early diagnosis which can lead to help before dependence is advanced or irreversible damage established is very much in the patient's best interests.

WHY THE DIAGNOSIS IS FREQUENTLY MISSED

There are several possible reasons for alcoholism so often remaining under cover, and several of these reasons conspire together. They can be listed as follows:.

1 Not knowing what we are looking for

The diagnostician may only be attuned to looking for alcohol dependence or the extreme case (with his ideas even on these presentations no more than vaguely formed), but with no real knowledge of the many different types of alcohol-related problems which may be daily impinging on his work. He must be familiar with the common diagnostic clues. Neither alcohol dependence nor alcohol-related problems necessarily declare themselves in direct terms, and the shrewd diagnostician has to be familiar with the wide range of signs and symptoms (physical, psychological and social), which can hint at the underlying drinking problem.

2   Lack of vigilance

The possibility of a drinking problem should *always* be borne in mind, for otherwise even the person who is armed with all the necessary book-learning is at risk of missing the obvious case.

3   Embarrassment at asking questions

The therapist may experience a certain degree of social inhibition in asking about drinking problems, very much related to society's general difficulty in facing up to alcoholism.

4   Not knowledge what to do if the case in uncovered

If the therapist lacks confidence in his ability to respond to a drinking problem if and when it is uncovered, he may be reluctant to make enquiries which threaten to put him in an uncomfortable position.

5   The patient's denial or evasion

A patient who is ashamed of his drinking will have difficulty in bringing the problem forward. That difficulty will only be overcome if the therapist can convey the message that no one is sitting in judgement. It must be safe to talk.

These five subheadings together point a need for much investment in relevant professional training, by educators who are themselves close to the realities of practice.

ENHANCING RECOGNITION RATES

The headings above which outline common reasons for failure in recognition point to how blocks on diagnosis can be overcome. The practical business of diagnosis will then further be aided by consideration of the following issues.

(i)   The use of disarming questions

It is useful to have as one's personal stock-in-trade a few disarming questions about drinking problems which can be fed into any history-taking in almost throwaway fashion. The scene is often best set by a casual introductory remark, such as, 'I always ask everyone about drinking – it can be important to feel that one can talk about one's drinking without being got at'. The implication is of course that it is routine to question in this area rather than the patient being singled out as a special case, and this is coupled with an immediate indication that anything the patient reveals will be sympathetically heard. The questions which follow are then usually best phrased in very open terms, for instance, 'Tell me, have you ever been worried about your drinking? Ever? In any way? I mean, has it led to any rows or troubles at home or at work? Health troubles? Ever thought you ought to cut down? Anyone criticized your drinking?'

Questions which thus feel out the possibility of worry or trouble are more likely to provide a way into fruitful dialogue than rather sterile and mechanistic questions along such lines as 'How much do you drink?'. The latter type of interrogation does not immediately reach across barriers towards what the patient is feeling and experiencing. It is too readily deflected by a bland answer, such as 'Just socially'. But if the preliminary questions about worries and troubles suggest that enquiry has to be taken further, it is then essential to construct the outlines of a 'typical drinking day' (see p. 150) and go fully into quantity and frequency of drinking.

(ii) Remembering who may be specially at risk

To bear in mind a list of who may be especially at risk is useful, provided the therapist does not as a result become blinkered to the wider truth that drinking problems can affect both sexes, and, either directly or indirectly, people of any age and every occupation. With that proviso, an awareness of particular occupational hazard is then important (see p. 17). The single person, the separated and the widowed (especially the recently bereaved) also go in this 'at risk' list. Certain ethnic groups are more at risk of drinking problems, with the Irish providing a familiar example. The person who is homeless and drifting might almost be presumed to have a drinking problem until proved otherwise.

(iii) Common social presentation

One should always be on the look-out for a hidden drinking problem with the patient who is frequently changing house, changing jobs or changing relationships. Family presentations are common – marital disharmony or family violence, the wife presenting with depression or the children with truanting, school failure, antisocial behaviour or neurotic symptoms. Any criminal offences also suggest the need to ask about drinking.

(iv) Common psychiatric clues

Here the essential background list derives from Chapter 5. In particular one should be alert to the possibility of alcoholism when the patient complains rather non-specifically of 'bad nerves', insomnia, or depression. Phobic symptoms, pathological jealousy, paranoid symptoms, and dementia or delirium may all at times be alcohol-related. A drug problem often implies a drinking problem. A suicidal attempt or gesture always demands enquiry into drinking.

(v) Common medical clues

A list of the medical complications of alcoholism is given in Chapter 6. In practical terms one should be particularly on the alert if a patient repeatedly asks for a 'certificate', is a frequent visitor to the doctor's office on a Monday morning, is suffering from malnutrition or obesity, is complaining of any gastro-intestinal disorder or liver problem, has otherwise unexplained heart trouble, has contracted pulmonary tuberculosis, or if the patient presents with 'epilepsy' of late onset. Bruising may be a clue, or burns which have resulted from a cigarette being dropped on the skin while the drinker is intoxicated. Accidents of any sort may be alcohol-related.

(vi) Not overlooking the obvious

The patient may declare the diagnosis by the smell of alcohol on his breath, by the bottle sticking out of his pocket, by his flushed face and bloodshot eyes, or by his tremor, but even the fact that he is obviously intoxicated can be surprisingly overlooked if the possibility of drinking is not held in mind. The patient who makes jokes about his drinking should have those jokes taken seriously. Similarly obvious presentations may be seen on a visit to the home: bottles and glasses lying around, decoration neglected and furniture reduced to a few sticks; the home may be a sad parody of a stage-set portraying decay. It would of course be a serious mistake to think only in terms of such flagrant presentations and therefore overlook lesser clues.

(vii) Having a word with the spouse

If there is any cause to suspect excessive drinking, a word privately with the spouse is essential, and particularly so if the patient says that 'the wife's too busy to come along'. It cannot, though, be automatically assumed that the spouse will be ready and willing to talk about a family drinking problem; loyalty, fear of reprisal, embarrassment or a determined unwillingness to face up to the painful truth may all stand in the way. Very much the same sort of tactful and open questioning may therefore be needed as with the partner who is drinking.

LABORATORY TESTS AND QUESTIONNAIRE SCREENING

(i) Laboratory tests

A number of laboratory tests are useful in the screening of clinical populations for possible drinking problems – within, for instance, a routine medical examination when staff are recruited or undergo annual health checks. These tests can also be confirmatory in the individual case where excessive drinking is suspected but has not been admitted. No one test by itself is of as much value as a battery of investigations, and it seems likely that a properly chosen array of tests should today detect over 80 per cent of patients with an at least moderately severe drinking problem. A negative result certainly does not rule out the possibility that excessive drinking has begun adversely to affect the individual's life, and false positives also occur. Laboratory tests therefore need to be interpreted shrewdly and no test results stand by themselves; they can only be read in the context of all those considerations that have been listed above.

Here we will not go into the technical detail at any length, but simply mention that the most useful contributions to a test battery are today probably made by measurements of MCV or Mean Corpuscular Volume (the size of the individual red cells in the blood may be increased by excessive drinking), by certain tests of liver function (serium gamma glutamyl transpeptidase or gamma GT, serum aspartate aminotransferase, and serum glutamate dehydrogenase levels), and by other tests such as serum uric acid and lipid levels. Lastly, clinching evidence may sometimes come from determination of a blood alcohol level. The patient says, for instance, that he 'only had a few drinks' the previous evening, but at 9 am next morning he still has a blood alcohol level of say 60mg per cent. If a patient has developed a high degree of tolerance to alcohol, the fact that he has a blood alcohol of even perhaps 120mg per cent may not be very obvious to the observer; the finding of a high blood alcohol level in the absence of evident intoxication is important presumptive evidence for habitual heavy drinking.

(ii) Screening questionnaires

A number of screening questionnaires have been devised which are intended to aid in the diagnosis of alcoholism. The test which has been most widely researched in terms of its reliability and validity is the 25-item MAST (Michigan Alcoholism Screening Test), which has also been published in a shorter 10-item form. The CAGE questionnaire is even briefer, containing only four items. These tests generally tend to pick up the more extreme rather than the early case. The MAST, for instance, has among its items experience of delirium tremens and hospital admission for drinking. Such instruments may be of some value for routine screening, for example, in the setting of a hospital ward or out-patient department where there is a more or less captive population which is reasonably attuned to the idea of filling in questionnaires. But these tests in general seem likely more to remain as research tools than to find a place in the front-line work of that wide range of medical and social settings where a paper-and-pencil test provides no substitute for vigilance, sympathetic questioning, and the very real skills needed for identifying drinking problems of all manner of degree, type and hiddenness.

REFERENCES

Holt S, Skinner HA and Israel Y (1981) Early identification of alcohol abuse: 2, Clinical and laboratory indicators. *Canadian Medical Association Journal*, **124**, 1279–1299.

Murray RH (1977) Screening and early detection instruments for disabilities related to alcohol consumption. In: Edwards G, Gross MM, Keller M *et al* (eds) *Alcohol Related Disabilities*, pp 89–106. Geneva: WHO.

Skinner HA, Holt S and Israel Y (1981) Early identification of alcohol abuse: 1, Critical issues and psychosocial indicators for a composite index. *Canadian Medical Association Journal*, **124**, 1141–1152.

Wilkins R (1974) *The Hidden Alcoholic in General Practice*. London: Elek Science.

PART III
TREATMENT

Chapter 13
Withdrawal States and
Treatment of Withdrawal

WITHDRAWAL IN PERSPECTIVE

DIFFERENT NEEDS OF DIFFERENT PATIENTS

Many patients who have sustained serious problems as a result of their drinking have not contracted the dependence syndrome and will experience no significant physiological disturbance on withdrawal. A further important sector of patients will be showing dependence to slight or moderate degree, but will not suffer from withdrawal symptoms which are to any major extent incommoding. On the other hand there are patients who are going to feel wretched on withdrawal, and a small group for whom withdrawal will precipitate life-threatening disturbance.

Given such a spectrum of possible withdrawal experience it makes no sense to approach the treatment of withdrawal in terms of a fixed regime for all-comers. A spectrum of likely withdrawal experiences suggests the need for a spectrum of treatment approaches as corollary. Many patients will need no medication at all to help them come off alcohol, while for many others withdrawal can be safely managed on an out-patient basis with minimum drug cover. In only the minority will withdrawal require admission to hospital, but for some of those patients the effective use of medication will be vital. The clinical significance of withdrawal is firstly, therefore, the demand it makes on the clinican to see the different needs of different patients, and to manage minor withdrawal states without unnecessary fuss while at the same time learning to recognize the necessity for very great care in treating the potentially dangerous situation. This chapter will therefore discuss treatment in terms of different regimes for different intensities of need.

SIGNIFICANCE OF WITHDRAWAL AS BARRIER TO 'COMING OFF'

Some patients will present themselves as unable to come off alcohol because of their incapacity to cope with the withdrawal symptoms. This plea may be entirely genuine. A patient who has previously experienced an attack of delirium tremens may know full well that when he is in a state of severe relapse there is a grave risk of precipitating a further attack of delirium if he attempts abruptly to stop drinking. His pleas for admission should be heeded. On the other hand, there are patients with less severe degrees of dependence whose belief that they cannot stop drinking without coming into hospital should be kindly resisted. It is important for such patients positively to learn that they can cope with withdrawal at home, with minimal ado, and without repeated admissions which reinforce the idea of incapacity to deal with relapse themselves. Unnecessary admissions which mean invalidism and time off work must be avoided.

WITHDRAWAL AND TEAM-WORK

Given that drugs may have to be prescribed for out-patient withdrawal, and given also the potential seriousness of the major withdrawal experience which demands in-patient admission, it is evident that the medical practitioner has an important role to play in treatment of these conditions. If the case is primarily being handled by non-medical staff, this implies the need for very good medical liaison. The social worker in a voluntary agency must, for instance, know when to make the quick out-patient referral, or call on the advice of the general practitioner with whom there is a working relationship.

DETOXIFICATION IN CONTEXT

Mere drying out is not by itself an effective way of helping a patient, and whatever is done about withdrawal only has its meaning within the context of other strategies for aiding the patient. When plans for withdrawal are being made at the same time as initial assessment and goal-setting, the withdrawal phase is easily placed within its proper context. When, however, withdrawal is being dealt with in response to relapse and in an atmosphere of crisis, it is easy to react precipitously and forget the context within which any decisions about withdrawal treatment ought to be made. Questions which ought to be asked in such circumstances centre on what *use* the patient is to make of this help (either as out-patient or in-patient), and what the patient's expectations are of this particular aspect of the contract to help. What plans has the patient got for the far side of withdrawal? Treatment of relapse is discussed further in Chapter 14.

CHECK-LIST FOR AN OUT-PATIENT APPROACH TO WITHDRAWAL

This section will consider the ways in which out-patient detoxification of the not too severely dependent patient can be managed.

DOES THE PATIENT WANT TO COME OFF ALCOHOL?

To put this item first in the check-list may seem an over-emphasis of the obvious, but it is not uncommon to see medical prescribing which suggests a confusion of logic. The doctor has given the patient drugs to treat withdrawal because the doctor believes that the patient *ought* to come off alcohol, rather than because the patient seriously *intends* to come off alcohol. The patient leaves the interview with a prescription for a bottle of tranquillizers which he will use to supplement his continued alcohol intake.

IS IT SAFE TO CONDUCT WITHDRAWAL IN AN OUT-PATIENT SETTING?

This decision is made without difficulty when, as commonly happens, it is obvious that the patient has not got a severe dependence syndrome. He is, for instance, suffering from morning shakes of only moderate intensity which have been present for not much longer than six months, and he came off alcohol for two weeks on his own initiative and without any untoward happenings a month ago. A brief review with the patient of such points as these will usually settle the question of whether out-patient withdrawal is appropriate. A similarly quick answer can be reached in the other direction if there is a previous history of major withdrawal experience and the patient has now reinstated dependence of very serious degree. It is decisions in the middle ground which set difficulty and which call for the most experienced skill. Handling this problem will, as ever, depend on a relationship with the patient which allows open discussion of the issues involved. Such a patient may come into hospital for an admission of only two or three days 'to see how things go', or alternatively he may opt initially to try detoxification at home provided he has good support.

IS THERE LIKELY TO BE A WITHDRAWAL EXPERIENCE WHICH REQUIRES TREATMENT?

If it is necessary to make sure that the patient is not so dependent as to preclude the out-patient approach, it is also necessary to ensure that he is indeed suffering at all from a dependence syndrome, or from dependence of more than minimal degree. Otherwise, one may fairly talk about treatment of his drinking problem and the strategies he may apply for abstinence or ameliorated drinking, but there is no sense in setting up a withdrawal regime when there is no significant withdrawal disturbance to be treated. This might again seem a too obvious point if it were not common to find patients routinely medicated with minor tranquillizers without any enquiry being made into their true needs.

WHAT IS THE BEST TIME?

It may be asking too much for a man or woman with a busy job to try to achieve successful withdrawal in the midst of engagements and in the full setting of usual drinking pressures. Discussion may suggest that the patient set aside a long weekend or take a holiday specially for this purpose. To suggest this degree of forward planning may usefully help to focus commitment.

IS THERE ADEQUATE SUPPORT?

Although there are plenty of people who at some time in their lives have been so determined to deal with their drinking that they have come off alcohol in such adverse surroundings as a drink-laden doss house, it is always useful to think through with the patient how environmental supports may be deployed to maximize the chances of success. If there is a husband or wife to give support, that person should be brought into the discussion and the active engagement of the spouse may have benefit for both partners. This may also be the moment when a patient will be particularly able to accept the usefulness of Alcoholics Anonymous: getting out, for instance, to an AA meeting and hearing how others dealt with this problem, or a phone call from an AA member giving a feeling of contact and fellowship, with a follow-through to more continuing involvement. The hospital doctor must also ensure that the general practitioner is kept in the picture. Support from the hospital may imply the offer of daily appointments over the period of a few days, and if there is no other social support available, day–patient facilities for a short period may be helpful.

USE OF DRUGS

Some practical aspects of the use of drugs in out-patient withdrawal will be briefly discussed in this section, both so as to provide background information for the person other than the doctor who wants to understand this aspect of the patient's treatment, and so as to emphasize some points of immediate medical concern.

Given that assessment suggests that a major withdrawal state is not a risk but that there is reason to believe that some degree of withdrawal symptoms is going to be experienced, then most patients within this band of the dependence spectrum are going to need a minor tranquillizer prescribed. The same drug may be used for daytime and night-time sedation. Within this spectrum there will, though, be a range of severities, so therapy may involve a range of drug doses with the emphasis always on avoiding needless over-medication.

There are a number of different drugs which are effective for this purpose. A drug of the benzodiazepine group would be considered as first choice by many practitioners, while others more usually employ chlormethiazole. It is best for the individual doctor to familiarize himself with one drug, so as to develop a sense of the likely needed dosages in particular circumstances, rather than his switching from drug to drug. Among the benzodiazepines, chlordiazepoxide (trade name Librium) may be prescribed in a dose of say 5 to 10mg three or four time per day. The usual out-patient dosage range for chlormethiazole (trade name Heminevrin) is in the region of 500mg three or four times per day.

The level of doses and how they are to be spaced should be discussed with patient and spouse, and instructions written down very explicitly. In the first instance a prescription should not be given for more than three to seven days, and prescribing should not then be allowed to trail on unnecessarily once the patient has withdrawn. The patient should be cautioned against the risks of driving when under the influence of drugs.

Prescription of vitamins is not a routine part of withdrawal treatment within this severity range, but may sometimes be indicated on other grounds.

CHECK-LIST FOR IN-PATIENT TREATMENT OF WITHDRAWAL (OTHER THAN DELIRIUM TREMENS OR WITHDRAWAL FITS)

In this section the treatment of the greater part of the spectrum of withdrawal states seen in the in-patient setting will be discussed, but treatment of delirium tremens and of alcohol withdrawal fits will be held over for discussion in the next section. The check-list here bears on medical and nursing practice.

REMEMBER THAT IN THE IN-PATIENT SETTING (AS WITH OUT-PATIENT), A WIDE RANGE OF WITHDRAWAL STATES WILL BE ENCOUNTERED

It is inappropriate for a ward to operate in terms of any fixed drug regime. At the time of admission a patient-specific withdrawal regime has to be set up for each case, and this regime must be flexible in response to unfolding events.

MONITORING IS VERY IMPORTANT

Competent routine ward monitoring provides the basis for treatment which is alert, flexible, and able rapidly to be escalated in case of need. There is much to be said for an in-patient centre designing its own supply of charts for this aspect of the work, with the nurses trained to complete the ratings in standard fashion. A simple way of handling these observations is contained in the Selective Severity Assessment Scale, designed by Dr Milton Gross.* Precise instructions are provided for rating 11 variables: eating disturbance, sleep disturbance, agitation, hallucinations, tremor, sweats, clouding of consciousness, quality of contact, temperature, pulse and convulsions. A sensible ward procedure

*Gross MM, Lewis E and Nagarajan M. An improved quantitative system for assessing the acute alcoholic psychoses and related states (TSA and SSA), *Alcohol Intoxication and Withdrawal: Experimental Studies*, ed. M.M. Gross (Plenum, New York, 1973), 365–76.

may be for the nurses to make at least eight-hourly observations on all withdrawing patients for the first three days, and for observation to be discontinued with the senior nurse's approval if all areas are normal. Every now and then a patient who has given an incomplete history and who is expected to show only mild withdrawal will unexpectedly develop much more severe symptoms. Routine observations over the first few days are therefore essential.

ENVIRONMENT

That the environment should be properly supportive is as important here as when the patient is detoxifying at home. General and psychiatric nursing skills have to be employed to help the patient through what may be a few unpleasant days, and the ability of the patient to tolerate this experience will depend in part on the sort of friendliness which he is being offered. To mobilize support from other patients and from visiting relatives can also be valuable.

DRUG TREATMENTS

The possible use to be made here of a number of different drugs will be considered separately.

(i) Minor tranquillizers

The same types of drugs can be prescribed here as for ambulatory treatment, but in a setting which allows close monitoring and where the severer grades of withdrawal are sometimes being dealt with, considerably larger doses may on occasion be employed. There is an old saying that the proper dose of any drug is *enough,* and that certainly applies in these circumstances. The skilled use of a drug with the intention of ameliorating severe withdrawal distress or aborting risk of delirium is a matter of titrating the drug dose against the symptoms. The withdrawal symptoms occur because the level of alcohol in the brain is falling, and these symptoms will be ameliorated when the level of prescribed drug is high enough to compensate for the fall in alcohol. What one is in fact doing is substituting a monitored drug intoxication for an alcohol intoxication, and it is in those terms necessary and rational in the severe case to press the drug dose quite boldly.

With a benzodiazepine one may with severe withdrawal have to give a dose of say 40 to 60mg three or four times a day, or even larger doses. If there is immediate need to bring severe symptoms under control, then chlordiazepoxide may be given by intramuscular injection, with an initial dose of, say, 50 to 100mg. If chlormethiazole is given, the dose may be pressed up to say 2g four times daily by mouth. It should, though, again be stressed both that what is 'enough' is determined by clinical observation of response rather than by any rule book. If the patient becomes excessively drowsy or if there is a large fall in blood pressure, drugs should be cut back or temporarily withheld. Such an approach is far more in the patient's interests than a blind reliance on heavy mixed drug schedules which will be unnecessarily extreme in many instances, and yet insufficient in other cases.

If it has been necessary in the acute phase to load the patient with a drug, one is then in effect subsequently carrying out a drug withdrawal rather than an alcohol withdrawal procedure. And this implies gradually tailing off the drug dose at a rate which will not produce significant drug withdrawal symptoms. The rate of reduction must once more be patient-specific and in accord with monitored symptoms. Problems may in particular arise if withdrawal from a large dose of chlormethiazole is carried out too quickly, with confusion or delirious symptoms arising.

(ii) Vitamins

With patients who have had a heavy alcohol intake there is the risk of an acute Wernicke's encepholopathy developing with disastrous suddenness (see p. 102), and it is therefore a wise prophylactic measure to give thiamine (vitamin B1), in a dose of 200 mg daily, with initial doses given intramuscularly or intravenously when there is serious cause for concern. It is then also useful to give a mixed vitamin preparation.

(iii) Major tranquillizers

Phenothiazines and other major tranquillizers have no part to play in the treatment of this spectrum of withdrawal, and only add to the risks.

(iv) Specific treatment to avert withdrawal fits

The effective use of minor tranquillizers should be sufficient to minimize the likely development of serious withdrawal convulsions, and it is neither necessary nor useful to give additional medication for this purpose.

THE TREATMENT OF DELIRIUM TREMENS

This section deals with technical issues which are mainly the concern of medical and nursing staff, but it may again be of interest to other professionals to acquaint themselves with at least the outlines of how such problems are handled.

The best hope here is in fact that the condition will not arise and not have to be treated. If severe withdrawal is adequately managed with appropriate drug doses the risk of delirium tremens will in many instances be aborted. However, despite the best efforts, ward admission and alcohol withdrawal will sometimes precipitate DTs, and cases of already established delirium will also sometimes present direct for admission. Once a fully developed attack of delirium tremens is underway, it is uncertain whether any treatment will actually shorten the attack, but there is persuasive evidence that the difference between competent and less competent tretment may be the survival as opposed to the death of the patient. The dangers of death from delirium tremens should not be exaggerated, but they exist.

Here is the list of matters to be kept in mind when treating this condition.

WHAT SETTING FOR TREATMENT?

Given the risks to life, patients suffering from this condition should have the benefit of being treated in a setting where the medical and nursing staff are as experienced as possible. When a case occurs on a psychiatric ward there may be uncertainty as to whether the patient should remain on that ward or be transferred to a general medical unit. The decision can only be made in the light of an appraisal of the skills and resources available in either setting.

But whatever the ward on which the patient is to be treated, the basic elements which the setting must provide are much the same. First–rate nursing is required, both for observation and for care. The situation must be one where a potentially disturbed patient can be cared for without staff becoming flustered, and there must be precaution against a patient accidentally hurting himself in a state of confusion. A patient who is only uncertainly in contact with reality is going to be helped by friendliness, positive reassurance and by good room lighting rather than a side-room with shadowy corners.

WHAT UNDERLYING OR COMPLICATING CONDITIONS MAY BE MISSED?

Those patients who die in delirium tremens perhaps most often do so as a result of a medical complication which has been overlooked. Such oversight, unless actively guarded against, can easily come about when all energies are being concentrated on dealing with the immediate and acutely worrying presentation. The patient is probably in no condition to give an accurate history or an account of other symptoms.

The conditions which may have to be recognized are many (and have already been outlined on p. 71), and no check-list can substitute for full initial examination and subsequent continued watchfulness. But conditions specially to be borne in mind must include the possibility of head injury, intercurrent infection (specially chest infection), liver disease and hepatic coma, gastro-intestinal bleeding, and the acute onset of the Wernicke-Korsakoff syndrome. The picture may also be complicated if the patient has been taking barbiturates or another depressant.

WHAT DRUG TO USE FOR SPECIFIC TREATMENT?

Much the same considerations apply here as with choice of drugs for treatment of less severe withdrawal symptoms. A great deal of research has been aimed at determining which drug is likely to be most useful in treating delirium tremens, and the evidence is still conflicting. On the whole it seems best to employ a drug with cross-tolerance to alcohol, and hence one which effectively *substitutes* for alcohol. Chlordiazepoxide may be given in a dose up to 400mg daily by mouth in divided doses, and initial doses may have to be given intramuscularly (up to say 100mg 4–6 hourly over the first 24 hours). If the patient is extremely disturbed a slow intravenous injection of diazepam maybe used (say a 10mg injection at a rate of not more than 5mg per minute and with careful watch on vital functions): as ever an intravenous drug should not be used if avoidable. The dose of chlormethiazole will usually be in the range of 2g four times daily, with higher doses employed with care if indicated. Chlorpromazine and other phenothiazines (major tranquillizers), probably increase the risk to life, although some clinicians have used promazine in this situation to control acutely disturbed behaviour.

FLUIDS AND ELECTROLYTES

Patients who are over-active, sweating and feverish (and perhaps also suffering from gastro-intestinal disturbance), are candidates for serious disturbances in fluid and electrolyte balance which must therefore be monitored. A dangerous fall in potassium level must be averted, and there have been suggestions that decreased magnesium levels are a particular likelihood in delirium tremens. Blood sugar levels should also be watched. Although a drip may have to be set up, so far as possible fluid and electrolyte correction should be managed by oral administration: keeping a drip in position with a delirious patient can set problems.

VITAMINS

Given the danger of an acute brain syndrome, there can be no doubt that the patient with delirium tremens should receive heavy doses of thiamine for a few days, with the first dose of 200 mg being given intramuscularly or intravenously.

LIFE SUPPORT

Emergency facilities must be available in the event of acute circulatory failure. A rare complication is hyperthermia with the temperature suddenly rising to 105°F or more. Hepatic coma is sometimes precipitated when the previously malnourished patient begins to take protein.

ALCOHOL WITHDRAWAL FITS

Fits usually occur within the first 24 hours of admission but they may also happen during the course of delirium (see p. 72). They are less likely to develop if the patient has been adequately sedated, and the same basic drug treatment as for withdrawal symptoms is in general the correct prophylaxis for withdrawal fits, rather than additional anti-convulsant medication being given. If a sequence of fits occurs or status epilepticus develops (a run of fits in continuous succession), intravenous medication will have to be given to bring the situation rapidly under control, and the usual measures deployed as for any patient suffering from convulsions.

WITHDRAWAL SYMPTOMS IN SUMMARY

From what has been said in this chapter it must be evident that the clinical skills required effectively to respond to the range of alcohol withdrawal pictures that will be encountered involve the ability to deploy a range of techniques apposite to varied presentations. The proper use of drugs can sometimes be very important, but this should not lead to any neglect of the importance of support and encouragement. The trust and the relationships established during the treatment of this crisis can be valuably carried through to the next phase of treatment.

REFERENCES

Annis H, Giesbrecht N, Ogborne A *et al* (1976) *The Ontario Detoxification System*. Toronto: Addiction Research Foundation.

Becker GE (1979) Pharmacotherapy in the treatment of alcoholism. In: Mendelson JH and Mello NK (eds) *The Diagnosis and Treatment of Alcoholism*, pp 283–303. New York: McGraw Hill.

Feldman DJ, Pattison EM and Sobell LC *et al* (1975) Outpatient alcohol detoxification: initial findings on 564 patients. *American Journal of Psychiatry*, **132,** 407–412.

Greenblatt DJ and Shader RI (1975) Treatment of the alcohol withdrawal syndrome. In: Shader RI (ed) *Manual of Psychiatric Therapeutics: Practical Psychopharmacology and Psychiatry*, pp 211–235. Boston: Little, Brown.

Hamilton JR (1977) Detoxification – the first step. In: Madden JS, Walker R and Kenyon WH (eds) *Alcoholism and Drug Dependence: A Multidisciplinary Approach*, pp 271–276. New York: Plenum.

Hore BD (1977) Setting up detoxification centres. In: Edwards G and Grant M (eds) *Alcoholism: New Knowledge and New Responses*, pp 313–320. London: Croom Helm.

Chapter 14
The Basic Work of Treatment

WHAT IS MEANT BY 'BASIC WORK'?

Special techniques, such as various psychotherapies, behaviour therapy, or the use of antabuse (disulfiram), can all at times make an important contribution to an individual's treatment programme. It is these approaches which catch the attention and offer the conventional headings for discussion, while the everyday and undramatic basics of the helping process tend to be passed by, or dismissed as the background to the application of specialized techniques. It is, though, vital that attention should be given to the subtle and important range of happenings which occur whenever patient and therapist meet and interact – the what, when and how of what is felt and said and done between them. Otherwise we are at risk of throwing out as packaging what is in fact the essential content of the parcel. Here is how a patient saw what happened between him and a particular doctor:

> 'I remember when I first met that doctor. She seemed friendly but when I tried to con her, she laughed and told me to get my priorities right. Typical alcoholic thinking – I just told myself that she didn't understand, and I didn't bother to turn up for the next appointment. What happened next? I get a letter, not one of those form–letters that hospitals send out, but a personal letter from this doctor saying something like, "I know it's difficult. I don't want to push you into anything, but I'll be in the clinic on Friday afternoon if you want to talk about things further." So I went back to tell her she didn't understand!'

Care for the immediate impression made at the first encounter, the ability to combine being 'friendly' with confrontation, finding a phrase like 'priorities' to sort out complexity, the way a letter is written – here are just a few immediate examples which point to the substance of what is meant by 'basic work'.

197

Therapeutic work is only likely successfully to produce movement when its efforts are in alignment with the real possibilities for change within the individual, his family, and social setting. The basic work of therapy is largely concerned with nudging and supporting the movement along these 'natural' pathways of recovery. We need a far more developed sense of people's innate capacity for recovery and the possible dimensions of recovery, rather than a belief that we can impose therapies on people who are to be marched along at our dictate. The clumsy therapist is like someone who tries to carve a piece of wood without respect for the grain. The basic work of treatment requires immense respect for that grain, and therapy must always be matched to individual needs.

This chapter will be written in terms of the patient who is aiming at abstinence rather than at modification of drinking, in so far as it is necessary at certain points in the text to refer to the treatment goal. But with due interpretation what is said in this chapter is very generally applicable, whatever the chosen goal.

THE RELATIONSHIP

The relationship between patient and therapist is fundamental both to what can be achieved in any one therapeutic session and to what changes can be achieved over time. This relationship begins to be built at the first moment of contact, is developed during the assessment interview (or interviews), is vital to the effectiveness of the initial counselling and goal-setting, and continues thereafter as the most basically important component of therapy. 'What is said' matters, but it cannot be abstracted from the feelings between the two people who are doing the saying and the listening. Take, for instance, the following remarks by the therapist which might be necessary at a certain stage of a particular individual's treatment:

> 'You know that I believe you can stop drinking and make sense of
> your life, but things can't just drag on. You've been coming up
> here regularly to talk about your problems for the last six months,
> and we are both aware that you're now becoming badly caught up
> in this business of tomorrow . . . the day after. Here's a
> challenge. I'm not giving you an appointment for next week but
> instead am going to propose that you come back in six weeks and
> show me that by then you have stopped these binges and started

instead to do some of those things with your family that you have been talking about. I want you to show yourself that you can succeed, and that will be a great feeling. It's time to make a start. You *can* make a start.'

That same form of words may have three very different types of impact. The impact may be negative, with the patient reinforced in his sense of hopelessness, going immediately on a drinking binge, and giving up all attempt at change or help-seeking. A negative relationship in which these words are rightly read as conveying the therapist's pessimism and disdain would certainly propose such an outcome. The second alternative is for the patient in effect not to hear what is said, because no words spoken within a meaningless relationship can matter very much; if he bothers to come back in six weeks' time, it will be with nothing having changed, and with what was said in that previous sesssion blandly neutralized. Lastly, there is the possibility that the challenge is taken and used as a turning point, but this outcome can only be expected when the relationship very positively matters. At worst, the word 'relationship' is devalued into a catch-phrase of professional jargon, and yet every now and then one senses again the intensely important reality of what is being talked about.

Work with drinking problems requires the development of a very practised awareness of how relationships are made and used. There is, of course, little which is unique to alcoholism in this regard. The same basic skills and awareness are needed in any area of therapy and the general nature of a therapeutic relationship will not therefore be discussed here in great detail. It may, though, be useful briefly to list a number of considerations which derive from general psychotherapeutic principles but which have to be especially thought through when working with drinking problems.

(i) Showing warmth

Warmth is not something which can be invented, and a show of pretended warmth will be transparent. The ability to express genuinely warm feelings towards the patient may be easy, or may be frustrated by what the patient or the therapist himself brings to the encounter, for instance, the patient's guarded expectation of rejection or the therapist's unease with deviant behaviour. Warmth is something that has to be felt out and worked towards, and it is possible positively to make the effort to reach this experience. When warmth is genuinely experienced, it still has to be conveyed, and there are skills in the use of voice and gesture, as well as in learning how to convey warmth in words which are not cloying.

(ii) Possessiveness and directiveness

The seeming helplessness of the patient who is caught up in drinking and his pleas for rescue, if not guarded against, may set up a relationship in which the patient is invited to slip into the regressed role of a child. The therapist takes on the role of the perplexed and guilt-ridden parent, loaded with responsibility to try and save the child from its wilful destructiveness. The patient's successes belong to the therapist and, at the same time, the patient's failures are felt as personal failures by the therapist. Such a relationship is the antithesis of one which encourages growth towards autonomy. Directiveness may seem to work in the short-term as the patient is carried along by the therapist's will and demand, but progress of that kind in unlikely to be sustained. The patient will sooner or later rebel and drinking is the obvious act of rebellion. There is an important distinction between the directiveness of telling the patient what to do and reinforcement of the expectation that the patient can meet the goals which he has himself set up. The difference is between 'Go and get a job' and 'Your commitment is to get a job and we agreed that this is a priority'. This issue will be discussed again at greater length in Chapter 20 (p. 305).

(iii) Conferring worth and giving hope

The way in which the patient's bad feelings about himself are to be handled within the relationship is another important question. Feelings of worthlessness, helplessness, pessimism and unresolved guilt are very common in the patient who has experienced years of excessive drinking, and can greatly handicap the attempt at recovery. Bad feelings have to be brought into the open and the covert as well as the overt statements which indicate these attitudes identified. The therapist's job is not then to give a cheery and false comfort which will carry no conviction at all, but to attempt, by many small strategies, to help towards better feelings. Much of what can be achieved depends on the central, unspoken, and yet very tangible qualities of the relationship itself: 'What really helped me to turn the corner was that this particular nurse seemed to have faith in me. She believed that I could do it and I couldn't let her down. She always had time to listen.'

The way in which patient and therapist are *feeling* about each other is very clearly at the core of the change process, but those feelings will, at many points, be fed by the well-timed ability to find words which reinforce the changes in self-image: 'Well done! A year ago if anyone had treated you like that, you would not have seen their point of view, but have gone straight off to the pub. Don't be shy about a bit of well-deserved self-congratulations.'

And these headings of course only indicate some few of the many possible aspects of the relationship.

THE INTERVIEW: SOME THERAPEUTIC PRINCIPLES

What actually happens when, after the initial assessment, formulation and goal-setting, the patient and therapist, on a series of later occasions, again sit down together and talk? Here are some principles which can guide the work.

MAINTAINING CONTINUITY OF PURPOSE

Both patient and therapist have to maintain a sense of progress and purpose, and avoid confusion and drift. This is achieved in a number of ways:

1 *Making use of the initial formulation and goal-setting.* The initial exercise in clarification of understanding and purpose in not afterwards something to be forgotten, but should be referred to as the continued basis for action.

2 *Checking on what has been achieved.* At each session, it is useful for the therapist to help the patient identify what has been achieved since the last meeting and thus reinforce the patient's own sense of achievement, for instance, so many weeks of abstinence, a difficult situation dealt with successfully, a new job started, an outing with the family, or some new aspect of self-understanding.

3 *Setting the next task for the short-term.* The meeting also has to identify what are to be the next steps, with the patient making a commitment to

attempt these steps. The work plan is of no value if it is only in terms of generalities, such as 'getting some other interests going' or 'trying to be more understanding of the wife's point of view'. Generalities cannot provide a programme for action. What is needed is a series of explicit, practical and attainable goals which can then be checked at the next meeting: 'When I came off skid row I suddenly realized I didn't *own* anything. With the next few weeks' wages I'm going to get myself some good clothes, and I wouldn't mind getting one of those alarm-clock radios,'

Although it is useful to concentrate on the short-term, patients will also to varying extent want to see rather further ahead, and be helped forward by thoughts of what things may look like in six months or a year hence. The person who thinks more concretely will be happier to plan his steps in such visible terms as the new clothes, while someone else may think more in terms of personal changes and changes in relationships.

IDENTIFYING SOME LEADING QUESTIONS FOR EACH SESSION

Each session is an occasion in its own right, but it is again useful to have a check-list at the back of one's mind as to the sort of issues which are likely to be covered.

It is a mistake for the therapist immediately to go into detailed questioning, particularly if those questions overemphasize concern with drinking to the exclusion of other problems which the patient has brought with him. The therapist has skilfully to handle the responsibility for defining some sort of structure for the session (otherwise very important matters will escape attention), but structure must not be prematurely imposed. Some very open-ended questions can start the interview – 'What's been happening?' – and the patient's concerns are then built into the wider structure as the interview proceeds.

AN EYE ON THE RELATIONSHIP

The basic importance of the therapeutic relationship has already been noted, and a continuing eye has to be kept on what is occurring in this regard. Is the therapist, for instance, being edged towards a too authoritarian role, or being moved towards argument and intellectual debate?

HOLDING ONTO THE FAMILY PERSPECTIVE

Despite good intentions it is easy to become too focused on the individual and suddenly to discover after some months that the needs of the family and the relevance of the home situation have been allowed to slip from sight, with adverse consequences. If the patient has a family, what is happening within the family and within other close relationships has therefore to be thought about on every occasion, and any needed plans made for continuing work with the people involved (see p. 215).

REINFORCING COMMITMENT

A patient is often more likely to achieve a goal if he has committed himself in so many words to attainment of that goal, rather than the issue being left to nebulous good intentions – 'So you are telling me that by next month you will have painted your house. Is that a commitment? Are you going to invite me round to see the results? All right, by 10th June?'

MONITORING

Implicit in the idea of commitment is the expectation that commitment will be met, but the process only works if the therapist remembers and checks on what is agreed. It is helpful for the patient to feel that his progress is being monitored, and periodic reporting to the therapist may usefully be supported by an element of self-monitoring. The patient may, for instance, be asked to keep a daily diary, with headings to deal with such issues as drinking, craving, 'tricky situations' and how they were dealt with, and the use of leisure time.

THE BALANCE OF DYNAMICS AND REALITIES

The treatment approach which is outlined in this chapter embraces a concern both with psychodynamics and external realities. There is danger in putting too heavy an emphasis on either area while the other is neglected. It is inappropriate to concentrate on exploration of, say, early relationships and go towards the form of an orthodox psychotherapeutic interview (with its relative lack of structure, undirectedness, silences and interpretations), while work problems take second place. But it would also be mistaken to concentrate on why a patient is in perpetual confrontation with his superior at work without exploring his lifelong difficulties with authority. The best balance is usually a close concern with realities and immediacies, combined with a lively awareness of the inevitable psychodynamic implications.

BALANCE BETWEEN DRINKING AND OTHER TOPICS

Each interview will probably to an extent focus on drinking, and will for instance reinforce the agreed drinking goal and monitor progress along the drinking dimension. But work towards recovery also has to be planned, pursued and monitored along other dimensions, often bearing on enhancement of the quality of sobriety (p. 205). No fixed balance can be promulgated as universally appropriate, and the balance of concerns is likely to evolve as recovery progresses. In general, though, it is best to retain a wary and continually adjusted attention both towards work on drinking and progress along other dimensions, rather than ever believing that either sector can be allowed to become the exclusive concern. It is when therapist or patient focuses too much on one sector to the cost of any other that things go wrong. This is an issue to which we again return in chapter 20 (p. 300).

WORKING CONTENT OF THE INTERVIEW

So much then for the discussion of eight working principles which can be seen as the warp of therapeutic work. They are not abstract concepts to be noted and put on one side, but considerations which directly relate to what actually happens at any meeting. With those headings in mind we can now go on to look at the cross–cutting weft of content, with headings given for a check–list that can be used as immediate work directions in any session.

WORKING ON THE DRINKING PROBLEM

According to which phase of recovery the patient has progressed, this heading will have different meanings. It should again be emphasized that this chapter is worded largely in terms of the patient who is aiming at abstinence, although with due modification much the same principles apply to work toward a controlled drinking goal. For instance, at the earliest stage the immediate question is how the patient who is aiming at abstinence is to come off drink and be helped where necessary with detoxification (see Chapter 13), while for the patient who has chosen the goal of controlled drinking the immediate task is indeed to get the drinking under control. Whichever the chosen goal, the patient has to be presented with the unambiguous message that dealing with the drinking problem is a high priority, and that the present is the time to muster the commitment to make a break with drinking or with excessive drinking. Success in achieving this initial break depends on a shared model of the nature of the problem, the overcoming of ambivalence, the awakening of a sense of personal commitment, the quality of the relationship which makes the therapist credible and his persuasion and cajolerly acceptable, and then also on a host of strategems which may be applicable to the particular case. Drinking or damaging drinking should not drag on and on.

But when the patient is off alcohol – focusing again primarily in the present discussion on the abstinence goal – there is still very important work to be done directly on the drinking problem, and this is the time for consolidation rather than for sitting back. The patient's basic understanding of the nature of his drinking problem (and the nature of dependence) has to be rehearsed and reinforced. This is not accomplished by the therapist giving a lecture, but by his pointing up a discussion – 'Just how do you *understand* this drinking problem? How would you explain to another person what's different between your relationship with drink, and his drinking?' Work on ambivalence is also a continuing task rather than something ever settled once and for all – 'What would you lose now if you went back to drinking? What so far looks like the best thing that's coming out of sobriety?'

Discussion will also then usefully focus on questions such as the degree to which the patient is thinking about or craving for alcohol, the cues and circumstances which trigger these subjective experiences, and the ways in which the patient copes with any such feelings. Personal coping mechanisms must be identified, and it is important to teach patients to think in these terms and rehearse the strategies which are going to be employed in difficult situations. He has to learn to sense the reality of these mechanisms as an important personal armoury to be kept in good repair and used whenever there is any threat to sobriety.

There may also be work to be done in terms of dealing with relapse (p. 211).

MENTAL HEALTH

The non-medical therapist may feel uneasy handling responsibility for mental (or physical) problems, but given that non-medical people are properly and inevitably going to be involved in working with alcoholics, they must be aware of the issues which may arise, be able to deal with health questions that come up during interview, and know when to look for back-up from a medical colleague.

A patient will often bring up problems related to his 'nerves' – anxiety, phobic symptoms, irritability, jealousy, depression, or difficulty in sleeping. He must be given the feeling that the therapist is listening and understanding, but what must certainly be avoided is the thoughless prescription of drugs. During the initial weeks (or even months) of sobriety, these symptoms may still be related to withdrawal, and can therefore be expected gradually to clear. It seems likely that the hyper-excitability of the nervous system, which is the essence of acute withdrawal, may continue for much longer than the few days typical of the acute withdrawal period. What at first appear to be handicapping phobic symptoms may, for instance, gradually fade out with two to three months of sobriety. But in practice the contribution made to the patient's 'nerves' by the biological processes of withdrawal will, over the initial period of sobriety, be inseparable from symptoms which may stem from the patient's rediscovery of what it is like to be his real self unshielded by alcohol. His real self may be anxious and irritable, but for years alcohol has blotted out, exacerbated, or generally confused these underlying propensities.

No matter which of the above factors may explain the patient's psychological discomfort, the best immediate response is not heedlessly to offer drugs, but to employ a very common-sense and supportive approach. That approach will, though, only be feasible within the context of a good relationship and the patient's immediate awareness that someone is listening to, rather than brushing aside, his complaints. Within these terms the message that has to be carried to the patient is firstly the optimistic one that such symptoms can generally be expected to ameliorate as the weeks go by, and secondly the realistic one that it may be necessary and possible for him to learn to live with his 'nerves' without resort to a chemical answer. A reflex assumption which has been reinforced over many years' drinking has to be overcome: psychic distress is part of the human condition and not something which has to be immediately and chemically ablated. The patient is, as it were, too anxious about being anxious.

The patient is then likely to be helped if, together with these basic messages, some ideas are offered as to how distress is to be ameliorated more constructively than by resort to tranquillizers. This may entail further effort by the patient to deal with circumstances which are generating stress, for instance, anxiety about debts, housing or employment, which can only be relieved by the problems being positively met, or tensions within the marriage which require resolution, and so on. The patient may be helped by learning a relaxation technique (p. 16), or by developing a variety of simple coping strategies, such as listening to music, going for a walk, or telephoning a friend.

But while the basic approach to many psychological problems is best made in this low-key fashion, the therapist must also keep an eye open for the emergence of more serious disturbances (see Chapter 5) which may require very active attention. To argue that the first line of response to the patient's 'bad nerves' should not reflexly involve prescription of tranquillizers or antidepressants is, though, in no way to suggest that the significance of these rather non-specific symptoms should be underrated or that therapeutic inactivity is the order of the day. Skilled support and identification of those stressful environmental circumstances which are amenable to change may indeed be required.

SOCIAL AND FAMILY ADJUSTMENT

A wide range of problems may need to be discussed and monitored under this heading, as the patient works towards agreed goals. If such topics are not spontaneously brought up by the patient during the session, it may be wise for the therapist on each occasion to make at least a general enquiry as to what is happening within the family, how things are going at work (or as regards looking for a job), and how leisure is being spent. Financial problems, housing or any court proceedings may also need to be checked on. Work along these lines is essential to the process of recovery, and the therapist needs to be as much interested in monitoring what is being achieved in these directions as in talking about the drinking itself or any psychological problems.

PHYSICAL HEALTH

Particularly in the early stages of sobriety, there may be problems in the patient's physical health which require attention or referral, and which must not be lost from sight because of all else that is on the agenda. A feeling of rediscovered physical well-being may be one of the prime rewards of sobriety, and work under this heading should therefore entail not only dealing with ill-health, but efforts positively to enhance good health.

SLOTTING MORE SPECIFIC TREATMENTS

The use of the more specific treatment approaches which are discussed in the next chapter requires discretion and timing. Only on the basis of an understanding of the individual and his progress, which will emerge from the type of contact which has just been described, is it possible to judge whether any added help is needed or likely to be effective. Questions of this type should therefore be in the therapist's mind from the first session onwards – is it appropriate to set up a behaviour therapy programme? Should disulfiram be prescribed? Is it now after six months timely to think of psychotherapeutic help? and so on. Decisions here demand an ability to utilize team resources and the therapist's knowledge of how to make use of skills other than his own. Thus every session, besides its immediate contact, is also potentially a routing point.

MAKING THE EFFORT WORTHWHILE

No one is likely to achieve long-term success in dealing with a drinking problem unless sobriety (or ameliorated drinking) proves to be a personally rewarding experience. Alcohol can only be given up very grudgingly if its surrender is a loss with no gain. If all that is won by the effort to stop drinking is a grey and empty existence, it will probably not be long before there is a relapse. When sobriety is unrewarding, there is also the danger that alcohol will be substituted by uncontrolled gambling or by excessive use of tranquillizers and sedatives.

Many patients move spontaneously towards discovery of rewards, and two general patterns of development can often then be seen – either a wide new engagement in life, or, alternatively, a much narrower substitute activity. It is important that the therapist should learn how to sense what headway the patient is making and the choice of pathways which is evolving. The first of these two pathways – the wide new engagement – is in fact more often a re-engagement in life than an entirely new series of moves, and is characteristic of the patient who had a positive involvement in life before the emergence of the drinking problem overwhelmed these enjoyments. The sense of physical and mental well-being which sobriety offers is rapidly capitalized; family reconciliations can offer happiness and very special closeness, neglected leisure pursuits are taken up again, and holidays are planned and enjoyed. The second pathway – that of narrower substitute activity – more often characterizes the recovery of the person who never, at any previous period, achieved any great base of enjoyment. In this instance, it is not that a happy pattern of living was overwhelmed by drinking, but, on the contrary, that the drinking problem initially developed in the setting of unrewarding relationships and activities. Recovery may be marked by an almost/frenetic commitment to one particular interest, often to the neglect of family or as defence against emotional contact. Familiar pictures may include a massive involvement in AA, with meetings attended every evening and holidays spent only at AA conferences, an addiction to work which the patient himself may identify as very similar to an addiction to alcohol, or an obsessional commitment to one particular hobby, for instance, the collecting of toy soldiers and endless sand-table battles.

A respect for natural processes and for individual strengths, needs, possibilities, and ways of going about things must mean that when the patient is moving towards his own approach to consolidation of recovery, the therapist's role is largely limited to that of information resource, giver of ideas, and sounding-board. This phase requires work and commitment rather than being left to luck. Drift does often need to be discusssed, and when someone is heading for the very narrow type of substitute activity, it may be useful to try to help him to see what is happening and to move him towards something more fulfilling.

When no rewarding pattern of new involvement develops in the wake of sobriety and as the months go by there is instead a continued complaint that 'it was better when I was drinking', thought then certainly has to be given to what can be done to obtain constructive movement. The therapist's role is firstly that of identifying the problem and encouraging the patient to identify small real steps towards a solution and to take those steps. This is often a stage where the family again needs to be very much involved. Beyond common-sense advice, there are then various other lines of approach. For instance, the passivity and pessimism which stands in the way of a determined attempt to find rewards seems often to have the characteristics of a learnt expectation of failure – 'I just can't get on with people, I'm no good at anything.' Even one small limited success may begin to offer a new sense of possibilities – success generalizes. Efforts may usefully be concentrated on finding reward in one relationship, or a sense of achievement can come from learning how to be a good cook or from taking the children fishing, and so on. One strand of activity suggests, enables and interacts with another. As ever with goal-setting, very detailed and factual planning of steps is likely to be required, rather than general declarations of intent which provide no real guidelines for action.

It may be useful also at this stage to look closely at possible anxiety about social situations. 'I suppose I just feel uneasy with people. I don't know how to chat to the other girls in the office, and if they all go out to lunch, I make some excuse and am the one left behind to answer the telephone. Couldn't possibly ask anyone round to the flat in the evening.' A formal approach to treatment of social anxiety may sometimes be indicated or social skills training (see p. 240), or much may come right through encouragement and shared planning of simple tactics.

On other occasions, the rewardingness of sobriety takes a turn for the better after a major life change which may be more or less accidental or very purposely brought about, such as a shift to a new locality, a new job, the break-up of a marriage, or a new relationship. These are precisely the kind of solutions which tend traditionally to be looked on with suspicion as 'geographical escape', with the problems in no way resolved but taken along to be acted out again in the new personal setting. Such strategies are, admittedly, in some instances no more than unprofitable escapism, but it is wrong automatically to take a negative view of what is likely to be achieved by these large shifts. At times the patient is precisely right in taking the bold and simple view that 'what is wrong is living in this street', and the move to the new house, with the decorating, furniture buying and pride in ownership, the shared family involvement, the escape from the old social environment and all the drinking friends who used to knock on the door, indeed marks the start of a new epoch.

Successfully to deal with the problems of rewardingness, the therapist thus needs a range of skills. He needs first a general awareness of the problems, and hence the ability in turn to help the patient towards the necessary awareness. A sense is also needed of the very different ways in which different people respond to these challenges. However, there are common patterns to be identified. Balance and timing are needed; it may be inappropriate in one instance to intervene too soon rather than let patient and family find their own way, while in another instance it may be vital to attempt constructive intervention before sobriety is abandoned.

WHAT TO MAKE OF RELAPSE

Relapse is a common event. This statement will be interpreted pessimistically if one has misread the treatment of drinking problems as being only about rapid and maintained 'success'. More often real success involves trial and error on the way. Dealing with and learning from relapse is, in fact, very commonly part of the process of recovery. But such a view is not to be read as favouring a *laissez-faire* attitude. Relapse has to be taken seriously by patient and therapist alike, but in another sense it has also to be demystified. It is a piece of behaviour to be objectively understood rather than a fall from grace. The relationship needs therefore to be trusting enough for relapse to be talked about rather than hidden and denied, and trust should be such that patient and family can turn for help if relapse occurs rather than their avoiding all contact because of shame and feelings of failure.

Relapse can take many different forms. It may be precipitate and explosive, or it may be a matter of a slow slide; the pace of relapse is often directly related to the degree of dependence. The patient may then stay relapsed for months or years, and the AA member of 20 years' standing may seem tragically to have lost all his gains. On the other hand, relapse may be short-lived, with the patient pulling back after a day or two. Beyond the surface description of these different patterns, there is then the question of the cause and meaning of the occurrence, and it is these inner significances which, in the individual case, have to be examined if there is to be profit from the experience and recovery is to move forward.

A list of headings is convenient for discussion, but in reality matters are, of course, seldom so unitary. To separate the impact of adverse events from diturbance of mood and insufficiency in coping mechanisms is, for example, artificial. The influence of the adverse event is mediated through emotional upset and is overthrowing only because the patient has not yet sufficient coping skills. Depression or anxiety may, on the other hand, arise from within the person without major evident external cause. In analyzing the individual story of relapse, the therapist should, therefore, think in terms of the multiple *processes* which may have led to the drinking, and the sequence and interaction of those processes. Some of the commoner circumstances of relapse are set out below, but the fact that in reality the determinants are likely to be multiple should be very much borne in mind.

An initial and ambivalent sobriety overthrown

Here one is dealing with the patient who relapses in the early days of treatment because he has not as yet satisfactorily sorted out the balance of his motivations. He is as yet in two minds as to whether or not he wants to stop drinking, and the relapse indicates that there is still important initial work to be done in sorting out these ambivalences.

Insufficiency in coping mechanisms

Here the same surface picture has a different inner meaning and different therapeutic implications. This type of patient has, to a greater extent, overcome his ambivalence, but he is unskilled in defending his sobriety. He knows what he wants to do, but is caught out and fails in his intentions. Effort has to be directed at better learning of coping mechanisms.

Failure to find sobriety rewarding

Sobriety has not been consolidated and no satisfactory substitutes have been found for drinking. This is the type of relapse which occurs after perhaps 6 to 12 months of uneasy sobriety. The need is obviously to work on the rewardingness of sobriety.

Disturbance of mood

Relapse is, in such instances, an indication that the patient has been unable to cope with an upset in mood. The patient may have experienced a transient patch of gloom, anxiety, or irritability, which has overwhelmed his defences, or he may be prone to definite cyclical mood-swings. Depressive illness is a not uncommon cause of relapse, and the possibility of hypomanic illness may also have to be considered.

Overcome by events

In such instances, an event or series of events proves too much for the individual's defences. Rather than drinking being a response to catas-trophic happenings, the more usual story is of an event which, to the outsider, might seem fairly trivial, or a cluster of seemingly minor troubles. For instance, the patient has had a row with her husband and, that same morning, the water tank in the roof has leaked, and the desire to bring back a bottle of gin from the supermarket is irresistible. To dismiss such a story as 'just a bundle of excuses' is unhelpful. Its analysis tells us that for this woman, fairly ordinary marital discord gives rise to feelings of insecurity which are hard to bear, and that when subjected then to a little extra stress, she will be without any means of coping other than resort to drink.

Failure in vigilance

Sometimes it seems that the patient has been careless. He was half aware that it would be dangerous to go to that party, but such considerations were less important than the prospect of fun. He knew that it would be risky to start drinking in such a setting, but by the time the party was in full swing, he 'thought he could get away with it'. This lack of vigilance is often related to a fading of memory; the pains previously experienced with drinking are now rather distant, while the pleasure of that glass of wine is immediate.

The study of a particular incident will thus often reveal the need and possibilities for further work with the patient. But it also frequently points to the need for further examinations of family interactions, rather than either the cause or prevention of relapse being issues to be analyzed only in terms of the individual.

Whether relapse is insidious or abrupt, it is therefore a happening to be *used* in treatment. The usefulness of the experience is, though, lost if the incident is met inappropriately, for instance, if it is passed by as trivial and unimportant, interpreted as reason for pessimism and surrender of therapeutic effort, or taken as occasion for abandonment of the patient's and family's responsibility, with an unnecessary retreat to hospital. Relapse is best met with no retreat from expectations of the patient's self-responsibility. That responsibility now includes getting out of the relapse, working out its meaning, and setting things up so that further relapse is less likely.

Many relapses are short-lived, with the patient regaining sobriety before harm is done. It is indeed potentially misleading to use the same word to describe the happenings when a patient takes a few drinks one evening and then stops drinking again completely, as opposed to his sliding into a rapid reinstatement of dependence and being once more in the grip of very threatening drinking. The casual slip may, of course, lead on to the major relapse, but this is not the inevitable march of events. And what the therapist too hastily stigmatizes as 'relapse' may be the patient's tentative move toward re-establishment of normal drinking.

But as well as therapy seeking to enable patient and family to learn from the incident, there may be immediate work in seeking to minimize the harm done by any such occurrence. Prevention of harm implies consideration of a number of different strategies. The patient should, for instance, already have talked through ahead of time the *possibility* of relapse and rehearsed the emergency strategies which should then be brought into play, rather than discussion of relapse with the sober patient being seen as a taboo surrounded by fears of self-fulfilling prophecy. The patient should have learnt that one drink can be dangerous, rather than his having been fed the idea that one drink spells inevitable disaster. Such a myth may harmfully perpetuate a self-fulfilling prophecy of a different kind, with the patient believing that after the one drink all is lost so that he may as well go on drinking. It is much better that he and his family should have rehearsed how such a potential situation will be coped with – the wisdom perhaps of taking a couple of days off work and staying indoors, an Alcoholics Anonymous phone number in the diary, and the need to contact the therapist before things get out of hand. The family should be trained and encouraged to act as an early warning system, and the helping agency must then have the capacity for a quick response rather than offering an appointment in a few weeks time. A home visit may be particularly indicated. It is desirable that drinking should be prevented before dependence is reinstated and treatment of withdrawal symptoms poses an added problem.

At one level the damage that has to be averted is to do with immediate realities. The patient has, for instance, to avoid losing his job and get back to work as soon as possible. The lone mother who is already living in very difficult circumstances may have to act quickly if she is to avoid having her children taken into care. Where there are particular dangers to physical health, such as may be present if the patient is suffering from pancreatitis or liver disease, then the sooner drinking is stopped the better. Relapse may sometimes pose dangers of suicide if the patient believes that 'the last chance has gone', for example, the doctor-patient who is already under threat of disciplinary action and who has had a last warning from his partners.

At another level, there are feelings and potential damage to relationships to be met. If prior to this episode the spouse has been working rewardingly with the patient on the drinking problem, relapse can readily be taken as occasion for further mutual work. But if the spouse has been left on the sidelines and has unreal expectations of immediate treatment success, she may then respond calamitously to a relapse. Anger can be appropriate and useful, but it will be destructive if the spouse's reaction is no more than punitive, or if she pulls out absolutely at a time when further shared effort would be likely to give results. Reference has already been made to the need to prevent a too pessimistic and despairing interpretation of a relapse, and this applies to the spouse's understanding as well as to the patient's. The spouse's readiness constructively to work through the meaning of relapse is likely, of course, to be contingent on the patient's own willingness to do more than shrug off the experience.

BASIC WORK WITH THE FAMILY

Throughout this chapter, an emphasis has been placed on the family perspective, and basic work on recovery must mean work with the family as well as what is being attempted with the patient. The importance of the family dimension in the initial assessment and goal-setting, and the value

of the initial interview with the spouse (p. 203) have already been
discussed. With that sort of groundwork accomplished, it is vital that the
family should not then be forgotten as therapy gets under way and the
months go by.

WORK WITH THE SPOUSE

The emphasis must be on how the wife is to mobilize her own resources,
on how she is to gain a framework of understanding rather than be
overwhelmed by the happenings around her. She needs to find some
optimism and encouragement, to see more clearly her own role in the
situation and be more aware of her own needs. In the initial counselling, it is valuable to discuss the significance of the way she copes
with the situation, which has already been identified in the assessment.
Behaviour patterns may have become stuck in a rut, and be producing no
benefit, and sometimes just trying a change can help. Constructive help-
seeking and constructive management seem on the whole to be more
effective than continued attack or manipulation, but it is impossible to lay
down any absolute rules as to how best a wife should cope in varied
situations. Much will depend on what that particular wife believes to be
within her resources. Coping behaviour can be usefully discussed and
alternatives weighed, but it cannot be prescribed mechanically. It may,
though, generally be beneficial if she can reach a decision as to what she
definitely will not do, and what are her limits. For instance, she may
decide as an act of definite policy that she will abandon arguing and
nagging, or that she will not give him money nor go out and buy him
drink. It is the open identification of a set of intentions, the sense of
something to do, the drawing up of a personal programme, which is often
helpful in such a situation.

Exactly as with the patient, what is favoured here is a rather conserva-
tive approach and certainly one less immediately energetic than has often
been favoured. The assessment with the wife and the initial counselling
can be completed in a few sessions. It is often helpful also to hold one joint
session to try to ensure that mutual goals are understood and that there is
some shared commitment to constructive change. This single session can
be used to give the sense of a new start, with an emphasis on the positive,
on identifying what is good in the marriage, what each in very practical
terms wants from the other and what each will give to the other partner.

The basic approach which is being proposed is therefore again low-key, but this should not be taken as a dogmatic rule and judgement is necessary to identify a range of circumstances where more must be done. For instance, if the wife is in acute danger, there must be an immediate response, and a crisis may have to be dealt with by providing shelter for the wife and children forthwith. Even faced with such a seeming crisis the experienced therapist should, though, be able to involve the wife in consideration of the choices rather than be caught in a panic response which may not be constructive.

Indications of the need for more active help should be detected if the idea of a 'watching brief' is operating properly. The danger of being drawn into too great activism must, though, be guarded against, and there is no evidence that a routine social-work intervention with such wives is of benefit. It is far better to develop the discrimination which allows deployment of resources where they are really needed.

HELP FOR THE CHILDREN

The best help for the child is restoration of the happiness of the home. The fact of a previously alcohol-dependent parent ceasing to drink, of rowing and violence no longer being the continuing experience, can be dramatically beneficial to the child's happiness and well-being. The extent to which a child can grasp and utilize the possibility of happiness depends on the degree of previous hurt, and on whether there have been continuing elements of warm feeling and good contact despite all the distress. Sometimes the changes are evident within a week. The teacher notices that the child is concentrating at school, the mother knows that a child has stopped bed-wetting or will say, 'It's lovely, they're talking to their dad again.' More often the changes are going to be seen over a longer period, and sometimes the restoration of confidence will take many months, with the alcoholic parent hurt and discouraged because his children have not sooner come towards him. The family atmosphere may be improved not only by the parent ameliorating his drinking, but by help and support for the spouse, which in turn allows greater affection and attention to be made available to her children.

Given that help for the alcoholic parent (and the spouse), may often be of enormous indirect benefit to the children, other ways of aiding the children have also to be considered, especially where there is no immediate treatment response by the drinking parent. There may be instances where urgent thought has to be given to removal of the child from the home as an immediate measure of physical protection, or where high priority has to be given to social work supervision of an intensity which can monitor the child's safety. The procedures of the 'at risk' register have then to be invoked. The decisions that have to be made call, as ever, for balanced judgement. Taking a child out of the home unnecessarily is to no one's benefit, while a careless decision in the other direction can be disastrous. What must, however, be borne in mind is the unpredictableness of a parent's drunken behaviour – the dangers of a sudden rage against a child (where the child has become a target of hostility) causing an accidental but appalling degree of damage. Such a problem is often best dealt with by a case conference which can quickly bring together everyone with know-ledge of the family. At a certain stage the decision may be made that temporary removal of the child from the home is desirable simply to allow escape from the continuing stresses, even if actual violence is not threatened. This is, though, likely to be a decision which is worked towards with the family, rather than one to be made hastily. As far as possible the alcoholic parent as well as the spouse should be involved in the discussion, so that the move is not seen as punitive.

As regards individual help for the child remaining in the disturbed home, much the same range of approaches is applicable as with a child facing any other disturbing home influence. The offer of a good and confident relationship is itself valuable, but with a child who is of an age to verbalize problems it is helpful to discuss very directly the parent's drink-ing – to listen to and offer understanding of the child's distress, to find some more satisfactory way of looking at the parents and of coping with the anger and hurt, to offer straightforward information, to discuss the child's role within the family, what the child 'can do to help' and the limits of those possibilities, and to aid towards good friendships outside the home. Children too have their coping mechanisms, which may be adap-tive or maladaptive. Individual help for the child is best given at the reality level as well as at the level of discussion, for example, a contact with a teacher who may be able to offer special help, or the introduction to a club.

There may sometimes be an indication that older children should be involved in family therapy in a formal sense, but the skills necessary to handle constructively the interactions of children and parents in such a forum should not be underestimated. More often what is useful is the home visit or series of home visits where children can experience a family discussion in a natural setting, and where family members drop in and out as they feel like it. The role of Alateen (a self-help group deriving from AA and Alanon) is discussed in Chapter 15.

SUMMARIZING THE BASIC WORK WITH THE FAMILY

The usual elements within the basic programme of work with the family can be summarized as follows:

(i) Monitoring

Continued contact with the spouse will give her the important feeling that there is someone interested in hearing what she has to say, and what she reports will indeed be useful to the evolution of the treatment programme. In many instances, a relatively brief visit to the home to enable this sort of flow of information to be kept going may be all that is required. Risk to the children may also have to be very carefully monitored.

(ii) Dealing with family problems in their own right

In other instances immediate help may be needed to deal with, for example, the wife's depressive illnesses, a child's school failure or maladjustment, or the urgent necessity for protection from violence. The most effective relief of family problems may well come in the long-term from the patient's recovery, but there may be acute problems which cannot wait for this hoped-for outcome. On occasions, there may be such real problems as unpaid fuel bills or rent arrears with which help can be given if the wife herself is not skilled or confident in dealing with official agencies, but in general it is anti-therapeutic to be lured into 'taking over'.

(iii) Aiding conjoint work toward recovery

Given that family relationships will often begin to improve at their own pace once the drinking problem has been dealt with, it is also true that there will be other families where, after the patient has stopped drinking, entrenched problems remain, painful in their own right and likely to hinder the consolidation of recovery. The patient may have stopped drinking, but he is not let back into the family circle, and, in consequence, neither he nor anyone else is finding his sobriety rewarding. He is still disgraced and a scarcely tolerated lodger. There may, at this stage, be a place for a series of conjoint interviews to try to open up possibilities of movement. A decision may in fact have to be made to go beyond what can be termed basic work, and specialized marital therapy undertaken.

(iv) Offering access

As important as any of the considerations listed above should be the basic message given to the family that their needs and views matter, that communication is going to be kept open, and that they have ready access to help rather than being held at arm's length.

As regards the staffing logistics, the same person may, on occasion, usefully be seeing both patient and spouse, and with work which is not intensively psychotherapeutic this should be feasible. But where possible, there is often benefit in patient and spouse each feeling that they have their own person with whom to talk. Exchange of information between staff is then vital.

THE USE OF THERAPEUTIC GROUPS

The place of group therapy as a special technique to be deployed at the stage when the patient is consolidating his recovery is discussed in Chapter 16, and the use of groups in the in-patient setting is considered in Chapter 18. Alcoholics Anonymous and Alanon also provide group experience (Chapter 15). But groups can also have their place in the basic work of treatment, and many therapists would see involvement in groups at an early stage of the treatment process as being useful for information giving, shared solution of problems, and support. There is no evidence that more intensive group work at these earlier stages brings special benefit.

SPACING OF APPOINTMENTS

There is no one rule for the spacing of appointments, and some patients will need to be seen more frequently than others. In general, the emphasis on autonomy and self-determination is best supported by giving more space rather than more frequent appointments, with escalation into an intensive intervention thus resisted. It is often appropriate after the initial goal-setting to offer little more than a kind of monitoring contact. A very general policy might be to expect to see most patients about once a month, with wider spacing as recovery progresses. Many therapists would probably feel uneasy with such relatively infrequent contact, especially at the early stage of treatment, but there is little evidence that greater progress is in general likely to be attained with more frequent sessions. It may be useful to ask the patient himself when he next wants to be seen, without accidentally implying that the therapist 'doesn't care'. Much must depend on the thoroughness and purposiveness of the initial assessment and exercise in goal-setting. It is better to put investment in that direction, with similarly purposeful but spaced follow-up, than to start from an incomplete assessment with a follow-through which lacks direction despite frequency of contact. But if more specialized treatment such as a behaviour therapy programme is underway, then the frequency of contact will, of course, be increased.

As for how long a session should last, this again must be individually determined. On many occasions, a 20-minute interview may give sufficient time for a focused monitoring of progress, while in other instances, it may be necessary to find 45 to 60 minutes for detailed discussion.

The treatment organization should also have the capacity to respond to emergency and be able to see the patient who experiences a crisis between his fixed appointments. The real needs for help of this patient have, though, to be assessed. It may, for instance, be unhelpful to agree to see a patient on a sort of free-demand basis if it is judged that his demands are witness to his over-dependence on other people; it would be better to encourage him to meet his own crises and keep to the schedule of appointments.

When a patient fails to keep an appointment there should be an administrative mechanism which ensures that he is not then lost from sight. A personal letter offering a further appointment should be written or a phone call made, and if contact is not then re-established a home visit should perhaps be made. When all else fails the patient should still be left with the indication that the door remains readily open.

DURATION AND TERMINATION OF TREATMENT

The duration of treatment may be proposed by the therapist but it is effectively determined by the patient. There are patients who appear to have benefited greatly from one or two sessions and who decide this is all they need, while at the other extreme there are patients who indicate that they want to maintain at least intermittent contact over years.

> A man aged 63 had first been seen for help many years previously when he was in severe difficulties with his alcohol dependence. He was at that time admitted briefly for detoxification, and was then in contact with a community-based counselling centre for two years. After that initial period he continued over many years to drop in for an occasional chat, and 12 years after initial contact he came along to discuss his son's drinking. A few years later he made contact again because his wife had died and he was finding it difficult to face life alone: he did not think there was any danger of his drinking, but he wanted to 'find someone who would listen'. Some acute feelings of guilt and remorse relating to his drinking days had been stirred up.

The use that this particular patient made of the counselling centre suggests that the image which he and the staff shared was of that place as a resource which could be called on over the years and as needed. It is difficult to see how the concept of 'termination of treatment' applies to such a story, or to many other instances where a patient forms this sort of useful long-term affiliation. In many cases it is therefore good policy never formally to 'discharge' a patient but rather to stress the continued availability of help as and when it should be needed, and to couple this with the offer of yearly follow-up appointments. Such an approach is obviously more appropriate for the patient who has had serious and multiple problems than the person whose initial problems were slighter and more quickly resolved.

The question is often therefore better rephrased in terms of *the duration of the more intensive treatment phase*, rather than the *duration of treatment*. A fixed course of so many sessions over so many months cannot meet the needs of an enormously varied patient population. Judgement certainly needs to be made in terms of the patient's progress along a number of dimensions of recovery, the likelihood of further useful work, the timeliness of a move which further emphasizes the patient's ability to handle his own responsibilities, and negotiation on timing between therapist and patient. Rather than there then being a 'this is the end of your treatment' type of announcement, what is said might often be something like this:

'We've been meeting each month for the last eight months, and you've achieved a great deal. If you agree, what I would now suggest is that we meet again just before Christmas – that's five months hence. But if for any reason you wanted to drop in and see me earlier just phone up and let me know. Does this sort of arrangement seem all right?'

The question arises in different form when making this decision not in relation to the patient who has made substantial progress but in a case where after perhaps six months of work the drinking is continuing un-abated. Does one 'terminate treatment' on the grounds that the patient is failing to benefit or show any real commitment to change? This sort of problem is discussed more fully in sections of Chapter 20, but in general rather than such a situation being an indication for termination of treat-ment, it more often suggests the need for reassessment of what is being done. There is certainly no profit in stumbling on aimlessly and without any therapeutic movement, but the response to continued drinking should be constructive and considered, rather than an angry discarding of an unsatisfactory patient.

BASIC WORK: BRINGING THE IDEAS TOGETHER

It would be misleading to present a carefully ordered flow chart or series of ordered steps to describe the basic work of treatment, for this would contradict the message that what is most required is the flexibility to meet the needs of the individual patient as his recovery evolves. But with that caution in mind, it may be useful at this stage to summarize some of the ideas expressed in this and previous chapters so as to provide a working check-list.

1 Assessment with patient and spouse is the initiation of therapy, and a shared experience.

2 The case formulation orders the material obtained in the assessment, and it is again shared with patient and spouse.

3 Goal-setting must be negotiated in similar terms. Goals must be specific and cover non-drinking as well as drinking. There must be an invitation to a tangible commitment to working towards those goals.

4 The therapeutic relationship is enormously important and must be skilfully fostered. The therapist must learn how to show warmth and give

hope, but on no account should he be lured into over-directiveness either with patient or spouse. Self-responsibility is very much to be fostered.

5   Some basic therapeutic principles should be borne in mind: continuity of purpose and sense of movement must be maintained; some leading questions must be identified at each interview, with the patient being allowed to define what is of importance; and the family perspective must be maintained. Therapy requires a continuous background of monitoring, and the patient may usefully engage in self-monitoring. Balances have to be struck both between focus on reality and dynamics (the two areas are much related), and as between drinking and other topics. Commitment may at various points need to be re-examined. An eye has constantly to be kept on the development of the relationship.

6   The actual content of the interview includes work on the drinking problem, and attention to problems in the areas of mental and physical health and social adjustment.

7   Each interview, as well as being concerned with the continuing basics of treatment, is also an occasion for deciding whether it is useful and timely to signpost the patient towards any more specialized type of help.

8   The effort towards recovery by patient and spouse has to be worthwhile. They must be helped to sense out the gains, for a sobriety which is only negative will not be maintained. The *quality* of sobriety is very important.

9   Relapse is not to be considered a taboo subject. If relapse does occur it should be possible to learn from the event. The many different patterns, causes and meanings of relapse must be understood.

10   Basic work with the family may also be very much needed. This includes meeting the immediate needs of spouse and children, as well as work which facilitates conjoint efforts towards the patient's recovery.

11   The pacing and intensity of help must be kept under review and ultimately tailed off, perhaps with the offer of an 'open door' rather than formal closure of the case. What must certainly be guarded against is an automatic escalation into heavy and continued intervention. Once there has been full assessment and careful and agreed goal-setting, much may then often be left to patient and family with occasional monitoring, checks on progress, and encouragement.

12   Basic treatment is an alliance with the natural possibilities for recovery; it is a matter of discovering rather than imposing directions.

REFERENCES

Baekeland F, Lundwall L and Kissin B. (1975) Methods for the treatment of chronic alcoholism: a critical appraisal. In: Gibbins RJ, Israel Y and Kalant H (eds) *Research Advances in Alcohol and Drug Problems*, Vol. 2, pp 247–328. New York: Wiley.

Bissell L (1975) The treatment of alcoholism: what do we do about long-term sedatives? *Annals of the New York Academy of Science*, **252**, 396–399.

Chaney EP, O'Leary MR and Marlatt GA (1979) Skill training with alcoholics. *Journal of Consulting and Clinical Psychology*, **46**, 1092–1104.

Litman GK (1980) Relapse in alcoholism: traditional and current approaches. In: Edwards G and Grant M (eds) *Alcoholism Treatment in Transition*, pp 294–304. London: Croom Helm.

Litman GK, Eiser JR and Taylor C (1979) Dependence, relapse and extinction: a theoretical critique and behavioural examination. *Journal of Clinical Psychology*, **35**, 192–199.

Janzen C (1977) Families in the treatment of alcoholism. *Journal of Studies on Alcohol*, **38**, 114–140.

Kissin B and Begleiter H (eds) (1977) The Biology of Alcoholism, Vol. 5: *Treatment and Rehabilitation of the Chronic Alcoholic* New York: Plenum.

Levy MF, Reichman W and Herrington S (1981) Abstinent alcoholics' adjustment to work. *Journal of Studies on Alcohol*, **42**, 529–532.

National Council on Alcoholism, UK (1981) *Counsellor's Guide on Problem Drinking*. London: National Council on Alcoholism.

Orford J and Edwards G (1977) Alcoholism: a comparison of treatment and advice. *Maudsley Monograph No. 26*. London: Oxford University Press.

Schukit MA (1979) Treatment of alcoholism in office and out-patient settings. In: Mendelson JH and Mello NK (eds) *The Diagnosis and treatment of Alcoholism*, pp 230–255. New York: McGraw Hill.

Smolensky WR, Martin DW and Lorimor RJ *et al* (1980) Leisure behaviour and attitude toward leisure of alcoholics and non-alcoholics. *Journal of Studies on Alcohol*, **41**, 293–299.

Chapter 15
Alcoholics Anonymous

Alcoholics Anonymous was founded in the USA in 1935, and first began to establish itself in the UK in the late 1940s. There are now about 1,500 groups in the UK and over recent years there have been as many women as men among new members. The estimated world membership today is upwards of one million. It has helped countless individuals (often when professional intervention has failed), is a repository of astonishing experience and subtle and often humorous wisdom, and has had a profound influence in humanizing social attitudes towards people with drinking problems. AA is thus an enormous potential resource, and it is a dereliction of duty if patients go through treatment without AA ever being mentioned, or worse still if they are deflected from AA involvement by some negative statement born of ignorance and misunderstanding – 'I think you would find it all too religiose.'

The therapist must be willing to find out how AA operates and what its beliefs are, and the best way of doing this is to pay a personal visit to an open meeting of AA – a meeting open to all-comers, as opposed to closed meetings which are restricted to AA membership.

AA MEETINGS

The AA meeting is of central importance to AA's functioning. It has a unique atmosphere, marked by a seeming informality but with an underlying and purposeful method of working. The number of people at a meeting will vary from group to group, but is typically around 10 to 20. Some of those present will have been attending AA for years, while the man or woman sitting in the back row may have just walked hesitantly through the door for the first time. A chairman will have been elected for that evening and he will probably be sitting at a table with one or two members who have been asked 'to give their stories'. The newcomer will notice a lot of friendly greeting and talking.

The meeting will start with the chairman saying 'My name is Tom' (only first names are used), 'I am an alcoholic'. These words carry immense implications: the speaker is not ashamed of his alcoholism, but without reservation acknowledges his condition as an inalienable fact. They also emphasize informality and the breaking down of social barriers. The starting point of the evening is thus one individual's reaffirmation, for all present, of what in AA terms must be the starting point of recovery for every individual – the admission that he or she is suffering from alcoholism.

The chairman will then read what is known as the AA preamble.

> 'Alcoholics Anonymous is a fellowship of men and women who share their experience, strength, and hope with each other that they may solve their common problem and help others to recover from alcoholism. The only requirement for membership is a desire to stop drinking. There are no dues or fees for AA membership; we are self-supporting through our own contributions. AA is not allied with any sect, denomination, politics, organization or institution; does not wish to engage in any controversy, neither endorses nor opposes any causes. Our primary purpose is to stay sober and help other alcoholics to achieve sobriety'.

With these preliminaries out of the way, the first speaker of the evening will then be called. His introduction will again be in terms of 'My name's Dick, and I'm an alcoholic'. He will speak for 20 to 30 minutes, giving an account of his personal background and then going on to describe the development of his drinking problem, the sufferings he endured or inflicted on others, the deceptions and prevarications of his drinking days, and then often some final turning-point or 'rock bottom' experience. He will go on to describe his introduction to AA and his recovery within the programme of that fellowship, and his evolving understanding of the meaning of AA as a way of life. Within this biographical format different speakers each develop their own approach, and the ability of the person who has never given a public speech in any other setting to make a personal statement which is both moving and convincing is no doubt related to the unwritten guidelines which propose that a personal *story* should be given, rather than any sort of abstract lecture. The story which is told in unadorned manner by the person with fairly recent experience of recovery seems indeed often to be better received than the highly polished performance by the person who has told his story many times, but who is by now rather distanced from the acuteness of his experience. And stories which deal with recovery, and which offer practical hints on how to work at recovery, are likely to be better received than long-drawn-out accounts of drinking days.

These life stories are followed by comments and personal statements from the floor. Themes are caught up and explored by the listeners, who often stress their identification with the speaker's story – 'That happened to me too ....' No one is forced to speak and it is realized that for weeks the new member may want to do no more than sit and listen.

Reference is often made during the meeting to 'The Twelve Steps', which enshrine the basic ideology of AA. These steps are as follows:

1   We admitted we were powerless over alcohol—that our lives had become unmanageable.

2   Came to believe that a Power greater than ourselves could restore us to sanity.

3   Made a decision to turn our will and our lives over to the care of God *as we understood Him.*

4   Made a searching and fearless moral inventory of ourselves.

5   Admitted to God, to ourselves, and to another human being the exact nature of our wrongs.

6   Were entirely ready to have God remove all these defects of character.

7   Humbly asked Him to remove our shortcomings.

8   Made a list of all persons we had harmed, and became willing to make amends to them all.

9   Made direct amends to such people wherever possible, except when to do so would injure them or others.

10   Continued to take personal inventory, and when we were wrong, promptly admitted it.

11   Sought through prayer and meditation to improve our conscious contact with God *as we understood Him* praying only for knowledge of His will for us and the power to carry that out.

12   Having had a spiritual awakening as the result of these steps we tried to carry this message to alcoholics and to practice these principles in all our affairs.

A speaker may comment on the meaning which any one of these steps has had for him personally and describe his efforts to achieve this step. For instance, the meaning to be given to step 2 with its idea of 'a Power greater than ourselves' often attracts discussion, with an interpretation in terms of a very open and individually determined concept of God – the 'God *as we understood Him*', of steps 3 and 11. This seemingly theistic formulation does not in practice debar an atheist from finding help in AA.

The formal proceedings end with the meeting saying together what has become known as the Serenity Prayer:

> 'God grant me the serenity
> To accept the things I cannot change
> The courage to change the things I can
> And the wisdom to know the difference'

The members then chat and exchange news over tea or coffee, and subtle but positive effort is likely to be made to put the new attender at his ease and draw him into contact. Frequently the new member will find a 'sponsor' who in the early stages will offer personal advice and a special degree of availability – a phone number to contact, an arrangement to meet in the evening to attend an AA meeting, and so on. The sponsor is also a role-model.

Besides the meetings themselves, much else is potentially on offer. Members may start to visit each other at home, go out to meals together or share other social activities. Old drinking friends are dropped, and new friends found who think and talk AA. In some localities routine meetings will be supplemented by study groups, and AA literature shared and passed around. Regional and national AA conventions may be attended, and the more experienced member may give much time to 'twelfth-stepping' (acting as sponsor and working with new members); he may help with prison or hospital groups, or make himself available as a speaker at meetings of community organizations.

ESSENTIAL PROCESSES

What are the essential processes through which AA operates? There have been many attempts to answer this question, and in summary the following dimensions can probably be identified:

Coherent, flexible ideas

A coherent but flexible set of ideas is offered (an *ideology*), which can relieve the individual's sense of hopelessness and explain the nature of his problem. He is suffering from 'the disease of alcoholism', which is pictured as metaphorically akin to an 'allergy to alcohol'. His constitution is such that he will react to this drug differently from other people. He can never be 'cured' but the disease will be 'arrested' if he does not drink again. Lifetime abstinence must be his only goal. It is the first drink that he cannot risk.

Action programme

AA offers an action programme, and 'The Twelve Steps' outline the actions which have to be taken. He must join AA and stay close to AA. He will be advised to take things 'one day at a time' and to work for short-term goals. The stories and discussions he listens to at AA meetings and the guidance from his sponsor will provide him with many hints on coping and problem solving. His first priority is to deal with his drinking, but the programme will also require him to examine psychological problems – his guilt, his 'resentments', his tendency to blame others, his 'stinking thinking'. AA is 'a selfish programme' and each individual is working for sobriety for his own sake and not to please anyone else, and he thus gives no hostages to fortune. If he relapses he is not rejected but may return any number of times to try again. The programme will finally include 'twelfth stepping', but by then a member should have learnt that by helping other people he will be helping himself and confirming his own strength; it is not, however, his job to proselytize, 'pull people down lampposts', or put his own sobriety at risk.

Rewards of sobriety

AA carries the message that sobriety is rewarding, and helps the individual to discover these rewards. AA gives him new friends, introduces him to a new social network, relieves his loneliness, helps him to structure and employ his time, removes a stigma and confers on him a sense of personal worth. If he has been sober for one day, he has been a success. Through AA he may ultimately achieve serenity, with sobriety a way of life.

Possibility of recovery

AA's ideology is persuasive and an approach to recovery is made to appear possible. This last heading bears on each of the previous headings. AA does not 'work' through an abstract set of ideas, but through those ideas being found persuasive by the individuals. The most apt theoretical definition of the disorder and the pathways to recovery would remain useless if AA did not have the ability to persuade the new member that AA is about him, can meet his problems, and show him personally the way ahead. AA can carry this conviction because its members so evidently know what they are talking about; they too have been through it all and know every stratagem of deceit and denial, while at the same time bearing tangible witness to the possibility of success.

WHO WILL AFFILIATE WITH AA?

Like other approaches to treatment, AA is not a panacea. Its membership is almost exclusively composed of people who have suffered from moderate or severe alcohol dependence, and group cohesion is therefore built around total acceptance of the abstinence goal. The person who is not dependent and who does not wish to aim for abstinence is unlikely to find AA compatible.

The alcoholic who goes to a meeting where everyone is of another social background is also unlikely to feel at home, although this problem can be met by the individual shopping around until he finds a group of people with whom he can identify. Different AA meetings vary in composition; some operate with a wide mix of social backgrounds, while others seem tacitly to have recruited their membership with a bias toward a particular socio-economic stratum. Also, some groups will emphasize the spiritual aspect of AA ideology much more than others. It may therefore take some time and perseverance for the new member to find the group which most suits his needs. Some groups may have a particular reputation for being helpful to the newcomer, and he may be guided in their direction.

It is always difficult to predict who will and who will not find AA helpful and patients should simply be advised to go along to meetings and see for themselves whether AA offers an answer.

THE THERAPIST AND CO-OPERATION WITH AA

As was stated earlier, the therapist should always be able, whenever appropriate, to signpost the way to AA. This not only means being able to provide the appropriate phone number (which is available in the local telephone directory), and perhaps being able to effect a direct introduction to an AA sponsor with whom the patient is likely to identify, but also means having the knowledge and sympathy which will enable him to convey to the patient that attending some AA meetings is likely to be eminently worthwhile. The therapist will know that only a minority of his patients (perhaps no more than 5 to 10 per cent) will enter into a full and prolonged relationship with AA, but even a lesser exposure may be beneficial. The therapist who, on occasion, finds time himself to attend AA open meetings will enhance his credibility as informant and build up valuable contacts with local groups.

Co-operation is, of course, a two-way business, and AA needs to understand the workings of the local services and to be able to make a direct referral for professional advice if assistance is thought necessary. Many centres have established a fruitful two-way relationship of this sort, and at the national level AA has set up mechanisms for liaison with hospitals and prisons. A centre which is offering a normal drinking goal for some of its patients will, however need to talk through this aspect of its work particularly carefully with AA, if misunderstanding is to be avoided. Another difficulty can stem from the anti-drug attitude of some AA members, which may result in advice to a new member that he should stop taking anti-depressant drugs, or his disulfiram, against the patient's best interests. At the extreme, some AA members may be so convinced that AA offers the only true pathway to recovery as to make any co-operation with other agencies very difficult. But such difficulties are rare, and with open communication and mutual respect, problems can usually be sorted out.

The relationship of AA to the in-patient unit is discussed in Chapter 18.

LEARNING FROM AA

Claims for the success and universality of AA can easily be exaggerated, and its emphasis on the disease concept may be out of tune with the model employed by some therapists. But there can be no doubt that as well as the direct benefit which AA offers to many individual drinkers, it also has much to teach the therapist about the processes which aid and influence recovery. There is wisdom to be borrowed from AA.

AL-ANON

Al-Anon is an organization which is independent of, but allied with, AA. It is a self-help group which caters for the families of alcoholics – for 'anyone who loves an alcoholic'. It has its own 'Twelve Steps' which mirror AA thinking. Quite often, an AA meeting will be going on in one room and an Al-Anon meeting in the next room, with everyone getting together afterwards over the tea and biscuits.

The functioning of Al-Anon will not be discussed here in detail, because its principles and methods of working have much in common with AA. That Al-Anon can fulfil an extremely important function does, however, need to be emphasized, and the therapist should again be able knowledgeably to point the way. Al-Anon often seems able to give immediate relief to the wife who has been struggling by every stratagem to stop her husband from drinking, and who has in the process been experiencing stress and frustration. Al-Anon will teach her to 'let go' and to give up the hope of trying to control her husband's behaviour or solve his problem for him. He must find his own answers to *his* own problem, and, similarly, she must examine *her* own behaviour: the only behaviour which she is directly able to control or alter is, indeed, her own.

AL-ATEEN

Al-Ateen is a self-help group operating along AA lines which aims to help the teenage children of families where there is an alcoholic parent. To date, this organization has become more widely established in North America than in the UK or other parts of Europe. That children living in such families are often experiencing much distress and conflict cannot be doubted (p. 52), and Al-Ateen potentially meets the needs of a group which the professional services involved with the parents may all too easily pass by.

REFERENCES

Ablon J (1974) Al-Anon family groups: impetus for learning and change through the presentation of alternatives. *American Journal of Psychotherapy,* **28,** 30–45.
Alcoholics Anonymous (1977) *Twelve Steps and Twelve Traditions.* New York: Alcoholics Anonymous World Services.

Alcoholics anonymous (1978) *Alcoholics Anonymous*, 4th Edn. New York: Alcoholics Anonymous World Services.

Bebbington PE (1976) The efficacy of Alcoholics Anonymous: the elusiveness of hard data. *British Journal of Psychiatry*, **128,** 572–580.

Robinson D (1979) *Talking out of Alcoholism: the Self-Help Process*. London: Croom Helm.

Trice HM and Roman PM (1970) Sociopsychological predictors of affiliation with Alcoholics Anonymous. *Social Psychiatry*, **5,** 51–59.

Tournier RE (1979) Alcoholics Anonymous as treatment and as ideology. *Journal of Studies on Alcohol*, **40,** 230–239.

Chapter 16
Special Techniques

In this chapter three approaches to the treatment of alcoholism are discussed: behaviour therapies, the use of deterrent drugs (disulfiram and calcium carbimide), and psychotherapy. The aim is to outline these techniques and discuss their value and limitations; no attempt will be made to go into details about their application. Anyone wanting to acquire the necessary specialised clinical skills will in any case do best to train under the guidance of someone already familiar with such methods, rather than try to learn the methods from a book.

What are described here as 'special techniques' may be considered routine by some practitioners, while others would certainly place a different emphasis on the approaches from that given. But the adjective 'special' is still useful to differentiate these methods from the basic approaches discussed in Chapter 14, and most experienced therapists would agree that whatever special approach is favoured, it is only valuable within the context of the general therapeutic work discussed earlier.

BEHAVIOUR THERAPIES

THE MEANING OF THE TERM

The term 'behaviour therapy' implies a model based on the assumption that it is the behaviour itself which is to be treated, as opposed to the psychoanalytic view that the behaviour is symptom or symbol of an underlying psychodynamic conflict or neurosis. Also implicit in this approach is the belief that all behaviours, however diverse, are subject to the same psychological principles of learning (and un-learning). Behaviour therapy takes note of the environmental cues as well as the cues arising from within the individual. To define behaviour therapy in these terms immediately suggests a polarity between it and the psychodynamic view, but the closer one gets to the care and understanding of the individual patient, the less meaningful does any confrontation between supposedly opposite philosophies become. The skilled behaviour therapist will know that in formulating the individual treatment plan he will inevitably have to take into account the *meaning* of drinking behaviour for that individual, as well as the behaviour at surface level.

The tradition which behaviour therapy brings to the treatment of alcoholism does, however, require understanding by those who have trained within other philosophies. There is firstly an emphasis on precise and detailed assessment of the immediate cues and circumstances which relate to drinking – *a behavioural analysis* (p. 257). Such an assessment provides the basis for *individual treatment programming,* and the behavioural philosophy suggests in effect that the treatment of each patient has to be seen as an experiment in its own right. This experimental tradition further emphasizes the need for precise *measurement of outcome,* with each patient's treatment monitored and the information fed back to enable the *flexible development of the treatment plan.*

Behaviour therapy may not in practice always live up to these scientific expectations, and it could also be argued that these expectations in no way fundamentally differ from the positions of other schools. But the considerable involvement of clinical psychology in the treatment of alcoholism over the last decade or so, must be welcomed not only for its techniques but also for the injection of scientific method and critical standards, together with a great deal of enthusiasm. It is still too soon to form a final view on the value of many of the reported methods but in the following paragraphs the more prominent of these techniques will be considered.

BEHAVIOURAL TECHNIQUES

(i) Aversion treatment

This first came to the fore in the 1930s, with a series or reports from the Shadel Sanitarium in the USA. Very favourable results were claimed, and the technique became widely used in other countries. The objective merits of this approach must today be viewed as questionable, but there can be no doubt that aversion therapy was of historical importance in fostering an optimistic interest in alcoholism treatment at a time when little else appeared to be promising. It should, though, be noted that the technique pioneered at the Shadel was employed only as one part of a wider treatment programme.

Aversion therapy was supposedly modelled on classical Pavlovian conditioning. The patient was given an injection of emetine, and then given a drink of alcohol just before the onset of the chemically induced nausea. The intention was that nausea would then be established as a conditioned response to drinking. The patient would often be administered a range of different alcoholic beverages so as to ensure the widest possible generalization of the reflex, and some therapists favoured a setting which was a mock-up of a real-life drinking situation – a bar-room for instance, or having the drinks displayed in an elegant cocktail cabinet. The patient would be given aversion sessions on five or six consecutive days, with subsequent booster sessions over ensuing months or years. Some later workers employed apomorphine as a safer substance than emetine, but apormorphine had the theoretical disadvantage of being in part a sedative.

There is little evidence that chemical aversion of this type does in fact establish a classical conditioned response. The favourable results which have been reported probably rest more on the artefact of patient selection than on any specific effect: a patient would obviously need to be highly motivated to volunteer for such an unpleasant experience in the name of treatment. The treatment might also perhaps be expected to have symbolic or ritual meaning – a flagellation or driving-out of devils – and to enhance the likelihood of 'conversion'.

All in all the dangers and unpleasantness of chemical aversion outweigh any supposed advantages to such an extent that this treatment should now be abandoned. And a variant of chemical aversion, which involves giving the patient an intravenous injection of succinycholine, should most certainly be discarded completely. Succinycholine is a drug which paralyzes muscular movement, and hence respiration. The rationale was to associate the terrifying experience of perhaps sixty seconds of cessation of breathing (apnoea), with the experience of drinking. Despite promising claims, this approach is ineffective. It deserves note only as a warning of what may be done in the name of healing when scientific enthusiasm outruns all else.

There are many recent research reports on the use of a conditioning model which uses electric shock rather than chemical aversion. The aversion which is established is probably to the taste of alcohol. Variants of this model employ classical conditioning or an 'escape' or an 'avoidance' model. From the experimental point of view, electric shock is easier to work with than chemical aversion, especially as regards the precise timing of the relationship between aversive stimulus and drinking, but there is again uncertainty as to effectiveness.

Attempts have also been made to employ 'covert sensitization' in the treatment of alcoholism. The patient is taught to associate the sight or taste of alcohol with unpleasant images, which he learns actively to conjure up. Post-hypnotic suggestion has also been used to instill a revulsion to alcohol.

(ii) Contingency management

By this phrase is meant a behavioural model which makes some sort of reward contingent on abstinence (or modified drinking) or on co-operation in treatment, or alternatively makes some kind of negative consequence contingent on drinking, excessive drinking, or failure to co-operate in treatment. There is no doubt that in the setting of an experimental hospital ward the patient's behaviour may be modified if ward privileges are made contingent on his drinking in a controlled fashion, for instance, if he knows that he will be barred from the television room if he gets drunk. Extension of such situational learning to the outside world is more uncertain, but contingency management has been used with some success to reinforce the taking of disulfiram and in other settings.

(iii) Community reinforcement

This might be seen as a variant of contingency management, with an emphasis on manipulation of real-life reward in the patient's environment. The family's positive reactions, aid with job-finding, membership of a social club and other positive social rewards are presented to the patient as contingent on treatment success, and the therapeutic team accepts responsibility to ensure that such reinforcing rewards are in fact on offer. Community reinforcement appears to be one of the more promising variants of the behavioural approach.

(iv) Self-monitoring of blood alcohol level

The aim here is to teach patients to recognize when they have reached a certain blood alcohol level, and not to exceed that level. Training may focus on recognition of external cues, such as number of drinks taken and speed of drinking, or on internal cues such as experience of flushing or the 'high' feeling. Training sessions may be run individually or for small groups. In a group an element of modelling may also be important: the individual learns to drink in the restrained manner that other people are employing, rather than modelling his behaviour on a heavy-drinking companion. A modification of this training procedure involves giving electric shock if the patient exceeds the stated limit.

Early reports on the efficacy of this approach appeared promising but later results have not always been as positive. Not all patients are adept at judging their own blood alcohol level within the necessary range of accuracy.

(v) Cue exposure

This interesting theoretical approach borrows from a treatment strategy which was developed for obsessional illness. The patient is exposed to cues which have previously precipitated craving or excessive drinking, and encouraged not to drink or not to drink excessively. For instance, he may be asked to carry around with him a bottle of whisky and sniff at it without drinking, or the therapist may accompany him on outings to a pub, or he may be asked to take sufficient alcohol to activate craving and then desist from further drinking. In terms of individual case experiment positive results have certainly been achieved, but this approach is still at an early stage of development.

(vi) Video feed-back

There are a number of different ways in which audio or video-tape feedback has been used in treatment. For instance, the patient may be shown pictures of himself drinking socially or, alternatively, be shown film of himself in an inebriated state. Some positive results have been claimed, but these approaches are probably only of rather limited value, and on occasion may cause harm.

(vii) Cognitive therapies

The application of a cognitive strategy will be discussed in Chapter 17, in relation to basic techniques for working towards a controlled drinking goal. The patient learns to identify risky situations, is taught to develop coping or avoidance strategies, and engages in self-monitoring. He may be provided with a brief self-treatment manual.

(viii) Social skills training, assertiveness training and relaxation

These approaches are not specific to alcoholism, but within the present context find their application as psychological treatments aimed at dealing with postulated psychological causes of excessive drinking. For instance, it is hypothesized (and there is some research evidence to back the hypothesis) that a proportion of patients with drinking problems are handicapped by an underlying inability to function confidently in social situations, and treatment by role-playing, desensitization, or other behavioural methods may ameliorate this problem. Assertiveness training comes under much the same heading: the patient who is unassertive may find it difficult to say 'no' to an offered drink, and one element in therapy may involve teaching him to rehearse saying 'no'. Teaching of relaxation by simple psychological techniques may be useful for a tense patient, and transcendental meditation and bio-feedback have also been recommended as adjuncts to the treatment of alcoholism.

(ix) Attitude change techniques

The techniques discussed under previous subheadings largely derive from learning theories and behavioural psychology. It is perhaps surprising that in comparison little work has been done on the application to alcoholism treatment of ideas from the social psychology of attitude change. There is not as yet a sufficient body of experiment in this area to allow confident appraisal, but one or two approaches can be mentioned as potentially promising. For instance, the patient may be asked directly to role-play persuading another patient not to drink, and be invited to confront the other person's acted denial and evasion. In the process his own attitudes may be expected to change. Similarly, he may be asked to prepare a taped message to explain the nature of alcohol dependence, the negative consequences of continued drinking and the benefits which will stem from abstinence.

(x) Multi-modal behavioural packages

The difficulties in reaching a firm conclusion as to what works best in this rapidly expanding field of treatment research are typified by the diverse appraisals of the value of a multi-modal approach. Some experts believe that trying several approaches at once or in sequence has no advantage over a single-minded application of some personally favoured technique, while others would argue that a drinking problem which probably has several dimensions (lack of social skills, lack of coping mechanisms, and lack of positive re-inforcements for changed drinking behaviour, for example) is best met by a multi-modal offer of treatment. Logic supports the latter interpretation, and research results also appear largely to support it. But rather than applying a uniform behavioural package in every instance, it is better to make the individual behavioural assessment and wider case analysis, and then set up the individual's multi-modal treatment.

THE PRESENT POSITION

What conclusions can be drawn from this brief review of behavioural treatments? It must be obvious that this field of experiment offers a great richness of ideas, many of which provide hints and suggestions for the everyday practice of the therapist who is not working primarily within a behavioural perspective. As for the substantive significance of this work in terms of relevance to general treatment planning, there are four broad conclusions.

1   There is as yet no formal behavioural technique of such proved efficacy that it should be adopted as an exclusive treatment approach.

2   There are many promising leads. A person-specific behavioural package may in particular provide a helpful treatment for some individuals.

3   In many instances a behavioural technique may be applicable to some particular facet of the patient's problems, and the generalist should develop the ability to identify when such techniques should be deployed.

4   The time and skill required for behavioural analysis and treatment by

behaviour therapies should not be underestimated, and only poor results can be expected from amateurish application of exact techniques. The therapist who is primarily working as a generalist in alcoholism treatment (a nurse or social worker, for instance) should, however, be able to apply some of these techniques competently; behavioural treatment need not remain exclusively the preserve of the highly trained psychologist. A treatment service should have a psychologist on its staff who can assist in training and case supervision, aid with case referrals, and conduct some treatment.

DETERRENT DRUGS

Since its introduction in the 1940s disulfiram (trade name *antabuse*), has been used very widely in the treatment of alcoholism. Citrated calcium carbimide (trade names *temposil* or *abstem*) was first marketed in the 1950's, with the claimed advantage over disulfiram of fewer side effects. It is a shorter acting substance, and only gives protection for 12 to 24 hours after the last dose, as opposed to the 24 to 48 hour cover provided by disulfiram. Disulfiram, which is given in a daily dose of 250 to 500mg, is more slowly absorbed than calcium carbimide (dose 200 to 400mg per day), so that a few days may be required to build up a satisfactory blood level, as opposed to the much quicker cover provided by calcium carbimide.

Of these two drugs, disulfiram gives the more marked reaction when alcohol is taken, but otherwise the two drugs are closely similar tools. Both block the breakdown of alcohol at the stage of acetaldehyde production, so that the patient will experience a transient poisoning with acetaldehyde if he takes alcohol after the drug. The accumulation of acetaldehyde is not, however, the total explanation for the drug/alcohol interaction, and other neuro–chemical processes are also involved.

The reaction is characterized by flushings, palpitations, breathlessness, headache, nausea, vomiting and general distress; and the characteristic odour of acetaldehyde appears on the breath. The reaction usually starts within 15 to 30 minutes of drinking alcohol, and its severity varies greatly. It may be so slight as to be therapeutically useless and the patient 'drinks through it', or so severe as to be life-threatening. The greatest threat may come from a profound fall in blood pressure. Patients with heart disease, cerebro–vascular insufficiency, liver disease or diabetes should not be given these drugs. Emergency measures for treatment of cardio–vascular collapse may be required if there is a severe reaction; the patient should lie down and the foot of the bed should be elevated; a vaso–pressor (blood–pressure raising drug) may be needed. Intravenous vitamin C or an antihistamine have also been recommended as antidotes. Patients who have been prescribed a deterrent drug should carry a medical card with emergency instructions. The practice of exposing the patient to a challenge dose of alcohol as a therapeutic test is not routinely justified.

The rationale of this treatment is that if the patient takes his tablets he will then know that he cannot drink while the protective cover of the drug lasts, and he will thus only have to make a daily decision to take his medication rather than have to resist the sudden temptations of any moment. The therapy is thus not primarily a conditioning treatment, though a variety of secondary learning processes may be involved.

Despite the many years during which these substances have been in use, it is still difficult to form a firm view as to their usefulness. The disadvantages include the dangers of the drug/alcohol reaction and, certainly with disulfiram, also the problems set by side–effects (which may include lethargy, depression, impotence, a delirious state, peripheral neuritis, dermatitis, an unpleasant taste in the mouth, and an unexplained breathlessness). This seemingly formidable list of potential complications does not, however, constitute grounds for abandoning use of either drug, but rather indicates a need for caution and adequate medical supervision. Another disadvantage may be that the prescription of the drugs can carry the covert message that all treatment can be dispensed in a tablet with other needed therapeutic work neglected, but this will occur only if the drug is deployed carelessly.

Some patients certainly find deterrent drugs a help, especially in the earlier stages of sobriety. Others will want to take a low maintenance dose over many years and will use the drug as their talisman. The spouse may also have her anxieties much relieved by seeing her partner take the daily tablet. Still other patients will use such a drug intermittently to give themselves cover over a particularly high–risk period, for instance, the businessman who is going to a conference where he knows that he will be exposed to much entertaining.

The best results are often obtained when one or both, despite their seeming contradictoriness, of the following conditions are fulfilled:

1   The use of the drug is explained to, and negotiated with the patient, so that the taking of these tablets becomes not only acceptable but wanted;

the patient is not being muzzled, or surrendering autonomy, but making a free decision to engage in this type of treatment.

2   A degree of acceptable supervision is set up (the tablet taken in the doctor's office for instance, or in the medical room at work, or under the eyes of the wife), or a contingency management plan or therapeutic contract established. Disulfiram has been used in this way within industrial treatment programmes, and in the USA within court probation programmes.

And as ever with a specialized treatment, the basics of therapeutic work provide the proper context.

A balanced conclusion might therefore be that where there is no physical contraindication and the patient is sufficiently sensible to be trusted not to drink rashly on top of the drug, one of these substances should at least be offered, and the nature of the treatment explained. It must be underlined, though, that this is an approach only to be instituted with medical supervision.

Over recent years disulfiram has been available in long-acting implant form. Pellets are implanted beneath the skin by means of a surgical operation conducted under local anaesthetic. This technique has been more widely used in Continental Europe than in the UK or North America, and the preparation is not officially approved in all countries. The pellets sometimes work their way to the surface and are scratched out, and unpleasant septic complications can occur. It seems likely that effective blood-levels of the drug are in reality seldom obtained, and success depends more on expectation than chemistry. The occasional patient may, however, be found who has great faith in this treatment, and who will regularly attend for a three-monthly implant – a patient who, for example, has experienced frequent imprisonment for petty drink-related crime, and who believes that only with this seeming extreme of external control can he avoid further trouble.

PSYCHOTHERAPY

INDICATIONS

A psychotherapeutic approach is inherent in everything which has been said about the helping process in this book. This particular section will briefly discuss the deployment of formal psychotherapy, not so much as treatment 'for alcoholism' but to aid adjustment and the quality of life when the patient has stopped drinking. It has previously been argued that formal and intensive psychotherapy is generally not indicated as a treatment aimed specifically at the drinking problem, and that such treatment certainly cannot be usefully initiated while the patient is still drinking.

With the drinking out of the way, the need for psychotherapy and the patient's suitability for it can be judged by exactly the same criteria as would be applied when deciding whether any other patient (with or without a drinking problem) should be taken on for psychotherapy, or for deciding the most suitable form of psychotherapy to meet individual needs.

The answer to those questions can only be determined by full assessment. Different therapists will have their own views as to whether suitability for psychotherapy is determined restrictively or more freely, but it would probably be common ground that only the minority of patients who have successfully dealt with drinking problems require at this later stage a major psychotherapeutic involvement. What should particularly be cautioned against is the danger of forgetting that suitability for psychotherapy does indeed have to be determined by careful assessment. The enthusiasm of those not specially trained in general psychotherapeutic working may lead to the prescription of psychotherapy for a patient whom no experienced psychotherapist would regard as a suitable person for such engagement – a well-meaning effort but with the patient's commitment untested, goals undefined equally by patient and therapist, and everyone heading for a muddle. It may in some circumstances be appropriate to make the offer of psychotherapy actually conditional on the patient's in the first place achieving a stable period of sobriety or other life change.

Here is an example of a referral to psychotherapy which was timely and proved useful:

> A woman aged 45 had presented three years previously with heavy non-dependent drinking in the setting of a painful marital breakdown. After a year's total abstinence from alcohol she had for two years been drinking in a moderate and controlled fashion. She was now contemplating remarriage, but was worried that she might in this new relationship re-enact what she sensed as being lifelong problems in close relationships with men. Her father had been a strong but distant figure whom she had been taught greatly

to admire, but towards whom her feelings had been very ambivalent. After two assessment interviews by a psychotherapist, she was offered a contract in terms of relatively short-term psychotherapy (six months with weekly sessions) which was to focus on her problems with key relationships, and her conflicting needs to be dominated together with her resentful and destructive responses to the people whom she manoeuvred into this role.

The type of psychotherapy which is most appropriate to the patient's needs must of course be decided individually. If group therapy is favoured, there is no. compelling reason why the patient should be in a group exclusively composed of people with drinking problems, and there may indeed be advantages in his being placed in a more mixed group. The plan may sometimes involve a few months of individual psychotherapy as preparation for 6 to 12 months of group experience. A relatively short-term and problem-focused approach is in practice most often the chosen treatment when individual psychotherapy is deemed to be indicated, and group work is usually best conducted at that sort of level.

Specialized or conjoint marital therapy may sometimes be appropriate, but the dangers should not be overlooked of bringing two people together with destructive feelings which they are narrowly controlling, and inviting them to admit those feelings. The result can be a sort of diadic abreaction with enormous outpouring of hostility, and the therapist (or therapists) may find it extremely difficult to control this so that the material can be used constructively. In such circumstances a drinking bout may be precipitated and drunken behaviour, charged with all the stirred-up feelings, may become aggressive or self-damaging. To note the possible hazards is in no way to counsel against the use of conjoint therapy in carefully chosen circumstances, but only to argue that where it is used, thought should be given to timing. It is generally useful to think of conjoint therapy as something for which the couple have separately to be prepared by individual work. They need to be sure that they can bring to the sessions some positive feelings and some commitment to change.

The alcoholism team may have appropriate psychotherapeutic skills within its own resources, or it may be necessary to make referrals to psychotherapy specialists. This type of problem may, however, also be ideal for training staff in short-term psychotherapy techniques, with the time of the experienced psychotherapist then devoted to case supervision rather than to the treatment of referred cases.

DRINKING AND ITS PSYCHODYNAMIC MEANINGS

Although psychotherapy is not here being viewed as a treatment 'for alcoholism' it is very probable that drinking will be discussed at times by the patient during psychotherapeutic sessions. Aspects of the previous drinking can at this stage often provide pointers towards important general dynamic themes, with the drinking *exemplifying* these issues rather than being a major focus in its own right. In the past some psychoanalytic writing has suggested that the dynamic meaning of drinking can be pronounced upon in universal terms – excessive drinking as always being a suicidal equivalent, for instance. Such a dogmatic view of the psychodynamics of drinking is as unhelpful to work with alcoholism as are any fixed formulae for dynamic interpretations in the general field of psychotherapy.

Drinking and excessive drinking will in fact have different meanings for different patients, and often multiple meanings for any one patient. Without in any way seeking to pre-empt the need to explore with the individual, there are some recurrent themes with which it is useful to become familiar. Some of these themes are set out briefly below, but this list is by no means exhaustive:

(i) Drinking may be an indicator of indentification with a heavy-drinking parent or other key figure in the patient's childhood. The patient is, as it were, destined to act out someone else's life rather than his own. Other people in his present surroundings are also being set up as actors in the old play, for instance, the wife is being forced into exactly the same role as the patient once saw his mother play in relation to his own alcoholic father. The father does not need to have been a drinker for such processes of identification and projection to be set in train, but the acutely traumatic early experience of the child in an alcoholic family, with the many unresolved conflicts of love, hate, rage, and pity, are particularly likely to result in the patient continuing to define relationships in terms of the play which he still desperately hopes to resolve. This rather complex line of explanation, which proposes the need to examine both self-identity and a series of relationships, generally seems to offer a more hopeful basis for case understanding than any unitary explanations in terms of 'alcohol is symbolically equivalent to . . .'.

(ii) Related to the general framework proposed above, one may identify a variety of fairly common sub-plots. The patient may, for instance, seek defeat, punishment or even destruction through drink, because he sees himself/his father as deserving such fate. He may be seeking to inflict punishment on others, believing that at some level his mother destroyed his father and that she (and now his ówn wife) are in a sense dreaded enemies. He may see drinking as giving power, because his father was only powerful when drunk. However, drinking may also point directly to interpersonal dependency conflicts: the patient wants to be powerful and independent but he also wants to be a dependent child, who is sick, erring and repeatedly forgiven.

(iii)   The patient sometimes seems to use alcohol as a way of entering a blissful state of reverie, where he can engage in fantasy and wish-fulfilment. The real world is too difficult. Alcohol is valued for its pharmacological effect, and it becomes symbolized as all-warm, mother-like, or milk-like. The drink is then an indicator of the patient's general difficulty in consistently maintaining an engagement with the real adult world.

It must again be emphasized that these examples are only to be taken as a few possible ways of looking at endlessly variable meanings and experiences. Psychotherapy cannot be practised in terms of any set phrase-book of symbolic translations. The meanings given to alcohol are not only individually determined and shaped by early personal experience, but also are often much coloured by particular cultural meanings of drinking and drunkenness. The need to be sensitive to the special meanings that a woman may give to her drinking also needs to be noted, for symbolic meanings may differ between the sexes.

Psychotherapy has thus something to offer the selected patient, and may on occasion be essential to that improvement in the quality of sobriety which is such an important adjunct to recovery. The therapist who, with modesty, open-mindedness and guidance, engages in such work is also himself going to benefit. Such responsibility will help to round out his understanding of the extraordinarily complex human processes which lie behind any drinking story, serve to persuade him that no single explanations are other than a blinkered denial of human experience, and further convince him that the task of understanding is never finished.

REFERENCES

Bailey MB (1968) *Alcoholism and Family Casework: Theory and Practice.* New York: The Community Council of Greater New York.

Bean MH and Zinberg NE (eds) (1981) *Dynamic Approaches to the Understanding and Treatment of Alcoholism.* New York: Free Press.

Blum EM (1966) Psychoanalytic views of alcoholism: a review. *Quarterly Journal of Studies on Alcohol,* **27,** 259–299.

Fehr DH (1976) Psychotherapy. In: Tarter RE and Surgerman AA (eds) *Alcoholism,* pp 637–653. Reading, Mass.: Addison-Wesley.

Gerrein JR, Rosenberg CM and Manohar V (1973) Disulfiram maintenance in outpatient treatment of alcoholism. *Archives of General Psychiatry,* **28,** 798–802.

Hill MJ and Blane HT (1967) Evaluation of psychotherapy with alcoholics: a critical review. *Quarterly Journal of Studies on Alcohol,* **28,** 76–104.

Hodgson R (1977) Behaviour therapy. In: Edwards G and Grant M (eds) *Alcoholism: New Knowledge and New Responses,* pp 290–307. London: Croom Helm.

Kwentus J and Major LF (1979) Disulfiram in the treatment of alcoholism: a review. *Journal of Studies on Alcohol,* **40,** 428–446.

Litman GK (1976) Behaviour modification techniques in the treatment of alcoholism; a review and critique. In: Gibbins RJ, Israel Y and Kalant H (eds) *Research Advance in Alcohol and Drug Problems,* Vol. 3, pp 359–400.

Madden JS and Kenyon WH (1975) Group counselling of alcoholics by a voluntary agency. *British Journal of Psychiatry,* **126,** 289–291.

Malcolm MT, Madden JS and Williams AE (1974) disulfiram implantation critically evaluated. *British Journal of Psychiatry,* **125,** 485–489.

McDonald DE (1958) Group psychotherapy with wives of alcoholics. *Quarterly Journal of Studies on Alcohol,* **17,** 227–238.

Miller WRM (ed) (1980) *The Addictive Behaviours.* Oxford: Pergamon.

Nathan P, Marlatt GA and Loberg T (eds) (1978) *Alcoholism: New Direction in Behavioural Research and Treatment.* New York: Plenum.

Steiner C (1971) *Games Alcoholics Play.* New York: Grove.

Chapter 17
Working towards Normal Drinking

Firstly, it is necessary to remember the varied nature of the population coming for help with drinking problems. Not everyone who turns for help because of his drinking is suffering from alcohol dependence and, with greater public understanding, earlier and lesser problems are increasingly likely to be represented. To propose one exclusive goal for everyone, be it normal drinking or abstinence, is not common sense. We need, as always, to plan treatment in terms of flexible responses to multiple needs. To claim that no–one who has experienced trouble with drinking will ever be able to drink in a trouble-free way is not true. On the other hand, it is unhelpful to make 'normal drinking' into a slogan or heedlessly to attack the validity of AA teaching.

This chapter discusses some of the basic ideas about 'normal' drinking which have been developing over recent years, and will outline a treatment approach. Much that was said in Chapter 14 about abstinence-oriented approaches is equally applicable to the normal drinking goal, for instance, the relevance of the patient-therapist relationship, and those general points will not be repeated.

In this chapter the phrases 'normal drinking' and 'controlled drinking' are used synonymously.

WHAT IS 'NORMAL' DRINKING?

If a patient is to aim for normal drinking, how is 'normality' to be defined in practical and recognizable terms? It is no good leaving the definition vague, for only when a goal is closely specified is goal-setting useful. The matter is made difficult by our society's latitude in regard to what constitutes an ordinary way of using alcohol. Getting drunk a couple of times a week is to some people the expected way to drink, while for others even one episode of mild intoxication would transgress expectations. For goal-setting, normality must be considered in terms of at least two different criteria.

1 *Objectively normal drinking: quantity/frequency dimensions*. The upper limit which is to be permitted needs to be agreed with the patient. About 40 g of alcohol on any one drinking occasion (two pints of beer, two doubles of spirits, four glasses of wine) is a reasonable ceiling, but may perhaps initially be rather too high. As for frequency, it is wise to agree that drinking should not be reinstated on a fixed daily schedule; there should be breaks and variation.

2 *Subjectively normal drinking*. Someone who is drinking alcohol normally should be no more apprehensive about this activity than if he were drinking coffee or tea. He should know his usual intake level without having to monitor his drinking behaviour and without a sense of effort. If at a certain point he says 'Not another, thank you', this should be without the conscious exertion of iron will. He should be able to think about the company and conversation rather than his thoughts being preoccupied with drinking, the next drink, or not having the next drink. Such easiness in the relationship between the drinker and what he drinks is characteristically lacking when moderate or severe alcohol dependence has been established. The patient who has progressed even to mild dependence will, when he has brought his drinking back to objective normality, often at first still experience subjective unease. Subjective normality usually therefore takes longer than objective normality to attain, and sometimes considerably longer. 'Normal' drinking in the true and complete sense has not been won until the two elements have come together, and when there has only been an objective change the patient's position remains precarious. This double aspect of goal-setting and the probable two-stage nature of recovery should be discussed with, and understood by, the patient.

Other dimensions could also be added to provide a more complex definition of normality, for instance limitations in the speed of drinking, or limitations on the circumstances in which alcohol is taken. These issues are, however, dealt with later in considering 'strategies for control'.

WHO IS CANDIDATE FOR A NORMAL DRINKING GOAL?

There are many patients for whom it would be manifestly inappropriate to attempt such a goal. For those with a long history of fully developed alcohol dependence, abstinence is at present the only feasible objective, although there are of course possibilities that in due time treatments will be developed which 'dismantle' dependence. Equally, there are instances where no one could doubt that for at least a trial period it is sensible to go along with and support the patient's wish to ameliorate rather than abstain, and this would often be true of the patient who has been drinking too heavily only recently and intermittently. It is the middle ground which again sets difficulties, and although a number of guidelines can be identified, it would be spurious to pretend that it is possible within the limits of present knowledge to make categorical statements. With those provisos in mind, the following considerations often contribute to the decision–making.

DEGREE OF DEPENDENCE

The importance of this factor has just been mentioned. In practical terms, if the patient has never experienced any withdrawal symptoms, then (other things being equal) normal drinking is an option. If the patient has experienced withdrawal symptoms but only for the last six months or less, normal drinking is still a possible, but more dubious, proposition – the more serious those withdrawal symptoms the more doubtful the patient's capacity to regain control over drinking. If for six or twelve months the patient has not only experienced withdrawal symptoms but has repeatedly engaged in morning relief drinking, return to normal drinking is improbable. The guidelines are, however, to be read as examples of ways in which the evidence may be examined, rather than as firm statements or fixed rules.

EVIDENCE OF RECENT SUSTAINED NORMAL DRINKING

If within the last couple of years the patient has been able to drink in a relaxed and controlled manner continuously for two to three months, this may indicate that he retains a capacity for a normal style of drinking, and that this capacity may now with due care be strengthened and extended. The circumstances in which this drinking occurred should be examined. The evidence must, though, be approached warily. Careful questioning may reveal that this previous period of 'sustained normal drinking' was less sustained and less normal than the patient at first suggested, and it may have been only a slide towards reinstatement of dependence.

THE PATIENT PERSONALLY WISHES TO ATTEMPT A NORMAL DRINKING GOAL

A patient who wants to return to normal drinking may in many instances be deluding himself in any such hope, and it is then the therapist's responsibility to try to help the patient to accept abstinence, rather than conniving in the delusion. Some patients will frankly declare that drinking other than for intoxication seems to them a purposeless use of alcohol. On the other hand a patient may be right in believing he can control his drinking, and be strongly committed to attempting this goal.

PERSONALITY

The mature and determined person who is good at exercising self-control is obviously more likely to succeed in drinking normally than the person whose capacity for self-control is in general not well developed – for example, someone who easily becomes angry.

UNDERLYING MENTAL ILLNESS

The patient who is suffering from any type of mental illness and as a result uses alcohol to relieve unpleasant feelings is not in a good position to attempt normal drinking. Whatever its nature, the underlying disorder has first to be treated, but there is always the danger that a relapse into that illness will precipitate loss of control over drinking, although of course equally it may overthrow the intention of complete abstinence. Underlying brain damage or mental retardation usually suggests that normal drinking will not be possible, and a concurrent drug dependence which has not been dealt with successfully probably also rules out a return to safe use of alcohol, so enquiry should be made into the possible use or misuse of psychotropics. Pathological gambling may also threaten maintenance of control over drinking; the euphoria of the big win, the depression of the big loss, or simply the tension associated with continuous gambling, all rather easily invite a return to heavy use of alcohol.

ALCOHOL-RELATED PHYSICAL ILLNESS

The decision in this instance must be made in relation to the actual type and degree of illness, but alcohol-related physical illness usually suggests that the patient would be wise to avoid any further drinking and risk of further tissue damage.

SOCIAL AND FAMILY SUPPORT

The patient who is socially isolated and without a family will probably find it more difficult to drink normally again than the patient whose behaviour is being monitored and influenced by close supports. On the other hand, a certain type of family network may positively encourage excessive drinking, with every weekend a family drinking party. Occupation has similarly to be taken into account. Someone who has no job, much time on his hands and no structure to his day may find it difficult to control his drinking, while jobs which involve exposure to heavy drinking may make it difficult to pursue a controlled drinking goal.

The clinical skill thus lies in knowing how to weight and integrate these and other factors when assessing the feasibility of a normal drinking goal, and in learning how to feed information to the patient to help his own decision-making. Our understanding of which patient can return to normal drinking is still changing and uncertain; a clinical judgement which to one person appears ultra-conservative may seem lax and risky to another. But whatever the therapist proposes, it is finally the patient who makes the decision.

AN INTERVAL OF SOBRIETY AS FIRST STEP

For some patients normal drinking emerges directly out of more chaotic drinking. Suddenly or gradually the new pattern supersedes the old. To begin with there may be occasions when drinking is at a social level with quite frequent circumstances where limits are broken, but after a few months the 'bad occasions' are averted. Alternatively, the story may be of a shorter or longer initial period of abstinence, followed by a tentative move towards moderate drinking. That move may have been planned at the outset as a step which would be taken after a certain interval of sobriety, or the patient may start to drink again feeling anxious about breaking the rules. When drinking follows a period of sobriety the therapist has the responsibility of working out with the patient whether this is a sadly familiar story of unguardedness and self-deception foreshadowing major relapse, or whether this is indeed the evolution of re-established control.

Whether the patient who is aiming at controlled drinking does best to do so directly or by the pathway of initial abstinence is not an easy question to answer. Different strategies suit different people. But if the drinking is chaotic and surrounded with problems, in general the patient is likely to do better if he starts out afresh from a less chaotic base.

TECHNIQUES FOR ESTABLISHING AND MAINTAINING CONTROL

Patients are themselves often very inventive in designing ways to keep their drinking within a limit, and it is always useful therefore to explore and encourage these personal strategies. The paragraphs below describe a variety of methods which may be employed, and the first heading – 'Full initial discussion with the patient' – is obviously the basis for therapeutic planning. The other approaches are going to be used in various combinations, and generally the more strategies the patient has available the better.

FULL INITIAL DISCUSSION WITH THE PATIENT

The first step in setting a treatment programme for the individual patient who is aiming at controlled drinking must be to clarify what is being expected of treatment, the methods of working, and the mutual level of commitment.

LIMITING THE TYPE OF BEVERAGE

Shifting from one type of alcoholic drink to another is often dismissed as the typical strategy of the alcoholic who refuses to face up to the fact that his problem lies not in the specific drink but in his relationship with any sort of alcohol – the whisky drinker who believes that 'beer will be safe' is classically warned that alcohol is simply alcohol, whatever the label on the bottle. The therapist has to distinguish between self-delusion and sound strategy, for the patient who is going to effect a successful return to normal drinking may often spontaneously discover that a change of beverage is helpful. He chooses what he may term a 'social drink' – beer instead of wine perhaps, or wine instead of beer, but in any case a beverage free of old associations.

LIMITING THE QUANTITY AND FREQUENCY OF INTAKE

The importance of strictly defining with each patient what is to count as 'normal' has already been mentioned. If the patient is making his definition in terms of 'a single of ...' or a glass of ...', or other such familiar but often rather vague measures (a 'single' is usually a very uncertain quantity of alcohol if the patient is pouring his own drink at home), then properly objective measures have to be agreed.

SPEED OF DRINKING

A patient may learn to 'pace' his drinking. This may be in terms either of not drinking faster than a companion or of pacing against the clock, for instance a pint of beer may be made to last 30 minutes.

MOTIVATIONS FOR DRINKING

The patient may discover that it is unwise for him to drink in response to mood, for instance, when he is angry, depressed or bored. He does better to drink only when he does not 'need' a drink.

CIRCUMSTANCES AND COMPANY

Drinking is at first often best limited to situations in which that individual's previous experience has shown that control is more likely to be maintained, while drinking situations which can be identified as dangerous are best avoided. For instance, the patient may decide that he will drink with his wife on Tuesdays in the pub at the corner, but will 'avoid the Saturday night crowd'. He will never drink at work during the day, and will not drink when he is on business trips away from home. When guests come to dinner at his own home, he will not drink before dinner or after dinner, but only with the meal (and within his explicit limits).

IDENTIFYING 'COMPETING ACTIVITIES'

The patient may usefully identify activities which can immediately be engaged in to prevent the risk of uncontrolled drinking. For instance, if a housewife knows that she is particularly likely to start drinking in an uncontrolled fashion when she is alone in the middle of the afternoon, then she has to find and plan activities which can divert her from drinking at this time of the day. She may decide on a simple strategy like doing shopping in the afternoon, or she may make this a fixed time for playing tennis, and so on. If the dangerous circumstances which particularly invite uncontrolled drinking can thus be neutralized by competing activity, practice in normal drinking can then perhaps be restricted to occasions when the chances of success are more real.

INDIVIDUAL BEHAVIOURAL ANALYSIS

The headings above provide ideas about the kinds of strategies which might be suggested for any patient. It may in addition be useful to carry out an individual and more detailed behavioural analysis of the patient's drinking. The aim is to identify the circumstances in which a particular patient tends to drink excessively, using particular recent instances and the experiences which evolve during treatment. General statements such as 'I drink when I am bored' are not to be discounted, but are usually of far less value to the planning of treatment than minute analysis of the immediate antecedents and circumstances of, say, last Friday's drinking binge. The analysis identifies the *cues* which are related to excessive drinking, both in internal (mood) and external (event and situation) terms. It is necessary to form an idea of how such cues interact rather than seeing them only in isolation, and to understand the sort of *pathway* that the individual is apt to move along when he indulges in excessive drinking. Such material is then used in planning the package of strategies which go to make up the individual drinking programme

HOW TESTING SHOULD THE PROGRAMME BE?

The patient must identify risky situations, although it may then be difficult for him to avoid many of these. He may, for instance, have to go away on business trips, knowing that a lonely weekend in a hotel is particularly likely to result in heavy solitary drinking. However, not only may exposure to such a risky situation be unavoidable, but for the real effectiveness of treatment, such exposure to temptation may be highly desirable. The patient should not make impossible demands on his own strength and determination, but the essence of therapy is that he should experience some sense of struggle, of temptation, and perhaps of craving to drink excessively, *and that temptation and craving should then be successfully resisted.* It is the repeated exposure to the relevant cues and the repeated resistance to an excessive drinking response which will in the end *extinguish* the potency of those cues. Without experience of craving there can be no long-term extinction of craving. In terms of a familiar analogy, a child who is afraid of dogs is unlikely to overcome that fear simply by avoiding all dogs; such a normal fear is dealt with in terms of ordinary family wisdom by introducing a dog to the child, and then by praise and close support persuading the child on this occasion not to run away. The objective behaviour towards dogs changes, and then more slowly the anxiety experienced at the approach of a dog begins to fade out.

In similar fashion the patient who only avoids risk will probably only achieve an objective recovery (see p. 251); his drinking will be objectively within acceptable social limits, but it will still be associated with much subjective unease. Subjective recovery comes about when there has been repeated exposure to cues, and repeated resistance to an excessive drinking response. Treatment will on the other hand suffer a reverse if on too many occasions the patient does in fact drink excessively; the potency of the risky cue is confirmed rather than extinguished.

The degree to which the patient is to be encouraged to engage in any sort of brinkmanship is therefore a theme to be carefully explored as therapy progresses. In the early phase the sum of risk should probably be curtailed and simple strategies of avoidance be the order of the day. But the patient should soon be grappling much more positively with risky situations, and testing himself out by drinking but not drinking excessively. Such a programme inevitably involves a degree of trial and error, and it is to be accepted that the patient may for some time occasionally overstep his limits. Acceptance of that reality is not, however, to propose a policy of *laissez-faire:* to resist craving is therapeutic while to yield to craving is anti-therapeutic, and if there are too frequent lapses into heavy drinking there is no therapeutic programme.

INVOLVING THE SPOUSE

The spouse has an important and practical part to play in supporting the patient's attack on his problem. The wife is often accepted as a direct and useful restraining influence, and as the person within whose company normal drinking may most safely be attempted. If, however, the wife's help and partnership is effectively to be enlisted, she should be properly informed of what is intended and she should be very fully consulted and made to feel that her views are taken into account. Therapy will be handicapped if the wife has reservations about her husband's normal drinking goal which have not been met and talked through, and she will be frightened and antagonistic if her feelings are ignored.

SEEING IT THROUGH

The patient who is attempting abstinence can after initial assessment and goal-setting, often be expected to need little subsequent help. He is best left largely to get on with things himself and to mobilize his own resources. In some ways normal drinking is a less clear-cut and more tricky goal, and the patient who is taking this course of action is likely to need quite close support over some months. Treatment which aims at return to normal drinking is far from being a cheap option in terms of service costs, and if such a treatment is to be given its place within the range of what is offered by a treatment service, it cannot be on a casual, unplanned and understaffed basis which fails to provide the proper follow-through of support and which risks irresponsibility.

Monitoring of progress must firstly involve the patient's own regular objective and subjective report at follow-up treatment sessions, and these sessions should probably be at not less than two-weekly intervals. Verbal reports may usefully be supplemented by asking the patient to keep a drinking diary, and thus to engage in self-monitoring. The spouse should also be seen regularly both for her to share in the discussion and planning of treatment, and for her contribution to monitoring.

One of two alternative decisions will then at some point have to be made in the light of progress and monitoring:

1 *Termination of successful treatment.* A successful outcome may be assumed when over about six months the patient has achieved both objective and subjective normality in his drinking. Judgement of 'success' is as ever provisional, but at some point treatment and frequency of visits should be wound down. The patient may be left with an open invitation to return if he encounters further difficulties, or it may be wise to offer widely spaced (say six monthly) follow-up appointments and 'booster' discussions over the next year or two.

2   *Termination of unsuccessful treatment.* The patient who is failing to make progress should not immediately and without review be told to abandon the normal drinking goal. Lack of progress is to be taken in the first instance as a matter for careful analysis of the causes of the difficulty, and on that basis some planned shift in the attack may be possible. But if the patient still fails in any way to progress, there comes a moment when there is no profit in encouraging him in a frustrating and perhaps damaging pursuit of normal drinking. He may now be persuaded by experience that it is better to opt instead for an abstinence goal, either as the short or longer term solution.

A FINAL WORD OF CAUTION

Many orthodox approaches to alcoholism treatment are not underpinned by research. The decision to advise the patient to aim for total abstinence may sometimes be ill-advised and result in the patient alternating sobriety with explosive relapses, rather than his learning how to control his drinking or attenuate his relapses. And the abstinence goal may involve a change in life-style which sets many difficulties for the patient. To suggest therefore that abstinence-oriented therapy is in some essential way more respectable practice than a normal drinking approach is not well founded, and it is better to admit that the treatment of every new case is an experiment which requires the patient's informed consent and the most careful ethical monitoring, and that is so whatever the drinking goal.

That having been said, there are certainly some special problems which may attach to work towards normal drinking. The greatest danger arises if the therapist's commitment to this approach drives the patient onward in pursuit of a goal which is manifestly inappropriate, with consequent risk and damage. If the patient is to take an enquiring and experimental approach to the solution of his own problems, he will need the help of a therapist of equally open mind.

REFERENCES

Davies DL (1962) Normal drinking in recovered alcohol addicts. *Quarterly Journal of Studies on Alcohol,* **23,** 94–104.

Ewing JA and Rouse BA (1976) Failure of an experimental treatment program to inculcate controlled rinking in alcoholics. *British Journal of addiction,* **71,** 123–134.

Finney JW and Moos RM (1981) Characteristics and prognosis of alcoholics who became moderate drinkers and abstainers after treatment. *Journal of Studies on Alcohol*, **42**, 94–105.

Heather N and Robertson I (1981) *Controlled Drinking*. London: Methuen.

Hodgson RJ (1980) Treatment strategies for the early problem drinker. In: Edwards G and Grant M (eds) *Alcoholism Treatment in Transition*, pp 162–177. London: Croom Helm.

Miller WR and Caddy GR (1977) Abstinence and controlled drinkng in the treatment of problem drinkers. *Journal of Studies on Alcohol*, **38**, 986–1003.

Orford J (1973) A comparison of alcoholics whose drinking is totally controlled and those whose drinking is mainly uncontrolled. *Behaviour Research and Therapy*, **11**, 565–576.

Pattison EM (1976) Non-abstinent drinking goals in the treatment of alcoholism: a clinical typology. *Archives of General Psychiatry*, **33**, 923–930.

Popham RE and Schmidt W (1976) Some factors affecting the likelihood of moderate drinking by treated alcoholics. *Journal of Studies on Alcohol*, **37**, 868–882.

Smart RG (1976) Spontaneous recovery in alcoholics: a review and analysis of the available research. *Drug and Alcohol Dependence*, **1**, 277–285.

Sobell MB and Sobell LC (1978) *Behavioural Treatment of Alcohol Problems: Individual Therapy and Controlled Drinking*. New York: Plenum.

Chapter 18
Treatment and the
In-patient Setting

This chapter discusses the part which in-patient care may take as a phase in treatment, and it starts by identifying different styles of in-patient care. The next section considers a range of factors which may affect the decision to offer admission; deciding whether a patient will benefit from coming into hospital is a recurrent question for staff discussion, and it is useful to have a check-list of ideas which can help frame a consistent policy. The chapter then moves on to a review some elements within the organization and working of a multi-purpose alcoholism unit – a look at the common problems that such a unit encounters and how those problems may be met. Finally, note is taken of the in-patient unit's potential as a base for professional education.

THREE STYLES OF IN-PATIENT CARE

There are many variations on the type of in-patient care which has been provided for alcoholics, ranging from the merely custodial to the intensive therapeutic community programme. The aim of this section will be to discuss three important alternative lines of development.

TREATMENT ON THE GENERAL PSYCHIATRIC WARD

Over recent decades the trend in many countries has been to try to take alcoholics out of general psychiatric wards and treat them instead in special units. It has been argued that the general ward is inappropriate for a patient who is not 'mentally ill', and who will not feel at home in an ordinary psychiatric setting. Furthermore, the emphasis on group therapy for alcoholism, which has also been a feature of recent decades, logically proposes an advantage in collecting alcoholic patients together.

But the pendulum may have swung too far. Given that a decade or two ago it was appropriate to try to get alcoholics out of the general psychiatric wards if their needs were misunderstood in that setting, in the light of what has since been learnt, efforts must now be made towards enhancing the competence of those general wards so that the needs of their alcoholic patients can indeed be understood and met. One very practical reason why general ward treatment should be encouraged as complementing the development of more specialized centres, is that patients with drinking problems will certainly go on turning up in the general setting, with their drinking often much intertwined with other disabilities. The generalist must be trained to recognize a drinking problem rather than overlook its presence, and to see how it is related to other apsects of the case. Even if, as is not the case, it were theoretically desirable to strive for entirely specialist facilities, it is extremely unlikely that this could be afforded within the health budgets or manpower resources of even the richest countries.

Advice on a particular patient from a staff member working full-time with alcoholism may on occasion be very helpful to the generalist, for instance, advice from a social worker with intimate knowledge of the local community resources available for this type of patient, a consultation on whether a psychiatric picture is or is not likely to be alcohol-related, an opinion on the general handling of a difficult case, and so on. It is one of the functions of the specialist team to act in this support role, but giving advice should seldom mean taking over the care.

As for the alleged 'unacceptability' to the alcoholic patient of the general psychiatric ward, an understaffed general unit which cannot mount an active therapeutic programme for most of its patients is no place for the treatment of drinking, but by the same token a well-run general unit should be able to provide as competent care for an alcoholic as for any other class of patient. That statement assumes that a mental illness hospital is able to offer a graded series of wards – a ward dealing with patients who are acutely ill and disturbed is not the appropriate milieu for treating any person who is not seriously ill, whether or not drinking is that patient's problem.

THE SPECIALIZED ALCOHOLISM IN-PATIENT PSYCHOTHERAPY UNIT

Since many specialized alcoholism psychotherapy units are today in a state of transition, no one description can do justice to their present diversity. What we will describe here might be termed the classical or orthodoc development which is still certainly functioning in some centres.

Typically, this kind of unit aims to admit patients with 'uncomplicated' alcoholism. Patients with severe depression or other underlying mental illness will be screened out. Personality disorder will often be taken as contra-indication, and the vagrant is also unlikely to be admitted. For purposes of homogeneity and group work, admission criteria are likely to favour the middle class and verbally fluent patient, although within this general model different centres will practise widely varying degrees of exclusiveness.

As already mentioned, there will also be many variations in the type of therapeutic programme which is offered, given that there will be a common emphasis on psychotherpy, group experience, intensiveness and a package approach which proposes that all patients during their hospital stay should go through the same basic group psychotherapy programme. Patients are often expected to stay for a uniform and stated period of weeks. Groups are likely to be held once or twice each day, perhaps with an elected group leader and with each new patient making a formal presentation of his life story. Regular family groups may also be organized. The AA influence will be strong, with attendance at AA often obligatory – patients may be regularly bussed-out to AA meetings in the locality. In addition to this general programme there may be an element of didactic teaching on the nature of alcoholism, aided by the showing of films, social skill or assertiveness training groups, and added individual psychotherapy or pastoral counselling.

THE MULTI-PURPOSE SPECIALIZED ALCOHOLISM UNIT

The style here is more rough-and-tumble. Admission policies are almost the opposite of the traditional psychotherapy unit: patients with 'uncomplicated' alcoholism will be treated in the out-patient clinic, while presence of underlying mental illness will be taken as a criterion for admission. Although all the patients who are admitted share in common the problem of alcoholism, the ward will have many of the characteristics of a busy general psychiatric unit. The staff will, for instance, commonly be treating underlying depressive illness or phobic states, making the differential diagnosis on a puzzling psychotic illness, offering admission for detoxification, or carrying out full assessment for potential brain damage. With such varied tasks there can be no fixed length of stay, and length of admission is determined by individual needs. Similarly, although there is likely to be a minimal basic timetabling of ward activities (some group meeetings, an occupational therapy programme, and so on), the programme for each patient must of necessity be more individually designed.

Within this perspective the unit provides a *phase* of care, and one to be recommended for a minority of carefully selected patients. The in-patient unit is the discriminatingly used back-up resource for out-patient, day care and community services, but it is not the centre of all activity.

Which of these models is to be preferred? Do they compete or has each its place? Different clinicians would give different answers. That the general in-patient unit should be capable of dealing with many patients with drinking problems has already been stated, and also that this style of care needs to be developed and strengthened. Some experts might dispute this and favour all-out specialism, but that extreme position would today be unusual. More often it would be agreed that there is a place for generalism as well as specialism in the treatment of alcoholism, and the debate would centre more on the model of specialism which is to be preferred.

What relative favour should be given to the development of specialized in-patient units of the psychotherapy type, as opposed to the multi-pupose style? There is no doubt that many countries (and especially perhaps the private care sectors in those countries) have heavily invested in the former – the fixed treatment period, the relatively programmed, psychotherapeutically oriented and AA influenced model. Such an approach had its historical determinants in a belief in the dominantly psychodynamic nature and genesis of the disorder which was being treated. The model was borrowed from a once popular fashion for in-patient 'neurosis units' and from the therapeutic community movement, as well as having more distant roots in the nineteenth century and the medico-moral treatment of the insane. Research evidence does not support the overall worth of intensive psychotherapeutic in-patient programmes, however, and as scientific understanding of the condition continuously evolves, so logically should the model of treatment which is to be employed, for otherwise our treatments will reflect institutional entropy rather than the best understanding of patient needs. Without in any way seeking heedlessly and precipitously to dismantle what may be the total or larger part of therapeutic operations in many countries, and certainly without brashly discounting the very considerably worth of what has been learnt from running psychotherapy units of this type, it could be argued that *evolution* must now be towards a more multi-purpose style of operation.

The remainder of this chapter focuses therefore on treatment within the general psychiatric setting or in the specialized multi-purpose alcohol unit. Considerations in relation to those two settings largely overlap, and the admission criteria are for instance nearly identical. Rather than repeatedly phrasing the discussion so as to draw out any similarities or differences between work in the two settings, it will be assumed that when direct reference is made to the workings of the specialized unit, by inference and with a little modification such statements can usually be made directly applicable to the general psychiatric ward.

THE MULTI-PURPOSE UNIT AND CRITERIA FOR IN-PATIENT ADMISSION

Whether a patient should be admitted to an in-patient facility or treated without being pulled out of his natural setting is a testing everyday clinical question. The pressures to admit from professional colleagues, from the patient's family, and from the patient himself can be extreme. There may be anxiety that not to do so is a denial of the patient's right to treatment, which will result in damage to his health or to the family's well-being, and may even carry risks of violence or suicide. However, unless the therapist assumes that diagnosis of a drinking problem automatically implies offer of admission to hospital, the responsibility to exercise clinical judgement and discrimination is inescapable.

Before admission is agreed the question should always be asked as to why in this particular case taking the patient into hospital will be more beneficial than patient, family and therapist working together in the natural environment. There is a skill in learning how to make this decision carefully and in the patient's best interests, rather than being blown off course by outside pressures or by the therapist's own anxiety. Such decisions can often usefully be discussed in a staff group, not only to arrive at the best decision on the immediate case but also to share learning processes. It is the more inexperienced, less confident or less well-supported therapist who most easily succumbs to unwarranted pressures and agrees to an inappropriate admission. Sometimes a quick decision has to be made, and insistence on a rational admissions policy does not mean procrastination in the face of manifest danger. Usually, though, there is time for a more leisured appraisal, and it may sometimes be useful to envisage a few weeks (or even months) of working with patient and family before a decision is made.

Listed under headings below are some of the issues which may affect the admission decision. The list is certainly not exhaustive.

DETOXIFICATION

The grounds which determine the setting for detoxification have already been discussed in Chapter 13, and all that need be said here in recapitulation is that most patients can be detoxified as out-patients, while some patients very definitely require the cover of the ward setting.

ADMISSION 'FOR TREATMENT OF ALCOHOLISM'

It is essential for the sake of patients, staff and referral agencies that this central aspect of policy should be explicit. As already stated, there are differing views as to whether diagnosis of a serious drinking problem by itself constitutes grounds for admission. The psychotherapy unit is likely to admit patients on that simple basis. But within the perspective of the multi-purpose unit, patients should not be admitted just 'for treatment of alcoholism'. The proper place to treat the uncomplicated case is in the community.

What then should be done for the patient who fails to respond to out-patient care? Admission to the ward on the grounds that nothing else has worked may be indicative of an out-patient service which is not being properly developed, supported and supervised. The fact that a patient is 'not doing well' may be exactly the occasion for challenging him to examine his commitment, an occasion for rethinking goals and methods, or a time for re-examining the family's role and involvement. Putting the patient into hospital may destroy the therapeutic opportunity, and may be a retreat both by patient and therapist from true engagement in the therapeutic process.

ADMISSION FOR ASSESSMENT

There are occasions when a patient should be admitted primarily for purposes of assessment, but these largely relate to questions of underlying mental or physical illness. It is a misuse of resources to admit a patient for general assessment of his problems, who could be assessed equally well or better as an out-patient or on a home visit. Such unnecessary admissions again tend to result if out-patient clinics are understaffed and resources concentrated on the ward – the staff member working by himself in a late-evening clinic all too easily feels he 'hasn't got time for a proper work-up', and puts the patient on the admission list. Once a patient is in hospital, assessement based on how he behaves on a ward or in a group is valuable (p. 272), but it is no substitute for the view based on how that patient behaves at home or at work, in the real-life setting.

UNDERLYING ILLNESS

A patient may have to be admitted for diagnosis and treatment of underlying mental or physical illness, and the handling of underlying or accompanying mental illness is indeed a very important function of an in-patient unit which is working in support of a busy out-patient service.

RISK OF SUICIDE

This heading is partly related to that of 'underlying illness' – the patient who is suffering from depression may clearly be at risk of suicide – but the problem is wider than that. A patient who is drinking excessively but is not suffering from depressive illness in any formal sense may nonetheless be at risk of, or threatening, suicide. The skill has to be learnt of differentiating between the threat which is empty and manipulative and the threat, even muted, which should be taken as a serious warning. The patient's circumstances (his social support, the pressures on him) have to be taken into account, as well as his mental state. The issues being raised here certainly involve some of the most difficult decisions which the therapist is called on to make. Taking the patient into hospital in the wrong circumstances may itself convey to him a message of hoplessness and reinforce the damaging idea that he cannot be held responsible for his own behaviour.

VIOLENCE AND THREATS OF VIOLENCE

Here again it is necessary to operate in terms of careful individual case assessment rather than by any rule of thumb. Violence is all too common a consequence of excessive drinking, and emergency admission may therefore sometimes be needed to relieve a dangerous situation, whether the threat is of violence between husband and wife or of assault on the children. But it has to be realized that on occasion hospital admission is no more than a deceptively easy and inadequate resolution of the real danger. The alcoholic husband goes into hospital, the danger is temporarily relieved, the wife drops the thought of separation or court protection, and the husband then goes home from hospital only for the violence suddenly and dangerously to be renewed. The cycle may be repeated, with admissions each time enabling the wife to avoid painful and necessary decisions.

Sometimes, therefore, the therapist may have to confront the threatened wife with the fact that she has to decide whether she will tolerate the violence or seek the protection which the courts rather than medicine provide. Such dangerous family situations can be extremely worrying, and great sensitivity is required in their handling. Hospital admission of the alcoholic partner (perhaps under a temporary compulsory order) may certainly have to be entertained as an option, but so, alternatively, has the possibility of rapidly getting the threatened wife into a women's shelter or away to relatives, or of her being put in touch with a lawyer. No neat formula will meet the case where the wife has five children and her Catholic faith makes breakdown of marriage particularly hard to accept, while her drunken and pathologically jealous husband refuses to obey any court injunction – and the wife's ambivalence makes her reluctant to have that injunction enforced.

LACK OF SOCIAL SUPPORT

If a patient is living in solitary lodgings and has no contact with friends or relations, can he be expected to deal with his drinking problem from that base, or is his social situation by itself an indication for admission? There may be occasions when extreme social isolation seems to argue in favour of in-patient treatment (a man sleeping under a railway arch), but in general these are gounds to be resisted. The patient who is admitted in such circumstances has after some weeks either to return to exactly the same environment, or the attempt has to be made while he is in hospital to improve the quality of his social support. That attempt often seems to lack impetus and to be enormously protracted once the patient is in hospital, and it may therefore be better to work with the patient within the reality of his own street and his own resources, with the expectation and invitation that if he stops drinking he will then be able by small steps to ameliorate his social situation.

But when the patient has become chronically homeless and is leading a skid-row existence, a short hospital admission may be needed for detoxification, followed by placement in a hostel or half-way house. Even the skid-row patient may, though, be able to come off alcohol with the help of daytime support and visits to a shop-front agency, and with the reinforcement of his knowing that if he stops drinking a hostel place will be available.

HOSPITAL ADMISSION AND THE COURTS

When a patient or his lawyers are pressing for hospital admission, the team must as ever respond as best as possible to individual needs, but hospital staff must in these circumstances be particularly careful not to be edged into an offer which is inappropriate. There is the familiar situation where, prior to the court hearing (and perhaps without it being admitted that court proceedings are in the offing), the patient tries to get into hospital in the belief that the judge will take a lenient view of someone who is hospitalized and 'sick'. On the other hand, the threat of a forthcoming trial may sometimes turn the patient toward a genuine willingness to accept help. But all the facts and motivations need to be in the open, and there is no therapeutic gain in an admission which is being contrived simply to dress up the defence plea.

Where, however, a psychiatric opinion has been properly sought by the lawyer for the defence and the history suggests that the offence was alcohol-related (perhaps with previous offences of the same nature), there may then be grounds for recommending treatment as an alternative to punitive disposal. Again, though, a recommendation for treatment need not be for in-patient care, and the psychiatrist should seek to keep his options for the handling of the case as open as possible, rather than being tied by the terms of the court's order.

Particularly difficult questions arise if the patient has a history of violence or other serious crime and the court believes that the need to protect society can only be met if the patient is admitted to hospital and held there under compulsory provision. If a violent patient is mentally ill, then secure hospital admission may of course have to be offered, whatever the drinking problem. An alcoholism treatment centre is unlikely to be the right place for the patient to be held, since it is improbable that such a centre could meet the court's expectations of custodial security.

So much for a review of some of the factors which bear on the decision whether or not to admit to an in-patient unit. In the section that follows we look at the workings of the unit and some of the issues which commonly arise once the patient is admitted. Again, many of those issues bear as much on the treatment of the alcoholic on the general psychiatric ward as in the specialized multi-purpose unit.

THE WORKINGS OF A MULTI-PURPOSE IN-PATIENT UNIT

GENERAL PSYCHIATRIC CARE

The multi-purpose alcoholism unit must not let its specialism lead to neglect of general psychiatric expertise. The nature of the problems with which it deals demands that it should function as a highly proficient general unit with added expertise in alcoholism, rather than as an over-specialized alcoholism centre with general psychiatric team skills neglected. The nurses must, for instance, know how to make out a general nursing plan for each patient, how to use relationships and act in a therapeutic role, how to deal with ward and group dynamics, how to record observations, how to nurse the ill or disturbed or suicidal patient, and how to head off or deal with violence or acting-out behaviour. The staff need to be very aware of the possible physical aspects of excessive drinking, as well as the psychiatric and social aspects.

ADMISSION

Coming into hospital must be seen through the patient's eyes. He may be frightened and defensive, and he may be confused as to what to expect of this experience. If the staff team is itself uncertain as to why this patient has been taken into hospital or more generally unsure as to the purpose of the unit, then confusion will be compounded.

To avert these muddles, before admission there should be discussion with the patient and between the staff as to the purposes and expectations of this hospitalization, and the family as well as the patient need to be clear about them. If there are rules which the patient is to observe, then these should be spelled out, and it may be helpful to have routine written notes which explain the unit's methods of working. When the patient arrives on the ward he should be personally welcomed by staff and by the patient group, and not left to feel a stranger.

ADMISSION FOR DETOXIFICATION

If a patient's degree of dependence is such that in-patient care is required for his detoxification, a multi-pupose unit should be able to cope, unless the physical dangers are such that the patient would be more appropriately treated on a medical ward. (The management of detoxification has been discussed in Chapter 13.)

To have a ward policy that some patients are admitted 'just for detoxification' (with a few beds especially reserved for this purpose), while the remainder of the patients are admitted for 'other purposes', is to make a too absolute division. If the aim is to offer relatively brief admission for detoxification, then the admission should not be allowed to drag on, but if in the event other needs become manifest, these must be met. It is therefore more useful to set up the ward so that detoxification is one of the activities it can competently perform, but without detoxification becoming an over compartmentalized function.

ASSESSMENT

The basics of assessment, which of course involve the family as well as the patient, are the same whether the setting is the out-patient clinic or the ward (see Chapter 9 and 10), but the in-patient setting also gives the opportunity for ward observation. Here the nursing staff have a special part to play and the routine recording of nursing notes is essential. Observations on interaction in patient groups can be helpful, and an occupational therapist's assessment of task functioning and skills in social interaction is also valuable. There are circumstances where it is useful to supplement clinical observation by the use of rating scales, or where patients may complete self-ratings. For instance, withdrawal symptoms should routinely be rated, and if a patient is suffering from depression, his own ratings of mood will enable his response to treatment to be monitored.

FORMULATION, GOAL-SETTING AND DESIGN OF THE INDIVIDUAL PROGRAMME

The general principles involved here have been discussed in earlier chapters. Very briefly, patient and staff need to know what the admission is about, and the task is to move towards a carefully thought out patient-specific therapeutic programme. There is nothing less helpful than leaving the patient to sit in a corner of the day-room and wonder why he is there. Time and opportunity must not be wasted.

POSSIBLE CONTENT OF THE INDIVIDUAL PROGRAMME

Everything which is discussed in other chapters of this book and which bears on the treatment of the individual patient is potentially relevant to this heading. The list of items given below is therefore by no means exhaustive (several of these ideas are taken up again later in this section), and the purpose here it to emphasize the range of skills, resources and working liaisons which should be available in planning the individual programme:

Detoxification

Treatment of physical complications or referral for expert medical opinion

Treatment of underlying or accompanying mental illness

Education as to the nature of the drinking problem, and basic work on goal-setting and achievement of goals

Psychotherapy within appropriate limits

Behavioural treatments of the drinking problem

Introduction to and understanding of AA

Exploration of family problems

Preparation of plans for social rehabilitation: work assessment, job finding, hostel placement

REMEMBERING THE FAMILY

In the in-patient unit the patient is obviously removed from his home environment, and attention is focused on his behaviour on the ward, in groups or in occupational therapy, in a way which may tend accidentally to reinforce this abstraction – the spouse and children are mentioned in the notes but are not part of the immediate scene. This neglect of the family may be sensed as very real by the family itself; they may feel alienated and excluded, and angrily take the position that the patient is having a rest-cure while they are left to soldier on. Neglect of the family is good neither for the patient nor for the rest of the family. The degree and type of family involvement which should be aimed at is in most essentials no different than in the out-patient setting, but some special features have to be borne in mind.

First there is quite simply the need for continued contact with the family, and an explanation of what is being aimed at on the ward. The spouse needs, for instance, to know what drinking goal has been chosen, and the logic which determines the choice, and she needs to know how long the hospital stay will continue, and why. There is then often a need to help the spouse explore her positive role in aiding recovery, with discussion of how she will manage the weekend leaves or prepare for the patient's discharge. A spouse who has for years been battling with the patient's drinking may feel lost and resentful if she now feels that she is left without a role.

Another possible development is that the temporary separation and relief of stress allows the wife to discover her own feelings and her own anger, so that she now suddenly brings herself actively to consider separation or divorce. She 'does not want to go through it all again'. Those feelings have got to be met. Rather than furtive plans being made for an injunction to prevent the husband from re-entering the house (with the ward staff being privy to secret moves which they are forbidden to reveal), it is best to arrange that husband and wife come together for open discussion of these problems, however difficult the business to be discussed.

RULES, EXPECTATIONS, CONTRACTS AND WARD ATMOSPHERE

An in-patient unit is a complex little society, and if it is without an explicit and agreed structure for its members' guidance, the therapeutic work cannot be done, and staff and patients will be under constant and needless strain. Limits must be visible. On the other hand, the extreme has to be avoided of a rigid, proliferated set of rules that turns the place into a barracks. Such a society largely works best (and learns most) by making the exploration of its own woking part of the positive business of therapy, and thus turning difficulty to advantage. It is unlikely that a busy multi-purpose unit can operate as a therapeutic community in the full and conventional sense, but the principles of such an approach are very relevant.

Experience suggests that an explicit rule is needed in regard to drinking, or things fall apart. There is however, a difference between setting up a ward structure in terms of rules which are seen as arbitrarily and externally imposed (and therefore to be defied) and rules which are seen as shared, rational, necessary and to be supported. Patients should be admitted on the understanding that they will not drink, either on the ward or while on leave, without prior permission. (The problem set by having mixed drinking goals among patients on the same ward is discussed below (p. 277).

It should ordinarily be agreed that if a patient then drinks without permission he will be discharged. Help can continue in the out-patient setting. Breath testing or urine testing may sometimes be necessary when there is suspicion that a patient is drinking but actively denying it, and such measures should be acceptable if their purpose is discussed with the patient group. The enforcement of such a seemingly harsh and rejecting rule can sometimes give rise to anxiety, but if the rule is endlessly bent the ward becomes very difficult to operate, and both staff and patients may become very insecure. That disscharge is purposely being used as a sanction is not to be fudged or denied, but it is emotionally truthful to insist that this policy is not in essence punitive. It is aimed to help the individual (as well as to protect the ward community) and may have a very positive therapeutic effect. The patient must be challenged to accept responsibility for himself.

On occasion there may, however, be a patient who drinks but who cannot safely be discharged (the depressed or suicidal person for instance), and staff and patients have to understand a variation of the rule in this case. Rules and expectations are for the guidance and support of the community, and not for blind imposition, but unless the particular circumstances are talked through, there may be a feeling that someone is being shown unfair favouritism and 'being allowed to get away with it'. If the depressed patient who has been drinking stays on the ward, it calls for very adequate nursing supervision to ensure that the drinking does not continue.

Another rule which must be made evident is that patients do not use any drugs other than those prescribed. The situation goes out of control if a patient is bringing in his own supplies of benzodiazepines or barbiturates, or using illicit drugs. If a patient is known to have a history of drug-taking, or there is suspicion that he is taking drugs, random urine testing may be necessary. Persistence in taking unprescribed drugs can be as disruptive to the individual and the ward as covert drinking, and undermines any therapeutic works. Such behaviour may well therefore again be defined as grounds for discharge.

Sometimes the problem of how therapeutic momentum is to be maintained in the face of various other kinds of patient resistance or non-co-operation has to be tackled. Every ward of this kind goes through bad patches where staff and patients no longer seem to be working together, for instance, two or three patients may decide to play billiards rather than attend a group meeting. One solution to this is to make another explicit rule – that patients will attend groups on sanction of discharge. But if difficulties are always managed in this way the list of rules will soon proliferate to frightening length and staff will find themselves edged more and more into a policing rather than a therapeutic role. A better solution is to define the general expectation as being that patients will co-operate in their treatment, and to deal with individual problems as they arise. There may also be benefit in drawing up individual treatment contracts with some or all patients. And if patients are, for instance, reluctant to attend occupational therapy or are otherwise failing to co-operate, staff should be open to examination of whether what is being offered is really meeting patient needs.

To devote this amount of space to a discussion of what could be dismissed as petty and regulatory issues rather than the real stuff of therapy might be seen as disproportionate. But a unit has to build and maintain a ward atmosphere which is therapeutic, and which is neither too controlling (the fulfilment of a patient's worst fantasies of unfeeling authority) nor so lax and unsupporting as to lead to chaos. The maintenance of that atmosphere is a difficult, skilled and continuing task for patients and staff working together.

DRINKING GOALS AND NON-DRINKING GOALS

Until quite recently the traditional view of alcoholism as a unitary condition dictating a rigid and universal need for total abstinence gave cohesion and unity of purpose to any in-patient group: the patients were all there not to drink, and not to drink ever again. To run a ward on the basis of that type of strong consensus is easier than dealing with the tensions which arise when highly dependent patients who are aiming at abstinence are on a ward with less dependent patients who as part of their treatment schedule are practising controlled drinking. It seems likely that exposure to alcohol will increasingly be used in behavioural treatments of certain types of drinking problem, but can a satisfactory ward atmosphere really be maintained with some patients drinking in permitted fashion and others knowing that they face discharge if they take on drink? Or is unity of purpose in the drinking goal so fundamental that patients pursuing different goals should be segregated?

There is so far not enough experience confidently to answer these questions. A ward that accepts the possibility of mixed drinking goals will, at least at the beginning, encounter difficulties and tensions, especially if the staff are insecure in newer approaches. On the other hand, benefit may accrue from working through such difficulties if in the process drinking can be seen more accurately in terms of its bearing on varied individual problems, and thus is demystified. Mixed policies need not detract from the absoluteness of the message for the patient for whom the message is indeed absolute, and seeing other people drinking may be a therapeutically useful rehearsal of what will have to be met in the outside world.

GROUPS

As already stated, the model of in-patient care on which this section focuses is that of the multi-purpose rather than the dominantly psycho-therapeutic unit. It is difficult to run traditional and intensive psychotherapeutic groups with a heterogeneous patient population, with varied problems, different goals, a mixture of backgrounds and verbal skills, and no fixed length of stay. An important but revised place nonetheless remains for group work. Without such a daily forum the community will find difficulty in holding together; uncontrolled and potentially anti-therapeutic group processes will evolve and patients and staff will all too easily drift out of touch. Such groups are therefore in part for dealing with the small daily problems of living together, and the resolution of those problems is in itself an important contribution to therapy. The groups are also useful for education; information is given about the general nature of the problems with which patients are dealing, and the problems which any individual patient is encountering are usefully shared and discussed. Mutual support is a valuable function of such meetings. That behaviour at group meetings may contribute material to patient assessment has already been noted. The work of such an open group with multiple functions has to be developed and led, and what is being dealt with will change from week to week. Staff and patients must understand the purpose and limits of what is being attempted.

THE ROLE OF ALCOHOLICS ANONYMOUS

The general and very important contribution which is made by AA has been discussed in Chapter 15. There is a major failure in the in-patient unit if the opportunity is not taken to introduce patients while in hospital to the working of AA, in terms of individual AA members visiting the ward for informal contact or AA meetings being held on the ward, or patients being encouraged to visit local AA groups. What the multi-purpose unit does well to aim at is the availability of AA rather than an AA dominance. On such a basis of mutual understanding a valuable and friendly working relationship can be operated between AA, with its special therapeutic vision, and the multi-purpose unit, which has to be willing to work in many different ways.

AVOIDING OVER-MEDICATION

The general dangers of over-medicating patients who have drinking problems, and the risks of substitute addiction, must be constantly borne in mind. A patient has been rendered a disservice if he contracts a drug habit as the direct result of a lax ward policy on the prescription of sleeping tablets or tranquillizers, with the patient rashly discharged with an un-needed supply of these. Quite often a patient will be admitted who is very reliant on sedatives or tranquillizers although not formally dependent. He may be reluctant to reduce or eliminate his drug-taking, and he is likely to importune for supplies. No amount of pleading or manipulation should, however, move the staff into prescribing or continuing to prescribe drugs which are not properly needed. When a patient is discharged (and the discharge letter written to the doctor), a check should therefore be made that the patient has by then been weaned off all medication which is not definitely indicated.

GOING OUT ON LEAVE

Patients should as far as possible themselves carry responsibility for deciding when and how soon they go home for an evening visit or a weekend. It may be a sensible expectation that a patient will not go home until he has been settled on the ward for a week or so, and special considerations obviously apply when the patient is depressed or suicidal or in an obviously unstable state. Otherwise the exercise of personal responsibility for decision-making is to be positively encouraged and usefully talked through. A very restrictive policy is again a way of denying autonomy and it is demeaning for a patient to have to plead for a pass.

LENGTH OF STAY

Length of stay is determined by individual need and must therefore vary widely – from a few days for detoxification to the many months which may be needed adequately to treat a severe and resistant depressive illness. Patients should of course be discouraged from leaving prematurely, but unless there is manifest danger there should not be great argument and battle of wills if the patient goes against advice. He has a right to make his own decision and may be able to make a more informed assessment of his ability to cope than can another person. The greater danger is of a hospital stay being too prolonged because of purpose and momentum having been lost.

DISCHARGE AND FOLLOW-UP

Discharge can be difficult for a patient. He goes out to face his problems without the comfortable support of the ward, and the longer the patient has stayed in hospital the more difficult this becomes. Thought should therefore be given not only to the detailed practical arrangements but also to the emotional meaning and anxiety attached to this transition.

As to the practical planning of follow-up, this again needs to be individually determined. The phrase 'intensive follow-up' has come into fashion to describe the supposedly appropriate blanket level of after-care to be offered in all instances. Many patients will indeed need detailed planning as to how each part of a complex treatment programme is to be carried through, but in other instances more infrequent contact may be entirely appropriate. Whether follow-up is more or less intensive, there is benefit in continuity of therapist, which must imply that the same staff work in out-patient and in-patient settings. The person primarily responsible for the individual patient's after-care must be identified, and it may often be evident that a particular member of the team has formed a relationship which can usefully be continued.

READMISSION

Each assessment for admission must to an extent be examined as a question in its own right, and the state of affairs at that particular moment considered. But if the patient has previously been in hospital, a decision on readmission must be made in awareness of what was gained or learnt on previous occasions. There should be no automatic bar on readmission, and for instance a patient with an underlying episodic depressive illness may usefully be offered multiple admissions over the years, with admission heading off the likelihood of relapse into drinking. A patient who is very dependent on alcohol may do well for stretches of time, but when intermittently he relapses, he may need brief admission for detoxification in order to abort a drinking bout which might otherwise be much more damaging.

If a patient is developing a history of multiple admissions (to one or a sequence of hospitals), the reasons for this development deserve scrutiny. Multiple admissions may be serving a good purpose, but on the other hand one bad decision may be piled on another. A policy of ill-judged multiple admissions, which is witness to the unit blowing before every breeze rather than ever confronting the patient constructively, breeds a sort of institutionalization by instalments.

USE OF THE WARD FOR DAY-CARE

A multi-purpose ward may also usefully offer day-care for some patients, either as a half-way stage towards full return to the community or as a substitute for admission. Day-care can be an important adjunct to the total range of helping facilities. Those patients who are coming on a daily basis should be able to function with the in-patients as one community, and it is necessary to apply the same rules and expectations. To have a day-patient dropping in only casually, with no planned programme and with the suspicion that he is drinking or taking drugs, is helpful to no one. If day-care is to be integrated within the unit's function it must be with forethought and purpose.

THE MULTI-PURPOSE IN-PATIENT UNIT AS BASE FOR PROFESSIONAL EDUCATION

Anyone who comes to work on such a unit should be given opportunities not only to give but also to learn about alcoholism and about multi-disciplinary team-work with alcoholism. Although the immediate concern of that ward is drinking problems, what can be learnt is more general: the skills, sensitivities and confident drawing of limits which make it possible to build and maintain a therapeutically constructive ward atmosphere. If people can learn to work successfully on such a ward at group and at individual level, they should certainly have learnt much both about group processes and the formulation and actualization of planned individual care. Learning goes on in staff groups and at case presentations, but also much more informally.

The only danger is if those engaged in this experience forget that the ward teaches only about the in-patient phase of care. It is easy for students to be attached to an in-patient unit, for visitors to come and see the arrangement of its rooms and attend a case conference. It is a betrayal of education if the seductiveness of team-work on that ward then leads the young nurse, social worker, psychologist, occupational therapist or doctor to sink back in an armchair in the group room and forget the world outside. That is a message to be remembered at all times, and the context within which to interpret this whole chapter.

REFERENCES

Glatt MM (1955) A treatment centre for alcoholics in a public mental hospital: its establishment and its working. *British Journal of Addiction,* **52,** 55–89.

Schukit MA (1979) Inpatient and residential approaches to the treatment of alcoholism. In: Mendelson JH and Mello NK (eds) *Diagnosis and Treatment of Alcoholism*, pp 258–282. New York: McGraw Hill.

Smith CM and Sommerfield EJ (1968) Managing alcoholics on an open psychiatric ward. *Quarterly Journal of Studies on Alcohol*, **29**, 703–708.

Welt J, Hynes G, Solmalow L *et al* (1981) Effect of length of stay in inpatient alcoholism treatment on outcome. *Journal of Studies on Alcohol*, **42**, 483–491.

Willems PJA, Letemendia FJJ and Arroyave F (1973) A two-year follow-up study comparing short with long stay inpatient treatment of alcoholics. *British Journal of Psychiatry*, **112**, 637–648.

Chapter 19
Organization of
Treatment Services

This chapter begins with a consideration of some general principles in the organization of alcoholism treatment. This is followed by a discussion, under headings, of a number of different types of treatment settings and treatment facilities. The intention is to provide a check-list and an outline of ideas, and the discussion is of necessity not detailed. No one organizational formula is appropriate, and much will depend on local resources, experience and habits of administration.

Health care planning is to many people a boring subject. It involves questions which we would often happily leave to yet another working party, while we ourselves get on with treating the next patient. The organization of services in order to help people with drinking problems more effectively is, however, profoundly important, and it is self-indulgent to rest content with efforts in our own parish, if in our city or stretch of country the majority of alcoholics who need help find no help available. The community requires services which are truly matched to its real and multiple needs as much as the patient requires individual treatment based on accurate assessment of his needs. In many localities treatment for alcoholism has grown piecemeal, with a review now very timely.

GENERAL PRINCIPLES

A RANGE OF RESPONSES FOR A DIVERSITY OF PROBLEMS AND A MULTIPLICITY OF INDIVIDUALS

The prime reason why the alcoholism treatment response cannot be allowed to be narrowed into any one mould (only in-patient units, only specialized services, only an AA orientation, or only anything else) is – as has been stressed repeatedly in this book – that the problems set by excessive drinking are vastly diverse. The job of providing help cannot be done well by, for example, by setting up one prestigious and specialized centre in one corner of the town. To reach people in need, help needs to be available at the primary level of health and social care, within the general hospitals, at the work place, and in many other settings and situations. The front-line of help for drinking problems should be available where people ordinarily go for help with their general health and social problems. A geographical area with a well-developed treatment response to alcoholism will rely on the skills and interests of all manner of generalists who are already in position within the community's health and social services, and this front-line must be backed by a range of more special agencies.

PLANNING AND INTEGRATION

Given that treatment must be characterized by variety and flexibility, the danger is always present that some aspect of the total scheme will be neglected or that a duplicate facility is set up. At worst no one is informed as to what others are doing, and the working liaison which could ensure that the right person reaches the most appropriate facility does not exist. A working party and a planning exercise at the community level is therefore often what is needed. The plan will not work perfectly and will soon be in need of updating, but it is the process of planning – the exercise itself, people getting to know each other – which is often highly productive. Planning has of course to place alcoholism treatment within the wider context of general and specialized services for other problems, and the most perfect co-ordination between all those engaged in alcoholism treatment will by itself be worthless if alcoholism treatment becomes isolated.

COMMUNITY PERSPECTIVE

From what has already been said, the position which is being taken here is clearly that dealing with drinking problems is a community endeavour. The word 'community' as used in health planning may sometimes and rightly be attacked by the sceptic as modish and often empty of meaning, but at best the organization of alcoholism treatment should lead to a rediscovery and confirmation of what 'community' means. Service planning has to be related to a defined geographical area, although there also has to be regional and national planning. Planning involves the mobilization of community resources more than the creation of new facilities. The attitudes of every person in the community to drinking (what counts as a problem, and what we can helpfully say to the person with a problem) will determine whether the planned resources are effectively utilized. There is therefore an important place for public education and community activism, which is often usefully carried forward by local councils on alcoholism and other community organizations. The fact that help is available has to be widely known, and any stigma removed.

FAMILIES AS WELL AS INDIVIDUALS

That drinking problems more often affect a family than the individual alone is again a position which has been stressed at various points in this book. Treatment has therefore to be a response to family as well as individual needs, and although everyone would no doubt applaud that sentiment, to translate sentiment into positive action is not so easy. Every agency does well to ask itself how this expectation is being met.

SUPPORTING THE HELPERS

If people who help with drinking problems are not supported and their needs to develop skills are not met, they will be much at risk of finding that what should be a very rewarding endeavour loses its reward. The problem of professional 'burn out' is well known in this field. How support and education are to be managed is once more a matter for local determination, but the meeting of these needs is not to be treated as a luxury. Lunch-time meetings, support groups, seminars and visits to other facilities have to be arranged at the local level, and staff should be seconded to training courses and summer schools.

SOME ELEMENTS WITHIN A TOTAL TREATMENT RESPONSE

DEVELOPMENT OF HELP AT THE LEVEL OF PRIMARY HEALTH AND SOCIAL CARE

What is meant by the 'primary care worker' must vary from setting to setting. In the Third World it may mean the medical auxiliary or barefoot doctor, the traditional healer, the priest or the political officer, and in those countries there is an awareness of the vital need to build on these resources rather than to put money and hope into expensive new health emporia and specialist training. And this Third World awareness has an important lesson for health planning in the urbanized West, where the question is how the resources offered by the family medical practitioner, the borough social worker, the community nurse, the health visitor, the clergy, and the street-corner pharmacist who dispenses hangover remedies are to be mobilized in the treatment of alcohol-related problems. The role of specialist agencies should increasingly be seen as aiding and abetting these primary resources, rather than the specialist centres taking everything to themselves and proclaiming a message which undermines the confidence of the primary level worker. Education, support, consultation and encouragement should for instance make the general practitioner expert in dealing with alcohol problems within his practice. Within that context he is the expert in early case detection, in giving an alcohol problem an unstigmatized place within a patients general health and life-style, in the good use of a few minutes' talk, in confrontation and the giving of hope, in the real meaning of the family perspective.

SERVICES OF GENERAL HOSPITALS

Alcohol problems will present in every department of the general hospital – in emergency, surgical, medical, and obstetric departments and in the whole range of specialized units. The needs are threefold: a heightened *awareness* of alcohol problems (and better history-taking); a competence to *treat and advise;* an understanding of *when and how to make referrals*. Here is a cautionary tale which illustrates the sort of consequences which may not uncommonly be expected if awareness is not cultivated.

> In the course of an epidemiological study of a general medical ward, a consultant physician declared that 'he never saw alcoholism'. There was on that day a patient on his ward, admitted for treatment of a bleeding ulcer, who was rapidly going into delirium tremens. The notes showed no evidence whatsoever of enquiry into the patient's drinking history, and a look at further case-notes showed that on that treatment service it was quite exceptional to ask about a patient's drinking.

To see drinking problems you have to look for them. Interesting experiments have been made in setting up alcohol problem clinics within general hospitals. Such clinics can foster useful liaison between psychiatric and medical staff, and serve to heighten awareness.

GENERAL SERVICES OF PSYCHIATRIC HOSPITALS

General units in psychiatric hospitals ought usually to be able to deal with drinking problems, whether on an in-patient or out-patient basis (see Chapter 18). There can be no doubt that staff in general psychiatric facilities are not sufficiently aware of drinking problems and that it is not only in the medical or surgical wards that such problems are overlooked. General psychiatric staff often admit to a feeling of 'not knowing what to do with the alcoholic', and to improve this situation may require very definite teaching. A psychiatric hospital, with its out-patient, in-patient and day-patient services, has a very important contribution to make to alcoholism treatment, and these capabilities must be fully developed.

SPECIALIZED SERVICES

The antithesis of an effective community-involved alcoholism treatment service is the specialized facility, which has a catchment area so wide that adequate follow-up is impossible, which ensures that patients with concomitant physical and mental illness are excluded and only severe cases of alcohol dependence admitted, and which consults with other services only to reject or take over the case. Few specialized centres today resemble that caricature, but we should heed the warning.

What a specialized service can offer is determined by its staff resources, the range of its facilities and the strength of its liaisons. The staffing must be multi-disciplinary and welded into a team, and there is likely to be constant debate as to how each team member should best deploy his specialist skills while also operating at a more general level. Nurse, social worker, medical doctor (psychiatrist or physician), clinical psychologist, occupational therapist and volunteer are some of the obvious contributors. Facilities are likely to include out-patient clinics (with opportunity for rapid consultation), and a multi-purpose in-patient unit. There should be a close working relationship with organizations which can offer half-way house accommodation, as an essential part of the total range of facilities. Further liaisons must be, on the one hand, with a range of specialized assessment and consultation facilities, whose resources should vary from X-ray or laboratory investigation, remedial help with reading difficulties and pastoral counselling to advice on sexual problems and difficulties and pastoral counselling to advice on sexual problems and dentistry. On the other hand liaisons are needed with other agencies which are the skills here would be, for instance, knowing how to offer the general practitioner a useful opinion on a case or how to hand that case back to GP care, and knowing when the patient must quickly be taken on by the specialized service.

The degree to which special services for drinking problems should be integrated with services for drug problems – the 'combined approach' as promulgated by the World Health Organization (WHO) – is another question to which there can be no formula answer. Ideas developed in one sector must be relevant to ideas in the other and patients themselves do not respect any substance boundaries. There are many alcoholics with drug problems and a significant proportion of drug addicts will also have used alcohol excessively either before, during or subsequent to their drug involvement. Such facts certainly point to a need for co-operation, but not necessarily to a forced marriage of services. A middle-aged patient with opiate dependence may, for instance, usefully be admitted to an alcoholism treatment unit, and a young patient with a drinking problem be given a place in a drug-free therapeutic community. But in many countries the differences in age and subculture will mean that the bulk of addicts and alcoholics require different treatment responses, and at the specialized level separateness with co-operation will be more in tune with patient needs than a combined service. Indeed, an over-emphasis on the 'combined approach' may serve to throw alcohol and drug services together at the cost of neglecting the much more important need for treatment of any substance to be 'combined' with general health and social services.

A substance problem which must not be neglected by an alcoholism treatment service is cigarette smoking. Many alcoholics are also heavy smokers. There is a temptation to excuse the patient who has dealt with his drinking from then thinking about his smoking; to suggest that the latter habit should also be tackled may seem too great a demand, with heavy smoking tacitly accepted as a necessary crutch. Some patients may indeed be unwilling or unable to contemplate a follow-through to an attack on smoking, but when the work on the drinking problem has been consolidated they should at least be offered the opportunity of help with their cigarette smoking. Skills in dealing with nicotine addiction may be developed as an ancillary within the alcoholism service, or it may again be a matter of establishing a liaison – a working relationship with an anti-smoking clinic.

TREATMENT ORGANIZATION WITHIN THE WORK SETTING

There has been interest over recent years in the mutual benefits to the employer and to the alcoholic employee which can result from the organization of work-place alcoholism programmes. For the employer such a programme means that ambiguities over what count as disciplinary and health problems are removed so that otherwise confusing issues can be handled without friction, that people in need can be reached early rather than their problems being covered up, and that valuable members of the work-force can often be returned to full functioning rather than lost by dismissal or premature retirement. In cash terms, the investment in setting up the programme is thus likely to pay ample dividends. From the employee's viewpoint there are manifest benefits from a routing towards help rather than a merely disciplinary response. The minimal necessary elements in such a programme are as follows:

1   An overt statement of policy on drinking problems – the rules of the game. This has to be agreed between trade union and employer representatives, understood by all parties and widely communicated. It is likely to be based on a clear definition of the terms on which help will be offered, with an explicit and mutual contract. For example, the response may be in terms of treatment rather than disciplinary handling, subject to review after six months, and provided the employee co-operates with treatment. There may be ancillary agreements on sick leave and protection of earnings.

2   There must be stated responsibility within the organization for implementing and monitoring the programme. This may for instance lie with the personnel officer, or with the personnel officer in conjunction with the firm's medical officer.

3   Help must be readily available, either through the organization's own medical and welfare system or through agreed methods of referral.

4   Questions of confidentiality must be defined and ethical issues dealt with carefully. If, as is likely, medical reports are at some stage to be made available to personnel who will potentially be involved in making de-

cisions affecting the individual's employment, this should be made clear at the beginning and agreement obtained in writing.

Such programmes have become common in North America, and in the UK there has been increasing interest in their development. Similar programmes have been set up for military establishments. Special education packages have been designed to aid the setting-up of work-place programmes.

TREATMENT ORGANIZATION RELATED TO COURTS AND PRISONS

A considerable proportion of people coming before the courts will be suffering from a drinking problem. Every effort should be made to organize resources so that the forensic presentation can, whenever appropriate, be a routing towards constructive help rather than mere punishment. As with work-place programmes there is a confluence of interests. It is in society's interests if effective treatment decreases the risk of recidivism or relieves overcrowding in prisons. And it is certainly in the individual's interests if he can be steered towards treatment rather than put through a process which may either achieve nothing, or worse still further destroy his social stability and reinforce his deviance. There are again, however, some ethical questions which deserve scrutiny. Treatment must not be allowed to become a synonym for restrictions on liberty by another name.

The four most usual issues that then have to be dealt with in this area are as follows:

(i) Organization of treatment services as an alternative to criminal handling of the drunkenness offender (the public inebriate).

This question overlaps with organization of services for the homeless alcoholic (p. 292), and with the functioning of detoxification centres (p. 294). In many countries there has been a realization that the 'revolving door' response to the drunkenness offender is ineffective and costly. There is little merit in fining a man or sentencing him to brief imprisonment for his hundredth drunkenness offence, when he has already been similarly punished on ninety-nine previous occasions without benefit to anyone. Various experiments have been made in different countries to mount a more constructive response: the street drunk being taken to a detoxification centre rather than a police cell, 'court probated' treatment with disulfiram taken under strict supervision, sentence to a farm community or semi-open setting where needs can be assessed and rehabilitation initiated, and so on. Whatever the local organizational solution, there should be an effective liaison between local courts and local skid-row or specialized alcoholism agencies, so that support can be given to the probation service and to court welfare officers, and screening and referral procedures evolved.

(ii) Organization of treatment response to the drunken driver

Here again there is an opportunity which should not be wasted for routing towards help. By no means every person who is arrested on such a charge is involved in serious excessive drinking or experiencing a wide range of alcohol-related problems. To mandate that everyone on a drunk driving charge should be referred to a therapeutic service is therefore inappropriate, but help should be on offer and a special approach made to those people most obviously in need of help.

(iii) The general problem of alcoholism and crime: treatment as alternative to punishment

The many different types of offence in which drinking may be implicated and the complexities of the drink/crime relationship have been discussed in Chapter 4. Besides help for the public inebriate or the drunk driving offender, what has treatment organization to offer for general alcohol-related crime as an alternative to punishment? No one suggests that a drinking problem should automatically mean the deflection of ordinary legal processes, while neither can it seriously be argued that the courts should ignore the possible implications of a drink problem. There has to be a middle way, with help offered in appropriate instances, and as always the organization of a subtle and appropriate response is far more difficult than a formula. The need is to educate judiciary and lawyers so that they think more often in terms of the treatment alternative, for more social workers and psychiatrists experienced in this sort of court problem (and able to provide practical and intelligible reports), and for treatment services which are willing to take court-referred cases. Treatment may be undertaken on the basis of 'probation with condition of treatment' or with some other leverage, or without court-imposed treatment conditions but with the court's knowledge and approval of treatment arrangements. Alternatively, probation may entail that the help is primarily provided by the probation officer, who then arranges any additional referrals as necessary.

Intoxication as a defence in terms of inability to form intent or of diminished responsibility gives rise to elegant legal argument (see page 75). But the large and daily business of the court centres much more on the undramatic question of what to do with the offender who has admitted his guilt or been found guilty, and where the social enquiry or submitted medical reports convincingly suggest that drinking is a factor in the offence.

(iv) Treatment organization within prisons

Many people who are admitted to prison as a result of an offence directly related to a major drinking problem will still receive no help for that problem. There is again a need for education, awareness and appropriate routing. Some prisons have experimented with setting up special alcoholism units. AA holds meetings in many prisons, and a degree of individual counselling may be available. There is, though, a limit to what can be achieved even by intensive efforts when the individual is not able to test any outside reality and when the release date still seems a long way off, but even in those circumstances a timely therapeutic intervention may aid reorientation and reinforce hope and determination.

The vital further task is then that of handling discharge and after-care, and making sure that resolve does not crumble at the railway station when the person finds himself with no support and seemingly no alternative to the return to drinking.

ORGANIZATION OF HELP FOR THE HOMELESS ALCOHOLIC

Services for the homeless alcoholic seem often to have an organizational base which is separate from the general alcoholism treatment services in the area. People working in the two sectors of endeavour may be strangers to each other, with no sharing of ideas (let alone of resources) or exchange of patients. The problems facing skid row organization are therefore again of two kinds: integration of the skid row responses, and organization of working relationships with other agencies (including alcoholism services).

The minimal elements that have to be developed within the skid row facilities can be listed as follows:

(i) A system of contact-making and patient recruitment

This may be through 'shop front' social work offices located in the city areas where homeless men and women congregate, through direct contact by outreach workers at street corners or at railway stations, or through regular contacts with courts, prisons and doss-houses.

(ii) Detoxification facilities

Facilities should be available either in terms of a detoxification centre (see p. 294), hospital beds, or supervised withdrawal facilities in the dormitory of a half-way house.

(iii) Hostels or half-way houses

Between them hostels or half-way houses can meet a sequence of needs from those set by the person who is just coming off alcohol to those of the individual who is achieving his first 6 to 12 months sobriety and who during this period will benefit from living in a community. Beyond that there are the needs of the person who is ready to move out from a residential community but who will still benefit from living in a flat or apartment managed by the rehabilitation service, which can thus offer some continuation of support.

(iv) Medical services

Medical services and screening have to be readily available to skid row agencies; these agencies are dealing with a group of people whose physical health may have been badly neglected.

(v) Special assistance with employment

The type of person with whom the skid row service is concerned often has a long history of unemployment or a fragmented work record, and no particular job skills. He may find it difficult to compete in a job market where the need for the unskilled worker is diminishing. As ever, humane treatment intention should not be allowed to teach helplessness, and even in the most adverse job market some people will show an extraordinary ability to find work. Others, though, may need special help: a job placement scheme specially organized with sympathetic local employers, assistance through statutory employment or retraining facilities (in the UK the local Disablement Rehabilitation Officer is likely to be helpful), or an imaginative self-help type of job-finding club.

(vi) Day-care facilities

Shop-front and residential facilities can to an extent provide an immediate element of day-care and contribute to support and follow-through; the ex-resident who is finding the going rough may come round for a meal with the other residents in the half-way house. Some treatment programmes have developed a more formal day-care organization and offer a wide range of assessment and rehabilitation facilities.

(vii) The 'wet shelter'

A city council will occasionally succumb to pressures of the 'get the drunk off the streets' variety and propose the cheapest way out; to set up a house where such men may doss down and continue to drink, but without offending public sensitivities by their unsightly behaviour. Such dubious political motivation may be allied with the genuine belief that anything is better than nothing, and that bringing men into a shelter where they can drink surgical spirits or rubbing alcohol offers hopeful possibility of contact. In the event such a hope is usually disappointed and the shelter becomes a destructive extention of a pathological system, rather than being in any way a place that gives help.

THE ORGANIZATION OF DETOXIFICATION CENTRES

General procedures for detoxification (with a stress on the management of ambulatory detoxification) have been discussed in Chapter 13, and in the present chapter the need for back-up detoxification facilities has been noted both in relation to treatment organization in general, and to the organization of treatment for the homeless alcoholic in particular. Starting in Eastern Europe and with the concept then taken up in the USA and Canada (and more uncertainly in the UK and other countries), there has been a move towards the establishment of specialized detoxification centres. As originally developed in Czechoslovakia and Poland, these centres were envisaged as places to which the police would take the public inebriate, rather than as centres to handle both that problem and general detoxification needs. Debate has therefore centred on at least four issues:

1 Whether the centres are to emphasize a medical approach and be under medical control, or alternatively whether they are primarily to provide a 'non-medical' detoxification, with medical help called only when needed. The decision has implications for staffing and for cost. Some case series suggest that the need for routine or intensive medical supervision may be less than might be expected, but this must depend on the type of patient being attracted.

2 The extent to which the facility will operate as a police–referral centre (taking mostly homeless alcoholic men), as opposed to more of an all-comers role. Should the centre serve the needs of alcoholics who are still socially integrated? Some champions of the homeless alcoholic's cause would argue that facilities to help that sector are so scant that monopoly rights on detoxification centres should be preserved, while others would plead that an exclusively skid row detoxification service once more institutionally confirms the stereotype of the vagrant alcoholic as a different human species.

3 Whether the separate organization of detoxification facilities sets the process of detoxification too apart from all the other processes of help and change, of which detoxification is an incidental part. The fear is expressed that detoxification centres may end up by offering a series of hurried and unprofitable admissions, and thus become no more than part of a latter-day and not much improved revolving door system, with very little real rehabilitation. Such dangers exist but they can be met.

4 The extent to which compulsion plays a part has also been a focus of discussion. The statutory basis for the organization of such centres may be founded in some countries on the idea of voluntariness, while in others compulsory placement in a detoxification centre is the alternative to the police cells. Questions arise about the usefulness of therapy based on compulsion, and the problems set by a mixed population of voluntary and compulsory admissions.

Those then are some of the current points of debate. A movement which started off with much humane commitment has more recently been subjected to criticism, partly because of the evidence of high relapse rates. Human concern is admirable, say the critics, but does this experiment actually *work*? It is possible that the need for specialized detoxification centres has in some localities been overplayed, that the facilities do indeed run the risk of becoming short-term and not very useful staging-posts, and that results do not always justify the costs. But against those contentions must be put the strong and central argument that police-court handling is manifestly ineffective, that leaving a drunken man in a police cell is a dangerous medical practice, and that the continued handling of the individual through the penal system damagingly confirms his hopelessness and degradation. Better solutions than the traditional penal handling must be sought, even if recent experiments are only tentative and imperfect.

THE NON-STATUTORY OR VOLUNTARY SECTOR OF TREATMENT RESPONSE, AND ITS RELATIONSHIP WITH STATUTORY ORGANIZATIONS

In many countries there has been a long tradition of work by voluntary agencies on alcohol problems – the world-wide activities of the Salvation Army and other charitable organizations provide historic examples of continuing importance. Work on skid row problems has in particular been a focus for voluntary concern. In North America and in Britain, local councils on alcoholism have established counselling services. Such counselling centres have often sought to get away from the exclusively skid row image, and have also tried to operate on the basis of an accessibility and informality which may be difficult for a hospital. AA is a self-help organization which offers another highly significant example of a non-statutory contribution to the range and quality of available help.

There is again therefore the danger of separate worlds developing. Small voluntary organizations easily become isolated, they are prone to high staff turnover, they can seldom offer career structures to people who work within them, and lack of 'institutional memory' can mean that what was tried unsuccessfully a few years back is now tried again. Network support between voluntary services is very important. Conjoint training schemes, shared meetings on organizational and therapeutic problems, between-agency rotations or holiday cover may all for example usefully link and strengthen the work of an otherwise all too isolated cluster of half-way houses. And apart from integration of different elements in the voluntary endeavour in order to prevent fragmentation, there is also the need to ensure that the two worlds of statutory and voluntary endeavour are in communication.

MONITORING AND ASSESSMENT

The problems that have to be faced here are not essentially different from those which relate to any other type of 'health care delivery'. But the problems in this instance are exacerbated by the extraordinary complexity of alcoholism treatment: the pressures and shortage of funding under which sections of this system operate, the difficulty in defining and measuring a multi-dimensional outcome, and the problems which beset attempts to set up controlled or random trials. Attempts to foist a set of ill-designed questionnaires on reluctant staff are clearly useless.

These difficulties do not, however, excuse those who are responsible for operating any part of the alcoholism treatment system from self-criticism. This is much aided by the regular collection of simple minimum data on the case-load and its characteristics, on itemization of services rendered, on length of stay in treatment, on outcome and on cost. The more complex the monitoring system, the more likely it is to break down. The process of self-monitoring does not, though, involve only data collection; it means continuing discussion and analysis of unfolding experience. Satisfied and dissatisfied consumers of the services should be listened to with care. There is obviously a place too for the formal research investigation, provided it is sensitive enough to ask the right questions. A several-sided review, with inputs deriving from some or all of the monitoring strategies described above, is most likely to be helpful to those who are giving time and energies to the business of care.

REFERENCES

Acres DI (1977) The primary health care team. In: Edwards G and Grant M (eds) *Alcoholism: New Knowledge and New Responses*, pp 321–327. London: Croom Helm.
Banham JMM (1980) Health services planning – does it ever work? In: Edwards G and Grant M (eds) *Alcoholism Treatment in Transition*, pp 264–272. London: Croom Helm.

Biegel A (1974) Planning for the development of comprehensive community alcoholism services: organisation approaches. *Journal of Drug Issues*, **4**, 142–148.

Blacker E (1977) Training for professionals and nonprofessionals in alcoholism. In: Kissin B and Begleiter H (eds) The Biology of Alcoholism, Vol. 5: *Treatment and Rehabilitation of the Chronic Alcoholic*, pp 567–592. New York: Plenum.

Blume S (1977) Role of the recovered alcoholic in the treatment of alcoholism. In: Kissin B and Begleiter H (eds) The Biology of Alcoholism, Vol. 5: *Treatment and Rehabilitation of the Chronic Alcoholic*, pp 545–563. New York: Plenum.

Coates M (1980) *Alcohol and Your Patient: A Nurse's Handbook*. Toronto: Addiction Research Foundation.

Costello RM and Hodde JE (1981) Costs of comprehensive alcoholism care for 100 patients over 4 years. *Journal of Studies on Alcohol*, **42**, 87–93.

Department of Health and Social Security, UK (1978) *The Pattern and Range of Services for Problem Drinkers. Report by the Advisory Committee on Alcoholism*. London: H.M.S.O.

Glaser FB, Greenberg SW and Barret M (1978) *A Systems Approach to Alcohol Treatment*. Toronto: Addiction Research Foundation.

Hore BD and Plant MA (1981) *Alcohol Problems in Employment*. London: Croom Helm.

Home Office (1971) *Habitual Drunken Offenders: Report of the Working Party*. London. H.M.S.O.

Otto S and Orford J (1978) *Not Quite Like Home: Small Hostels for Alcoholics and Others*. Chichester: Wiley.

Plaut TF (1967) *Alcohol Problems: A Report to the Nation by the Cooperative Commission on the Study of Alcoholism*. New York: Oxford University Press.

Robinson D and Ettorre B. (1980) Special units for common problems: alcoholism treatment units in England and Wales. In: Edwards G and Grant M (eds) *Alcoholism Treatment in Transition*, pp 234–247. London: Croom Helm.

Room R (1980) Treatment-seeking populations and larger realities. In: Edwards G and Grant M (eds) *Alcoholism Treatment in Transition*, pp 205–224. London: Croom Helm.

Schramm CJ (ed) (1977) *Alcoholism and its Treatment in Industry* Baltimore: John Hopkins University Press.

Shaw S, Cartwright A, Spratley T *et al* (1978) *Responding to Drinking Problems*. London: Croom Helm.

Smart RG (1976) The Ontario detoxification system: an evaluation of its effectiveness. In: Madden JS, Walker R and Kenyon WH (eds) *Alcoholism and Drug Dependence*, pp 321–330. New York: Plenum.

Williams RL and Moffat GH (eds) (1975) *Occupational Alcoholism Programs*. Springfield, Ill: Thomas.

Wiseman JP (1970) *Stations of the Lost: The Treatment of Skid Row Alcoholics*. Englewood Cliffs, NJ: Prentice-Hall.

Chapter 20
When Things Go Wrong, and
Putting Them Right

Every attempt has been made in previous chapters of this book to present a perspective on drinking problems which is close to reality, and not to give an idealized view of the therapeutic process as a logical operation smoothly and inevitably moving forward to success as each patient obligingly responds to our wise and well-planned interventions. This chapter seeks to correct any such accidental caricature and considers some workaday clinical problems as they often arise in anyone's office or consulting room, and in the homes of our patients.

GOING WRONG

The person who wishes to treat alcoholism must develop an appreciation of the ways in which treatment may go wrong. He must train his eye quickly to recognize these situations, and he must be aware of the familiar patterns of events against which to interpret the latest instance of something going wrong. He must learn to examine the extent to which the therapist is going wrong, and the extent to which it is the patient, and most particularly to analyze what is amiss in the interaction. He must learn not to be discouraged or defeated by such events, but to turn them to good therapeutic advantage. One cannot treat alcoholism without things very often going wrong and the essence of treatment is usually a series of trials and errors rather than a straight-line advance. Such a statement is not to be read as a license for complacency – true, things will go wrong and we must not be too flustered by that fact, but equally true the insistence that the situation is recognized and an effort made to put it right.

This chapter does not attempt to give a comprehensive list of what might go wrong but seeks to provide only broad headings under which such happenings can be placed. No doubt anyone who has experience of alcoholism treatment would see ways in which the list might be extended, and a personal listing of cases where therapy went wrong (a list kept, as it were, on mental file) is a valuable working tool.

LOSING THE BALANCES

Much of therapy is a matter of finding balances (and of readily shifting balances), and things quite often go wrong because balance has been lost. To give this assertion meaning, balance can be considered in terms of a number of different dimensions.

EMPHASIZING THE DRINKING/EMPHASIZING ALL ELSE

It is possible to go wrong because the treatment has become so exclusively focused on the individual's drinking that the man or woman doing that drinking in a complex personal and social setting is quite overlooked; the drinking is everything. The complementary imbalance is a sensitive awareness of that individual's total life situation, with the reality of alcohol as a destructively pervasive aspect of that situation discounted; the drinking is hardly anything. This problem has already been noted in an earlier chapter (p. 204). To set the balance right is often difficult, and at a certain stage of learning and experience it is particularly the sensitive, open-minded therapist who is apt to fall into the trap of underestimating the seriousness of the drinking problem: the very proper desire to see the 'whole person' and to respect the complexities of that individual's life must not be put in opposition to awareness of the true threat of the drinking.

A man aged 44 had experienced a deprived and troubled childhood. Despite this, he managed to contract a seemingly happy marriage and for 16 years all had appeared to go well. Then his wife had an affair, and his world fell to pieces. All his fearful beliefs as to the inevitability of separation and betrayal were proved to be well-founded. His feelings towards his wife were unforgiving. He determined that an unhappy episode should be the occasion for catastrophe and he divorced, threw in his job, sold his house, gave up his friends and moved to a new city. A couple of years later he overdosed with barbiturates and consequently came under the care of a social worker who was interested in psychotherapy and who spent a year exploring with this patient his problems relating to a rejecting mother. He frequently turned up for interviews drunk, and this was duly interpreted. He was then admitted to hospital after a further and more serious suicidal attempt. The psychiatrist who saw him forthwith instituted a course of ECT for what he diagnosed as a severe and untreated depressive illness, and held up the story of the social worker's analytical meddlings as a dreadful warning. He noted that the patient had 'recently engaged in some secondary relief drinking'. The evening following the first ECT the patient developed an acute confusional state: it was one of the night nurses who made the diagnosis of delirium tremens.

Both the analytical social worker and the physically-oriented psychiatrist had focused on important aspects of this man's diagnosis, but each had overfocused, each had seen things comfortably in terms of their own predilictions, and each had therefore unhesitatingly prescribed their own panacea. Neither had bothered to take a drinking history. It seems likely that the patient was not so much covering up the seriousness of his drinking as that those who came in contact with him were almost wilfully turning a deaf ear to what he was telling them. A careful reconstruction of the history later suggested a drinking problem going back to the early days of marriage, a marriage much affected by drinking, and a wife who finally moved out because she could no longer tolerate the drinking and the violence. The next move must not of course be the substitution of an exclusive alcohol focus and a new imbalance for old, but ensuring that treatment of this man's alcohol dependence is accorded its balance place within the total strategy of his treatment.

There are of course many different ways of falling into error through seeing the patient as 'an alcoholic' and believing therefore that all his problems are to be understood and treated within that definition. A short extract from another case history should correct any notion that the error is always in one direction.

A 33 year-old labourer had been admitted to an alcoholism treatment unit, where a diagnosis of alcoholic hallucinosis was made. It was noted that he had previously been admitted to another hospital with what was now deemed to be the mistaken diagnosis of schizophrenia; the case-notes were not borrowed. He was put into the ward therapeutic group but seemed to spend more time listening to imaginary voices than participating. After six weeks or so he was thought to be 'somewhat improved' and was discharged to a hostel for alcoholics which was run on intensive therapeutic community lines. He was put into an encounter group on the evening of his arrival, and shortly thereafter again developed florid schizophrenic symptoms and was readmitted to the first hospital rather than to the alcoholism unit. Their case-notes recorded a clear initial attack of schizophrenia at the age of 17, in a man who did fairly well provided he was not too stressed and could find a supportive environment. But this was certainly a patient who over recent years had begun to overmedicate himself with alcohol.

The staff on the alcoholism treatment unit had so specialized a perspective that when a classical case of schizophrenia presented to them they reacted in terms of a predetermined psychological set, and the consequent diagnosis led to a package of group therapy and confrontation being given to a man whose needs were quite otherwise.

So much for two rather extreme cases to illustrate the poles of imbalance which can occur. No doubt the errors are usually on a smaller scale and more subtle. Perhaps the mass of general agencies tend to underrate the importance of the drinking, while the specialized alcoholism agencies not unexpectedly run the risk of being too alcohol-focused. Each individual has to develop a sense of the direction in which he personally is likely to be in error, and to remember that directions of error change with time.

TOO AMBITIOUS/TOO UNAMBITIOUS GOALS

Sometimes things go wrong because the therapist (and the patient) have got the balance wrong as to reasonable expectation of what changes may be achieved, or the pace of such change. This dilemma may occur at any stage of treatment. The mistake can be that too great a therapeutic pace is being set which can readily force the patient into breaking contact, but equally the problem may be in the direction of inertia.

A 60 year-old man stopped drinking but continued to treat his wife in a curmudgeonly fashion, was at cross purposes with his grown-up children, and had no leisure activities other than watching television and grumbling about the quality of the entertainment provided. At the end of a further year he was still sober and still regarding the world with unrelenting enmity.

What is the social worker to do next time she calls round on this family and the man purposely turns up the volume control on the television, while otherwise angrily staring ahead and not acknowledging the caller's presence? The wife offers a cup of tea in the kitchen, and says, 'He's always been that way and I suppose he won't change – a real old misery I call him.' What is the right balance of treatment ambition?

The reality may indeed be that a man of 60 who has for most of his existence defined the world as antagonistic, and who has built up his self-image largely in terms of afflicted righteousness, is unlikely radically to change his ways. His wife's assessment of the situation may be just about right, and she does not seem too put out by his ill-grace. Her father was much like that anyhow, and this husband's behaviour is much in accord with what she expects of any man. She is happy enough that he is no longer running her short of money.

And yet it seems sad to leave it at that. There is the lingering feeling that the goal is being set too low, that more happiness for two people should be possible than is seen here. The answer is perhaps for that social worker to try setting a moderately more ambitious goal on a trial and error basis. The goal had better be expressed concretely, and the starting point must be the identification of something which patient or wife themselves at least half-hint at being wanted, rather than the goal being invented by the social worker on her own. In this particular instance the wife let drop 'and he never takes me on holiday of course'. The 'of course' was an important part of the statement; it was clear that the wife's communication with her husband often carried the implication that she expected his response to be negative. A modestly realistic goal in these circumstances was to see if this couple could go away for a week's holiday together and come home with the feeling that they had enjoyed themselves. Working at first through the wife and suggesting that she might for once expect the answer 'yes' from her husband, the holiday was booked. The couple went for a week to the seaside, and although the holiday provided much cause for grumbling, in sum the week seemed to provide some real sense of shared reward. Beyond the immediate happening, some small shake-up had occurred in set negative patterns of interaction, and the basis established for the possibility of further, small change.

The case illustration giving under this heading has purposely been set in a minor key, and it contrasts with the more dramatic problems of alcohol dependence remaining undiagnosed or the schizophrenic patient being mis–diagnosed, which were discussed in the previous section. Judging the best balance on therapeutic ambition is often a matter of tentatively raising the expectations and seeing what can be achieved. The question which is being dealt with here obviously relates to the issue of the 'quality of sobriety' (p. 208).

TOO INDULGENT/TOO HARD

There is a balance to be struck regarding the degree to which the relationship offered by the therapeist to his patient is to be supportive and non–judgemental, as contrasted with a relationship which emphasizes elements of tough-minded expectation and hard confrontation. An effective therapeutic relationship will therefore often be one which embraces the skill to more confidently and appropriately choose between ability to support and timely willingness to confront with reality. To put the matter in terms of absolutes and contradictions is an oversimplification but it may be useful to examine this particular idea in terms of two very contrasting examples. Firstly, imbalance in the direction of indulgence:

> A social worker of rather little professional experience became
> highly committed to helping this family. The 30–year-old man was
> not alcohol dependent, but seemed to use drink to enhance his
> passivity and incompetence. He seldom worked. He borrowed,
> pawned and stole. The wife who was faced with this chronically
> difficult situation tried to prop up the family as best she might.
> When the social worker arrived on the scene she soon became no
> more than a provider of gifts, and she protected the man from the
> consequence of his having cheated on welfare payments. She found
> him good second–hand clothes so that he could go for a job
> interview, and when he pawned the clothes and didn't go to the
> interview she treated him as an amusingly naughty child.

The social worker was operating on the hypothesis that this patient was deprived and was testing out her 'goodness'; she believed that she 'must not reject him'. Where she may have gone wrong is in her assumption that the opposite to indulgence is rejection.

As an example of the tough-minded imbalance, the following case is illustrative: it relates to consequences of a stance which is quite commonly taken by helping agencies in their attempt to screen-out the 'unmotivated' patient.

> An alcoholic was to be discharged from prison and it had been agreed that he should then be admitted to hospital. He was homeless. However, the decision was made 'to test this man's sincerity'. The consultant in charge of the treatment unit decided that the man would not be admitted straight away but should find himself lodgings, go to AA, and then present at a ward goup for assessment by the other patients. Coming out of prison after four years the man was anxious, a little bit elated, very lost, and he immediately made his way to old friends. He was drinking again within hours, and within days had once more committed his familiar offence of breaking and entering. The consultant was confirmed in his sense of wisdom, and took these events as evidence that the patient was 'insufficiently motivated'.

There are occasions when it is therapeuticlly useful to be indulgent and other occasions on which it is kind and constructive openly to challenge. There are no fixed guidelines. This is simply another dimension where the question of balance has to be kept under review in all therapeutic dealings.

TOO DIRECTIVE/TOO AFRAID OF A POSITION

The alternative to forcing one's opinion on a patient is not necessarily the pretence of having no opinions at all. A therapist may have difficulty in treating drinking problems because he gives his patient the impression of lacking confidence at a time when the patient badly feels a need to borrow some certainties; an orthodox therapeutic detachment is for instance inappropriate in a situation where someone needs very practically to be helped by the therapist's knowledge of how to deal with a drinking crisis. while a dictatorial attitude will be equally counter-productive. Here is an example which bears on this particular and difficult aspect of balance:

> A 40-year-old woman who over a two-year period had begun to move towards severe alcohol dependence in the setting of a depressive illness was visited on the ward by her husband. The husband made himself unpopular with the staff by his unsympathetic and scolding attitude towards his wife. One of the junior nurses exclaimed to the patient, 'I don't see how living with

that man you could ever stay sober – you should go and live with
that son of yours who seems so fond of you.'

In the treatment of alcoholism more than in the treatment of many
other conditions, the therapist is faced with the problem of directiveness
because it often appears glaringly obvious that the patient is engaging in
wrong-headed and self-destructive behaviour, that he is revealing a
chaotic inability to make good decisions and order his life well, and that he
manifestly does not know what is best for his own good. Alcoholism
treatment seems therefore to pose a specially acute challenge to the
orthodox notion of the therapist's need to maintain neutrality. The nurse
felt that she knew what was good for the patient, and said what she
thought.

Perhaps the solution to this dilemma comes again from reminding
ourselves that a polarity must not be allowed to be put in false terms. It is
essential that the therapist should convey to his patient an unmuddled
re-inforcement of the treatment goals, once those goals have been agreed.
As has previously been stressed (p. 203), there is a difference between
imposing a view and setting the expectation that an agreed goal will be
met. With more open questions the balance is got right by bringing to the
patient's awareness the likely consequences of his behavioural choices and
by not then seeking to force one choice upon him. The therapist may in
any case be wrong, and even if the therapist is correct, the attempt crudely
to force his views may be an inept way of presenting them.

Returning, however, to that nurse's remarks to her patient, discussion
of this incident in the staff group would usefully bring into the open wider
issues related to the limits of directiveness, but the conclusion in this
particular instance could only be that the balance had gone wrong. The
nurse knew too little about the marriage to give such directive advice and
she certainly knew toolittle about that patient's son.

DEFEATED BY DEFENCES

That the patient's defences have to be identified, their usefulness to the
patient understood, and their existence adequately dealt with as part of
general therapeutic work are ideas common to the treatment of many
problems other than alcoholism, and the defences which the alcoholic may
deploy are by no means specific to this condition. The therapist who is

going to work with alcoholism would, however, do well to cultivate a particularly lively awareness of how defences usually manifest themselves on this scene. An inadequate response to the patient's defences is one of the more common reasons for things going wrong.

DENIAL IN PURE OR MIXED FORM

By *denial* is meant a defence against the threat of reality which is based on a refusal to admit the existence of that reality; it is oneself rather than others who have to be deceived. In pure form the mechanism is pictured as operating at a subconscious level, with denial thus differentiated from a conscious untruth which is aimed at the deception of other people. Often, though, the patient's initial difficulty in facing up to the threat of his drinking is a manifestation both of denial in the classic sense and of prevarication. The therapist will learn to be familiar with many variations in degree and weighting of this familiar combination, and dealing with this problem is a routine part of the work of recovery. In practice it is often difficult to determine the extent to which the two different elements are contributing to a given presentation, and conscious and unconscious processes often seem to merge.

In the popular image the alcoholic is frequently pictured as someone who insists on drinking himself to death while maintaining that no drop of alcohol ever passes his lips. Such crude and primitive defensiveness is relatively uncommon, but when it reaches extreme proportions it can be extremely baffling and a block to all progress, despite every therapeutic stratagem. Skill and patience is needed in dealing with this sort of situation. Here is a case abstract which shows the kind of problems that can be set by really entrenched denial in the face of a manifest problem.

> A 50-year-old accountant was brought along to a psychiatric clinic by his partner, who said that unless something was done his colleague would have to be pensioned off. The patient's breath smelled heavily of drink, his liver was mildly enlarged and he had bruises from several recent falls. He charmingly acknowledged his gratitude to the partner for taking this trouble, but said that the poor man was overworked, worried and getting things out of proportion. The patient admitted to having an occasional beer at lunch-time, but that was the limit of his drinking. He was then seen

again with his wife, who said that he was permanently intoxicated, that he was frequently incontinent, that he had recently fallen down stairs when drunk and that empty bottles were falling out of every cupboard. He said that his wife was a dear woman but a terrible worrier, that of course he was often tired at the end of the day (who wasn't), and that as for falling down those steps there had been a loose stair rod.

Given that one does not at this point surrender hope entirely, the best approach might first be to try to get some insight in to the reasons which could lead a patient to engage in this stonewalling. Usually of course there are several reasons rather than one. For instance, some people make lifelong use of certain favoured defensive systems (in sickness and in health), and this man may under stress simply be reaching for his personally most available coping mechanism out of a very limited repertoire. Another explanation may be that this stance is in effect a very angry response to what the man conceives as an attack on his integrity. He sees his partner and his wife (his father and mother) as out to dominate him, and he reacts with angry and childish stubbornness. It may also be that he very much wants to continue to drink, and cannot conceive of any alternative.

With these guesses in mind the therapist might then sit down alone with the patient, with the other actors out of the room. With no implication of attack, the therapist will start a discussion on the basis of an openly stated assumption that both he and the patient know that reality is being denied. The therapist will furthermore immediately lay ground-rules for the interaction by stating that the interview will not be allowed to degenerate into a useless cross-examination which could offer no fruitful result but only further entrenchment. The aim is thus not frontal assault on the defensive position, but to get behind the defence. It can be put to the patient that a lot of people find difficulty in talking openly about the degree of worry and trouble which their drinking is causing – they may be afraid of attack and afraid of being demeaned – and in such circumstances to try to insist that the worrying facts do not exist can be a natural response. The therapist must try to convey that he sees this situation from the patient's point of view, and then offer possible alternative solutions. It can be put to the patient that if a man drives his car off the road and someone comes up and asks questions, the driver may well respond defensively if he thinks it is a policeman who is questioning him, but it will make no sense to treat the person who is offering first-aid as if he were a policeman, and hence bleed to death.

The defensiveness may still remain absolute. The patient may take the line that the therapist is a nice fellow whom it is a privilege to meet, but that the clinic's valuable time is being wasted on the basis of a most unfortunate mistake – everyone is getting hold of absolutely the wrong end of the stick. What to do next?

It may as a temporary measure be possible to leave the defence in place, as it were, but to take no notice of it – to allow the patient to hold to the assumption that he has no drinking problem, while the therapist works on the assumption that there is a serious problem which has to be treated. Such a peculiar agreement to differ is unlikely to continue happily for long; either the patient will slide into accepting the therapist's definition of reality or contact will be quite unprofitable. Another and rather simple approach which may sometimes be promising is to concentrate for the time being on the patient's physical health. He may find it acceptable that he is in deed of advice on his physical health (an alcohol-free diet for his liver's sake), without any of the loss of face which he fears would result from fully admitting his dependence on alcohol.

If none of these approaches pays dividends, the only course may be to leave the patient with an unambiguous message as to the need for him to open his eyes, and a factual warning of the dangers which will stem from the denial and prevarication continuing, and then not to make any offer to see the patient again for a period of some months, unless he so asks. The wife may well need help or support in her own right.

The occasional baffling intractableness of really entrenched denial should not itself be denied. The temptation is of course to almost literally raise one's voice in the hope that he will actually hear, or to confront him with every sort of proof positive and hope that the high walls of his defences will then dramatically collapse. The temptation is in short to resort to the battering ram. Sadly, the consequence of that attack will probably only be the patient strengthening his wall of defence.

THE 'DEFENCE' OF SICKNESS

Sometimes a patient will claim that he continues to drink because he is indeed an alcoholic. He is suffering from an illness which is the explanation of his behaviour, and the responsibility for curing this illness rests with the therapist. Things go wrong if this position is accepted, but they go equally wrong if the therapist automatically assumes that the patient is playing games or working some sort of intentional trickery. That type of explanation may occasionally be correct, and the patient may be intending to continue his drinking with the position nicely established that the therapist is to blame. This same presentation may, though, have a meaning which is not so easily contained in the language of games analysis. The patient may be taking up this particular version of the sick role because he truly believes that he is sick, damaged and no longer able to control his own behaviour. He is not then so much displaying a defence as manifesting symptoms of learnt helplessness. The two very different possible meanings of outwardly similar presentations have therefore to be distinguished. In the wrong circumstances, simply cutting the patient down with an aggressively neat analysis of the game he is playing is likely to result in the therapist being rid of a rather difficult patient but nothing else. In those circumstances it is more useful to examine the therapeutic relationship with particular care, and to try to move the patient towards a realization that he can indeed start to take responsibility for not drinking, that he has more resources than he supposes and that it would be misleading if any one else were to pretend to be able to take his responsibilities from him.

ABSOLUTION

A patient may be able to defend himself from the pain which would otherwise force him to change his behaviour if he can find a doctor or social worker who can be persuaded to offer him regular absolution. At the same time he may present a picture of psuedo–insight. Intellectually he knows what suffering he is causing to himself and others, but he is able to divorce this insight from any deep feelings provided he is given regular doses of forgiveness. He is, in fact, seeking the therapist's connivance as actor in a repetitive and quite unproductive play. Here is a case extract which illustrates one such presentation.

> The patient sat down and puffed on his pipe. He said that he knew he was an alcoholic, had been going to AA for years and knew that all he now had to do was to get through one day without drink. His

wife was threatening to leave him, and after this last 'slip' and all
that she had been through, he entirely saw her point of view and did
not blame her in the least. He was the most dreadfully sorry and
knew that he had behaved to her like a swine. Furthermore, he had
let the doctor down again, and was thoroughly ashamed of
himself. He had in fact said exactly the same thing on at least a
dozen previous occasions with a similar show of contrition coupled
with detachment from real feeling.

Things go wrong if the therapist falls into the position of aiding and
abetting the cycle of this man's behaviour. Such a story is not uncommon
and the patient may sometimes be a long-term AA attender who has
managed to get little out of AA. One may suspect that he has used the AA
meetings in much the same way as he would employ the interview with
the psychiatrist, and he is nowhere near grasping the real AA message. For
the therapist to continue contact on this non-therapeutic or anti-
therapeutic basis is useless. It is more helpful to throw the responsibility
back on the patient and refuse to be his confessor. An element of challenge
and confrontation may produce new possibilities, but there is always the
risk that the patient will instead go off and find some other therapist who
will at least temporarily provide the absolutions.

THE ROMANTIC DEFENCE

Alcoholism peculiarly lends itself to a romantic defence, an identification
with famous drinking poets and playwrights. The following is an abstract
from a referral letter:

> This lady is a well-known artist and you will certainly know of her
> husband who is the novelist. She has led a truly amazing life, and if
> she gets round to telling you about her years in Paris you will find it
> fascinating. Everyone in her set drinks, and I think one has to
> accept that drinking is for her essential to the creative life. Recently
> she has been hitting the bottle and she was seen by someone last
> year who rather annoyed her by calling her an alcoholic. She cannot
> accept help which is conditional on her giving up drinking.

In this instance the patient's defence had overwhelmed the judgement of an experienced physician, who had been seduced into accepting drinking as symbolizing 'the creative life'. That the drinking was profoundly affecting this woman's ability to work and threatened actually to destroy her was being screened out.

If this position is accepted things very certainly go wrong, for the patient continues to drink and the therapist is effectively neutralized. He is invited to become an amused and admiring spectator of this fascinating way of life, and he will never then recover the therapeutic position. At the start of the contact the therapist has therefore to be reasonably on his guard and hold to the position that drinking must be de-symbolized and seen in its reality. The patient may have an immediate sense of relief if he finds that he can discard the act that self-destruction is romantic fun.

ENDLESS ARGUMENT

The problems set by intellectual defence are familiar in any area of psychotherapy. In work with alcoholics the intellectualization is likely to go off in certain special directions – the patient will divert the discussion away from any real therapeutic content towards making the interview a symposium either on the definition of alcoholism or on the determinants of alcoholism, or both. The therapeutic response should be to steer the patient away from the consideration of generalizations and back to the immediacy of his own position. Otherwise the therapist will find himself engaged in a lengthy analysis of 'the disease concept' while the patient continues to drink.

THE PATIENT WHO KNOWS SOMEONE WHO
DRINKS MUCH MORE

A block to treatment which can be no more than a minor distraction but which may sometimes be employed as a major stratagem to escape the reality of the threat which drinking poses is the claim made by the patient that he knew someone who drank much more than he ever did himself, or who drank a great deal and never came to harm.

> All right, I drink my share. But I'll tell you this, my old father
> died at 86 and he drank much more heavily than I have ever

reached. Absolutely routine, he'd never go outside the house without putting a bottle of whisky in his pocket, just like picking up his tin of tobacco.

To enter a debate with such a patient as to whether his drinking is more or less than his father's is bound to be defeating. The data on the patient's drinking is probably at that stage uncertain and the data on the father's drinking much falsified, so the patient is in a position to prop up his defence by revising all elements of the comparison at will. If one agrees to enter this debate, one gets involved in a sort of pub conversation, with wildly unlikely but incontravertible assertions being heaped one on the other. 'Look at Winston Churchill. He had the best part of a bottle of brandy every morning before he got out of bed. Greatest Englishman who ever lived . . ..' The best way to avoid entanglement in this unproductive sort of argument is to say quite simply that it is not the patient's father or Winston Churchill who has come for the consultation and that they will be left right out of it.

THE DEFENCE OF BEING GROUP LEADER

Hostels or in-patient units may work on the formal basis that a particular patient is elected or appointed to a special position of leadership, and even if the position is not thus formalized, a patient may come to assume this role *de facto*. It can sometimes become apparent that the assumption of leadership was a defence with which the staff have connived.

A 30-year-old man had been referred to a hospital with a letter which described him as 'really a very impressive fellow'. Before long he was editing the hospital's magazine, was group leader and effectively co-therapist, and had acquired various informal marks of privilege, such as being allowed against hospital rules to keep his car in the grounds. He eventually crashed his car when drunk, and it then transpired that he had been drinking for the entire period of his hospital admission. Several members of staff then admitted that they had half suspected this fact but had never brought the matter into the daylight: they had invested a great deal emotionally in this patient's success and were themselves now being forced to engage in denial, thus illustrating rather vividly the commonality between all of us in relation to the types of psychological mechanisms which we may at times deploy.

The patient had always shown a propensity to defend himself against his sense of inadequacy by becoming the prefect, the head-boy, the club captain, etc. He had the social confidence and the plausibility repeatedly to attain such positions, and would then repeatedly compromise himself by some disastrous piece of behaviour. It is unfortunate when a man with this particular type of stereotyped defence meets up with a treatment setting which invites the play to be played again. The way in which this defence is best coped with may be not to set up artificial and rather dangerous positions within treatment institutions, or very carefully to review the manner in which such a system actually works. If the therapeutic community model is being employed, it may be better to organize the treatment setting so that many people bear small responsibilities, rather than heaping large responsibilities on to one person.

WHEN EVERYTHING GOES WRONG

There are times in alcoholism treatment when everything seems to go wrong at once, and this not just in terms of happenings relating to one particular patient but with several patients getting into serious difficulties over the same few weeks. One's most hopeful patient relapses, another seems bent on destroying himself with his continued drinking, and a patient for whom the therapist had especially warm feelings dies and there is an element of self-blame. Such periods do indeed occur, and it is necessary for the therapist who runs into such a patch of troubles to remind himself (or be reminded by his colleagues) that the treatment of alcoholism will inevitably at times be a very fraught and perplexing business. Sometimes the therapist may have been selecting for himself all the more difficult cases, and there is the possibility that the therapist has become over-stretched, overtired or in some way careless. But it is more probable that events have randomly clustered and that the therapist needs his self-confidence supported more than being invited to blame himself for lack of omnipotence. Sometimes things go wrong because of forgetfulness and oversight: the need for a physical examination is overlooked, the spouse is not seen, what the patient is really trying to say is not heard. Perhaps most dangerously, things go amiss when the therapist becomes over-confident, fails to entertain doubts and assumes that he knows all, and that if the patient fails to respond what is needed is more medicine of the same kind. On occasions the way in which the treatment system is working may also need to be scrutinized, and it may for instance be evident that some of the difficulties stem from staff liaison being in poor repair.

This final chapter ends therefore with a reaffirmation that treating the person with a drinking problem is about moving that individual by every available strategy towards alliance with his or her own recovery. This book has sought to discuss some of the skills and understandings which can assist the thereapist in that task, but the only final arena for learning is the actuality of contact, the experience of things sometimes going wrong, and the discovery that with patience, flexibility and mutual effort things often very happily come right.

Author Index

Subject Index